NEWS
Revolution

NEWS
Revolution

Political and Economic Decisions about Global Information

MARK D. ALLEYNE

ST. MARTIN'S PRESS
NEW YORK

ISBN 0–312–15894–7

Library of Congress Cataloging-in-Publication Data

Alleyne, Mark D., 1961–
    News revolution : political and economic decisions about global
information / by Mark D. Alleyne.
        p. cm.
    Includes bibliographical references and index.
    ISBN 0–312–15894–7 (cloth)
    1. Foreign news—Political aspects. 2. Communication,
International—Political aspects. 3. Government and the press.
4. Foreign news—Censorship. I. Title.
PN4784.F6A45 1996
070.4'332—dc20   96–28129
                                                          CIP

Interior design by Harry Katz

First edition: January 1997
10   9   8   7   6   5   4   3   2   1

Dedicated to

Reudon, Angela, Andrei and Nicole Eversley

Contents

List of Tables and Figures

List of Abbreviations

AFP   Agence France-Presse
ALASEI   Latin American Features Agency
ANN   Asia-Pacific News Network
ANPA   American Newspaper Publishers Association
AP   Associated Press
BBC   British Broadcasting Corporation
CAME   Conference of Allied Ministers of Education
CANA   Caribbean News Agency
CCPJ   Canadian Committee to Protect Journalists
CHR   United Nations Commission on Human Rights
CNN   Cable News Network
COPUOS   United Nations Committee on the Peaceful Uses of Outer Space
CPJ   Committee to Protect Journalists
CPU   Commonwealth Press Union
CSCE   Conference on Security and Cooperation in Europe
DBS   Direct Broadcast Satellite
DPI   Department of Public Information
FANA   Federation of Arab News Agencies
FIEJ   International Federation of Newspaper Publishers
GATT   General Agreement on Tariffs and Trade
GII   Global Information Infrastructure
IAPA   Inter-American Press Association
ICCPR   International Covenant on Civil and Political Rights
IFEX   International Freedom of Expression Exchange
IFJ   International Federation of Journalists
IFP   International Financial Printer
INGO   International Non-Governmental Organization
INS   International News Service
IOJ   International Organization of Journalists
IPDC   International Program for the Development of Communication
IPI   International Press Institute
ITAR   Information Telegraph Agency of Russia (ITAR-TASS became the new name for the reorganized old news agency, TASS)

ITU	International Telecommunication Union
MBC	Middle East Broadcast Center
NAM	Non-Aligned Movement
NANAP	Non-Aligned News Agencies Pool
NGO	Non-Governmental Organization
NIEO	New International Economic Order
NII	National Information Infrastructure
NWICO	New World Information and Communication Order
OECD	Organization for Economic Cooperation and Development
OSCE	Organization for Security and Cooperation in Europe
PANA	Pan-African News Agency
PR	Public Relations
RFE	Radio Free Europe
RFTV	Reuters Financial Television
RIA	Russian Information Agency
RL	Radio Liberty
ROSTA	Russian Telegraph Agency (Rossiyskoye Telegrafnoye Agentstvo)
RSF	Reports Sans Frontières
SWAPO	South-West African People's Organization
TASS	Telegraph Agency of the Soviet Union (Telegrafnoye Agentstvo Sovietskavo Soyuza)
TBDF	Trans-Border Data Flow
UDHR	Universal Declaration of Human Rights
UNCTAD	United Nations Conference on Trade and Development
UNDP	UN Development Program
UNESCO	United Nations Educational, Scientific and Cultural Organization
UPI	United Press International
UPU	Universal Postal Union
USIA	United States Information Agency
USTTI	United States Telecommunications Training Institute
VOA	Voice of America
WIPO	World Intellectual Property Organization
WPFC	World Press Freedom Committee

Preface

Work on this book actually began in the academic year of 1993-1994, which I spent in New York City as a research fellow of the Freedom Forum Media Studies Center. I completed it two years later in Chicago while on the faculty of the Department of Communication at the College of Arts and Sciences, Loyola University Chicago. I am especially thankful to Everette Dennis, former director of the Freedom Forum Media Studies Center. I thank the Loyola University Office of Research Services, and the members of the committee on Faculty Research Support Grants for supporting my successful application for the funding that allowed me to complete work on the book.

A special expression of thanks must go to three faculty members at three different institutions for being very good friends over the years. They are professors Jannette Dates (Howard University), James Miller (Hampshire College), and Larman Wilson (The American University, Washington, D.C.).

Some students at Loyola University were significant sources of inspiration and help during the final stages of writing the book. I could not have wished for a more loyal, efficient and enthusiastic research assistant than Natalie Leone. Angela Baker and Colleen Carpenter put in several hours on the computer working on the indices.

The comradeship of friends in Chicago, especially my tennis buddies, sustained me during the long months of work. That cohort includes Angie Deppe, Larry Labow, Barb Meyer, and Niren Saldanha. The friendly, intellectually stimulating conversations with Theresa Amato and Kimberly Gordon were very important. Thanks are also due to my very good friends the Greens from Gary, Indiana—Eugene, Lavada, and Ray Green.

At St. Martin's Press, Michael Flamini was the one who expressed faith in the book from the start and I thank him for his confidence.

All the representatives of the human rights and press freedom organizations who participated in the International Journalism Survey were essential to the completion of this project. My hope is that this book is very relevant to their work.

Considerable help was also given by Dorothy Delman of Reuters America, Inc., New York.

Finally, as always, I must pay homage to my family and the extended family of Barbadian society that gave me the core values that account for whatever success I might achieve. These values include: a profound respect for education; self-discipline; honesty; and a rating of the spiritual and intellectual above the material.

The usual caveat applies. All who have helped are only responsible for what is best in this work.

NEWS
Revolution

INTRODUCTION: THE EVOLUTION OF NEWS

This is a book about the international politics of news. It originated with another book, my *International Power and International Communication.* In chapter 4 of that book I sought to explain how news flows were linked to the configuration of international political power. But it was clear, even as I wrote that chapter, that the topic of news and international politics deserved an entire book of its own.

There could be no better time than now to put down in one place my set of ideas about how transnational news flows have been problematical in international politics. New technologies have made global communication extremely efficient, and concurrent political transformations—such as the demise of authoritarian governments in Latin America and the Communist Bloc in Eastern Europe—impel a sophisticated understanding of how news media play a role in the international dialogue on democratic government.

This book is built on the bold assertion that news, the news media, and journalists have been problematical in international relations in four ways: (1) their potential as conduits for international propaganda; (2) their role in the unbalanced flow of global news; (3) their claims to be protected from censorship; and (4) the difficulty in ensuring the safety of journalists. Each one of these issues is examined in turn in a separate chapter.

The role of this first chapter is to provide the basic foundation on which the succeeding chapters build. It will answer a number of the following questions. What is news? What is the history of global news flows? What is the relationship between news and international politics?

In beginning to answer these questions, it is necessary to repeat, and expand upon, some of the ideas in chapter 4 of *International Power and International Communication.* In that chapter I began the discussion of the international politics of news by quoting a telling newspaper report from a press conference with United Nations (UN) Secretary-General Boutros Boutros-Ghali:

"Why should the United Nations pay attention to what is going on
in Yugoslavia and pay no attention to what is going on in Somalia
when people are getting killed in Somalia in a higher proportion
than Yugoslavia?" he asked. "One explanation is that public opinion
was aware of what was going on in Yugoslavia. The limelight of
media attention was on Yugoslavia, and nobody paid attention to
Somalia.

"The day that [the media] began to pay attention to Somalia, we
began to receive the support of the member states. Then they were
ready to give us planes for transport and to provide more humani-
tarian assistance and the forces to protect it."

He warned that the same kind of situation could recur in the former Soviet Central Asian republics, which many fear are moving
toward major ethnic warfare. "Tajikistan or Armenia or Uzbekistan
have the same problem as Somalia: They don't know how to reach
the media or to do the lobbying," he noted.[1]

The secretary-general's observations illustrated vividly why the news
media are so significant in international relations. In addition, he provided an
insight into the hierarchical structure of global news flows. Although he used
the neutral terms of "public opinion," "media attention," and "the media," he
was really speaking about specific media, catering to specific public opinion[2]
in specific parts of the world. He was not talking about the news media of
Zambia, St. Lucia, or Ecuador. If news media in those countries covered
Somalia's suffering it would be a bonus; however these media do not have the
audiences of *The New York Times* or *Le Monde*, with circulations in excess of
1,000, 000 and 300,000 respectively. Also, *The New York Times* and *Le Monde*
are examples of media published in countries with the resources to make a difference in places of need. The news media—and the elite media of powerful
countries especially—help to shape the agenda of international relations for
governments, organizations, and common citizens.

Early in their rule, political authorities of various ideological complexions
all devise positions on news media and use their legal, police, and military systems to control the press. [3] This has meant that journalism is one of the most
hazardous professions. Expulsion, arrest, detention, kidnapping, disappear-
ance, and murder are unfortunately common dangers for journalists around
the world.[4] However, news media are able to project and protect their interests
in ways not readily available to those who question their performance.
Therefore, the power of the press and the power struggle between the press and
those who want to control news media are the reasons why global news flows
are the most controversial aspect of international communication.

NEWS DEFINED

Because politics is about power, we say that the global flow of news is political because it reflects and determines the international configuration of power. But what is news? And on whose definition of news do we base our own definition?

The definition of news, or news values—what mass media see fit to report—is a key variable in understanding the politics of global news flows. Government officials and common citizens from small states often accuse the main disseminators of international news—that is, the international wire services, the global TV networks and the Western elite press—of concentrating on "negative" news about their countries. It seems that most of the news circulated about countries in Africa, Latin America and some parts of Asia concerns natural and man-made catastrophes, a phenomenon that has been called a "coups and earthquakes" syndrome.[5] It sometimes seems that there is a malicious attempt to stereotype these countries, and this attitude might be propelled by various factors, including racism, political ideology and ethnocentrism. In this way, international news can be seen as a weapon of those with power in the international system, a tool to maintain the status quo, at least in regard to the inferior status of some peoples and nation-states.

But an alternative way of viewing the problem is to focus on the dominant definition of news. Such an approach locates the problem with the power of news values rather than with particular prejudices towards certain countries or groups of people. According to a study commissioned by the United Nations Educational, Scientific and Cultural Organization (UNESCO),

> News in most media systems seems to be defined as the exceptional event, making coups and catastrophes newsworthy wherever they occur. It is not so much that the developing world is singled out for such "negative" attention, but that the developing countries tend to be reported only in this manner. These countries are neither the source of, nor themselves apparently particularly interested in, presenting "softer" news items. Third World media systems concentrate heavily on "hard" news, and the tendency is that the smaller the amount of general coverage, the more it concentrates on a few topic areas and reflects the specific events of the time. News tends to stereotype all regions in some way or another.[6]

This particular definition of news controls the way in which journalists decide what is important. Regardless of where the definition first was devised, it has created a peculiar situation in which all journalists working for, or using material from, the major international media can be seen as accomplices, whether they be in New York or Lusaka. One writer described this mix of contradictions by explaining that

> Third World papers pay as much attention to the private lives of American celebrities, to the problems of drug-taking among American students, to the health of the American President, as they do to the comparable personalities and issues of their own societies. The news sent out from Latin America, Africa and Asia to the international agencies is sent by local agency offices and representatives who are often natives of the countries concerned. Yet the local journalist will send the New York office the material which he knows it wants; this is then retransmitted with the agencies' bulletins to the newspapers of the same region according to the presumed news priorities of those papers.[7]

The logical extension to this line of thinking is that even if the personnel and organizations relaying international news become more diverse there is no guarantee that the coups and earthquakes syndrome will go away. What also must be changed is the definition of news.

The observation quoted above also points to the relative lack of freedom that journalists in many regions of the world have in reporting about local personalities, issues and events. To avoid the sack, censorship, or even harassment and murder, many media organizations in small countries devote much time and space to the readily available news from North America and Europe because such news is considered "safe." In contrast, investigative reports on government corruption, the private lives of local personalities or exploitation of consumers by merchants are "unsafe" stories because they are too close to home. This situation is the product of a rather schizophrenic attitude of elites in many small countries to local and international news. An illustration of this is provided by a journalist from Ghana who noted that

> Castigation of the Western media is a regular feature of the state-owned media, for the anti-Ghanian views, supposedly directed by their governments. Yet ironically, when the Ghanian press criticizes the Western leaders and system of government, it is with facts published in the same Western media. The fact that similar information published in Ghana about the government would be considered treason is conveniently overlooked. Most interesting of all, the least praise in the same Western press is proudly cited and broadcast.[8]

The recognition of the power of news values and the role of restrictions does not mean, however, that other factors such as ethnocentrism, racism and ideology do not color international news. After news values are determined to select what is to be news, journalists often use vague, shorthand terms to describe complex issues and regions. The power of such parlance has become so strong that, ironically, to express the anger that many feel, a journalist used one such woolly generalization—"Third World"—when he declared: "Third World states are persistently upset about being portrayed as poverty-stricken countries that are either pro- or anti-American."[9]

THE EVOLUTION OF GLOBAL NEWS FLOWS

The preceding analysis suggests that the distribution of news will always be problematical, regardless of the media used. However, within a decade the use of new technologies produced drastic changes in the character of global news flows. These transformations coincided with (and, some argue, helped cause) major transfigurations of the international system. Not only did the Cold War end and the Soviet Bloc collapse, but also military dictatorships were replaced by civilian governments in Latin America, and, in southern Africa, majority rule came to Namibia and South Africa.

The coming of global satellite TV networks was revolutionary for the structure of global news flows but, before discussing their impact, it is necessary to paint a picture of the structure of global news before their creation.

Before Cable News Network (CNN) was created international news circulated mainly through transnational news agencies and government-owned shortwave radio stations. That old structure provided governments and domestic media organizations with opportunities to censor, edit or control flows of news into their countries or regions. Wire service copy could be edited, and even when news was provided in the form of video it was often in the form of videocassettes or "feeds" for rebroadcast.

International Wire Services

Until the advent of global TV and computer networks, the so-called "Big Five" news agencies were the dominant purveyors of international news. The story of why they were created, how they related historically with their home governments, and how they evolved does a lot to explain the relationship between international politics and global news flows.

International news agencies were established not so much to create an informed international citizenry but to make money. Their histories are characterized by struggles to secure and expand markets for their news, markets often delineated by the territorial limits of their home countries' empires or spheres of influence.

Of the five largest international agencies, three—Agence France-Presse (AFP), Reuters and the Associated Press (AP)—were started in the 1800s, and of these AFP is the oldest.[10] It celebrated its one hundred and fiftieth anniversary in 1985 and claims to have been the world's first international news agency. AFP's origins date to 1835[11] when Charles-Louis Havas (1783-1858), a French entrepreneur, bought the Correspondence Garnier—a company that translated foreign newspapers—and started converting it into a news agency.

By the late 1800s Havas was to encounter competition when rival international news agencies—in the form of Reuters in London and Wolff in Berlin—were set up. His competitors were the Germans Paul Julius Reuter and Bernhard Wolff, both of whom Havas had employed earlier and trained. These three agencies—Havas, Wolff and Reuters—would remain the premier news agencies of the world well into the twentieth century. But Reuters and Havas outlasted the Wolff agency, which disappeared with the rise of Nazism in Germany and the coming of World War II.

The Associated Press (AP) was set up as a cooperative among six New York newspapers in 1848. The "United Press Associations" (later to become United Press International, or UPI) was formed by prominent American newspaper entrepreneur E.W. Scripps in 1907 to break AP's dominance of the news agency business in the United States, a position that agency enjoyed because it was the only national news agency in the country at the time.

Havas, Reuters and Wolff had established an international news cartel between themselves by signing the Agency Alliance Treaty in 1869, under which they delegated to each other regions of the world for exclusive coverage and service. Reuter got the entire British Empire and the Far East; Wolff covered Scandinavia, Russia, Austria and its surrounding territories; and Havas gained the rights to the French and Portuguese empires, Italy and Spain. Reuter and Havas agreed to penetrate South America jointly. The agreement was made in an attempt to offset rising telegraph costs. It was the first of a series of contracts between the three agencies that would last well into the 1930s. AP joined the cartel in 1893 and got exclusive rights from Reuter to distribute news within the United States and U.S.-controlled territories, and to supply the European agencies with news from the U.S. The de facto end of the cartel came in 1930 when the Japanese agency Rengo agreed to distribute the AP service in Japan and AP declared that it would end its agreement with the European cartel.

Unlike the Western agencies, the Telegraph Agency of the Soviet Union (TASS) did not originate as a private, entrepreneurial venture. It had its origins in two agencies: the St. Petersburg Telegraph Agency and the Press Bureau of the All-Russian Central Executive of Workers', Peasants' and Soldiers' Deputies. Conflict between the two organizations after the 1917 revolution caused them to be merged into the Russian Telegraph Agency (Rossiyskoye Telegrafnoye Agentstvo, or ROSTA). ROSTA had two departments—one for news and one for propaganda—Vladimir Lenin was among those who wrote for it. ROSTA became TASS after the declaration of the Soviet Union in 1925.[12] TASS was directly controlled by the Council of Ministers of the USSR. Its director was appointed by the Presidium of the Central Committee, and all its international contacts and agreements had to be approved by the foreign affairs ministry. Mikhail Gorbachev's liberalization of the Soviet press made TASS's reporting less doctrinaire, and, after his departure, the very unusual occurrences in the former USSR profoundly affected the fortunes of TASS even more. On January 22, 1992, Russian president Boris Yeltsin signed Decree Number 37, creating the Information Telegraph Agency of Russia (ITAR) by merging TASS and parts of RIA-Novosti. RIA, the Russian Information Agency, set up in March 1991, was intended to be a joint-stock company. Private investment failed to materialize, however, and RIA was merged with state-supported Novosti, established by the Soviet government in 1961, as a second official news agency. Thus, rather than subsidize both RIA-Novosti and TASS, and to "remove the unjustified duplication in work," a single agency, ITAR, was established by Yeltsin's decree to serve as "the central state information agency of the Russian Federation whose activity is designed for the inner state and international audiences."[13] It was decided that the TASS logo would remain in its news reports, as in "ITAR-TASS," due to its worldwide recognition. In a separate agreement, the heads of 14 national news agencies of former Soviet republics—also former branches of TASS—decided to cooperate in preserving ITAR-TASS's extensive information and communication structures in the post-Soviet era as well as to maintain its central data bank.[14]

When governments of poorer, small states made calls at the UN in the 1970s for reform of the structure of international news, the influential media of North America and Europe dismissed these initiatives as raising the ugly specter of government control over news. But the history of the international wire services reveals that these news organizations never have been able to be completely free of relationships of some sort with their various home governments, for ensuring telecommunications links or for needed financial support. The agencies have patterned their international reporting very closely to the contours of power of their home governments, as the specializations established at the time of the cartel reveal. And, in times of war especially, the strategic value of the wire services has not been lost on governments that have completely taken over some of the agencies.

Although TASS's ties with the Soviet government have been obvious, the European agencies and UPI have at various times in their histories not had the adversarial relationship with their governments that is supposed to exist in liberal democracies where the press is assumed to be a watchdog on government. About the time of the United Press Associations's merger with William Randolph Hearst's International News Service (INS) in 1958 to form United Press International, Frank Bartholomew, the UPI chairman after the merger, said "private enterprise with a profit incentive is the best guarantee of objective coverage of world news."[15] According to this view, there is nothing inconsistent with the profit motive and the liberal-democratic ideal. However, there are contradictions in a news agency's aspiring to liberal-democratic principles (in particular the principle of autonomy from government control) while relying on its home government for financial support.

Charles-Louis Havas had personal connections with French government officials, and this more than likely played a part in the government's decision in 1838 to employ the agency to relay ministerial news to state agencies. In the interwar years the Foreign Ministry subsidized Havas in the wake of its losing markets due to competition from TASS, shortwave radio revolutionizing the international transmission of news in the 1930s, and the end of the cartel. After the outbreak of World War II it was turned into the French Information Office. The agency was revived as Agence France-Presse (AFP) after the war by former London correspondents and journalists of the Resistance. However, the turning point was in 1957 when French law granted it editorial independence and financial autonomy. Nevertheless, AFP has not been able to shrug off allegations that it is linked to French government interests, both domestic and foreign.

Reuters entered an agreement with the British authorities during the First World War under which it "transmitted a service of Allied war communiqués and official news financed by the government but kept separate from Reuters own service."[16] The agency was more successful than Havas during the Second World War in resisting official pressure. It reorganized itself in 1941 as a private company owned by the British provincial press. The ownership body became the Reuter Trust, which "provided that Reuters should never pass into the hands of any one interest group or faction, and that its integrity, independence, and freedom from bias should be preserved."[17]

As part of a move to turn the company's financial fortunes around, UPI entered a $2.5 million contract with the U.S. government in 1987 to relay official releases outside the United States.[18] The agency had not turned a profit since the early 1960s and, after the Scripps family sold it in 1982, had gone through a succession of owners. Although AP has never been in as desperate straits as UPI, Jean-Luc Renaud has documented U.S. government assistance to AP's global expansion.[19]

A major reason why the international wire services have had to resort to government help is that international news in the form of mere printed words is not a very profitable commodity. That also explains why all the agencies diversified their output during the course of the twentieth century to include news photos, radio reports and new information technologies, such as facsimile. But, with the expansion of international trade and financial flows, the most lucrative arena for diversification became financial information. Of the Big Five, Reuters exploited this area most. By 1986 the traditional media market accounted for only 9 percent of Reuters's revenue, and although the company still ran one of the world's largest wire services, it was open to question whether Reuters could be defined as a news agency or a multinational corporation that sold news as just one dimension of its business. Over 50 percent of Reuters's revenue in 1986 came from its very extensive dealing in financial data.[20] There were over 34,800 subscriber contracts for Reuter Monitor Dealing Service, involving about 71,500 computer terminals worldwide.[21] (See the case study of Reuters in chapter 2.)

Global Satellite TV News

By the 1980s, satellites were getting more powerful and therefore required increasingly smaller reception dishes, a situation that enabled average citizens to buy dishes and receive transmissions from direct broadcast satellites (DBSs). Global news seemed to be no longer a hierarchical, mediated structure dominated by the international news agencies to one in which CNN came to symbolize for many the coming of a "global village." In the days when the international wire services were dominant, news came in the form of words, but the global TV news networks improved the quality of news by adding sounds and pictures. The qualitative flow of news also was made better by the fact that "breaking" news events—such as the collapse of the Berlin Wall, the release of Nelson Mandela and the student demonstration in Tiennamen Square—could be relayed live, uncensored and seemingly unmediated by the prejudiced opinions of reporters. The live TV camera appeared to be a global mirror, an objective tool for the collection and dissemination of the potentially volatile information called "news."

Time magazine was so impressed that it made CNN's founder, Ted Turner, its "Man of the Year" for 1991. It described the viewers of CNN around the world as having witnessed "the awakening of a village consciousness, a sense that human beings are all connected and all in it together, wherever on the planet they may be. How else to explain Kenyans who lined up six-deep in front of

electronics stores to watch footage of a war they had no soldiers fighting in? . . .
What we are seeing is not just the globalization of television but also, through
television, the globalization of the globe."[22]

This ability of live television news by satellite to involve so many in a seem-
ingly communal affair did not necessarily mean that it made international
politics any more democratic. Reporters for the mass media were not allowed
to be present, or were present under very controlled circumstances, during
Israel's operations in Lebanon and Britain's war in the Falklands in 1982, the
United States's military actions in Grenada in 1983 and Panama in 1989,
France's intervention in Chad in 1988, and the Persian Gulf War in 1991–92.
In the case of the Gulf War, the live relays via CNN of reporters speaking while
explosions were going off did not speak favorably about the capacity of the
"information revolution" to sustain peace. In the words of Marc Raboy and
Bernard Dagenais, two communication professors at Laval University, Quebec,
Canada, "we are allowed to see only that which we can no longer do more than
absorb" and "media become not a forum for public discussion of policy issues,
but a means of massaging the public with reassurances that the authorities
have the crisis well in hand."[23] And, as we will see in chapter 3, the Gulf War
was only one case in which governments used international public relations
firms to manipulate global broadcast media, public opinion and legislators.

Because broadcasting obviates the problem of illiteracy there is no question that it can reach even greater audiences than the international news
agencies, and that the direct broadcast technologies used by CNN mean this
contact is often direct. Global news broadcasts via TV also mean that the
flow of international news, depicted in figure 1.1, has been expanded in both
quantitative and *qualitative* terms. However, although CNN introduced a "World
Report" program that allowed foreign TV crews to air their reports over the
network, it has not been able to escape the criticism that it replicates the traditional prejudices and imbalances that have been characteristic of transnational news flows.[24] For example, the majority of the network's foreign
bureaus are still concentrated in the rich, industrialized countries and in
1996 there was still only one bureau in Kenya to cover all of Black Africa.[25]
The decision-makers and correspondents of CNN well into the 1990s also were
predominantly white, reflecting neither the diversity of the network's home
country nor of the world.[26]

The ability of live television news to provide a world audience and to send
information to both elites and common citizens unmediated except for the
cameras has meant that the medium became even truer to tested propositions
about the impact of TV news on foreign policy. One proposition is that TV news
is a participant in foreign policy because it sometimes serves as a direct con-

duit of communication between government officials and might be a catalyst for acts orchestrated to play to the cameras. Communication researcher James Larson found this to be true with the Iran hostage crisis even before the global TV news networks and it was most certainly the case during the Gulf War when Iraqi, Israeli, Libyan, American and Saudi Arabian officials all used CNN as a medium of political communication.[27] Other features that Larson found in the 1970s and seem to ring truer with the coming of CNN include: television's ability to relay emotions and consequently to change public perceptions of issues; the tendency of television coverage to be ahistorical; and difficulty in conducting private and secret negotiations about issues subject to intense TV coverage.[28]

Due to the success of CNN—it was reaching 78 million households and 250,000 hotel rooms by 1994[29]—the British Broadcasting Corporation (BBC) was encouraged to start its own competing international TV network, even though the new network broadcast more programs than just live news and initially was beamed to Asia.[30] Similarly, when the Middle East Broadcast Center (MBC) network was set up in 1991 its owners expressed the desire for the service to be "CNN in Arabic."[31]

Multimedia Information Networks

Exploiting the profitability of financial news and utilizing new technologies, a new dimension to the provision of international news came in the 1990s with the Bloomberg network. It was started in the early 1980s as a securities data service by former Solomon Brothers trader Michael Bloomberg. In 1990 he expanded the service to include business news. By the mid-1990s it was the fastest-growing company in the financial information field, with 30,000 subscribers around the world receiving via interactive, multimedia computer terminals quotes on stocks, currencies, commodities, bonds and other securities, as well as breaking business news. Most of the world's central banks were subscribers, in addition to insurance companies, pension funds, banks, large corporations, U.S. government offices, and other news organizations.[32] In 1993 Bloomberg was adding up to 25 news services to the system each month, including even horoscopes, sports results and help-wanted advertisements. The information flowed in numbers, words, pictures and sound. Although Telerate (with 95,000 subscribers in 1993) and Reuters (200,000 subscribers in 1993) competed with Bloomberg in the provision of financial information, the Bloomberg service used multimedia technologies the most. A gauge of the profitability of the enterprise was the company's revenues, which were estimated to be in the region of $400 million in 1993. Michael Bloomberg was in the Forbes 400 in 1992 and 1993.

The rapid growth and profitability of the financial information field was seen in the performance of Reuters. Its 1993 pretax profits of $651 million were 15 percent better than those in 1992.[33] (See chapter 2.)

THE STRUCTURE OF GLOBAL NEWS

Figure 1.1 illustrates this hierarchy in the structure of global news flows that still has not been threatened by the evolution in the technologies for global news distribution—from the international wire services to global satellite TV networks and to interactive, multimedia systems. The new technologies have increased the quantity and quality of information flows but they have not subverted the basic hierarchical structure of those flows. The new financial information networks have merely mirrored the patterns of world trade and investment flows and these are still concentrated in the richer countries of North America, Europe and Japan. In other words, the tempting assumption that more efficient international communication has produced "globalization" is rather incorrect. What is more precise is that there is "uneven globalization."[34]

FIGURE 1.1
THE STRUCTURE OF GLOBAL NEWS FLOWS

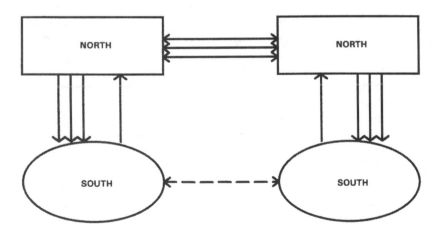

North: = the richer, industrialized states concentrated mainly in the Northern Hemisphere's regions of North America and Europe, and also including Japan.

South: = the smaller, poorer states located mainly in the Southern Hemisphere and concentrated in such regions as Africa, the Caribbean, Latin America and Asia.

The flow of news between regions varies *quantitatively* and *qualitatively*. The quantity of news flowing from the richer countries of the North to the South greatly exceeds the quantity going in the other direction. The quality of news from South to North is lower than the reverse flow. In contrast, there are high quantitative and qualitative flows of news between the richer countries. The "Big Five" international news agencies, the elite newspapers and magazines of North America and Europe, and now the global TV networks, such as CNN have the vast majority of their foreign news bureaus concentrated in the so-called major capitals of the world, especially London, New York, Paris, Washington, Brussels, Tokyo, and Hong Kong. Every day these offices disseminate millions of words, pictures (still and moving) and sounds to their head offices where they are packaged for evening TV newscasts, radio reports and daily and weekly editions of newspapers and magazines. Also, important distribution points for news in these countries are financial news services supplied to computer screens by such networks as AP/Dow Jones and Reuters.

The high quantitative and qualitative North-North flow is in contrast to the South-South flow, which is relatively low in quantity and quality. Unless there is a major natural or man-made catastrophe the average consumer of news in, say, New Delhi will hardly have available to him or her as wide a choice of news about, say, Latin America, Africa or even other Asian countries, as he or she has about Western Europe or the United States. And even when the consumer of news in New Delhi gets news from other countries of the South the quality of this news is often low. By this we mean that a news story about a hurricane in the Caribbean, for example, might come only in words, without still or moving pictures. The quality of news flows is determined by how news is covered, and if there are few international news bureaus in these regions then it is less likely that information will be relayed in more ways than just written reports from sources called on the telephone.

South-South flow is peculiar not only because of its very different quantitative and qualitative character, but also because it has a higher propensity to not flow directly. We can draw an imaginary triangle in the middle of Figure 1.1 with the tip of the triangle pointing upwards. Because all the major international news organizations are based in the North, news from Africa to the Caribbean, for example, often comes via London or New York. In the 1970s the Non-Aligned Movement (NAM) and UNESCO encouraged initiatives, such as the Pan-African News Agency (PANA), the Caribbean News Agency (CANA) and the Non-Aligned News Agencies Pool (NANAP), to give journalists in these regions more editorial control over news from their regions and abroad, but none of these organizations have the resources to set up their own bureau in distant capitals to obviate the triangular South-South flow, and the best these agencies can do is to mediate and reedit the news supplied by the international wire services.

The journalists who define what is news not only see news as the exceptional event, but also define news as what is important. So our description of the global flow of news is also a view of the perceived important sources of news and the major points of exchange for such information. Those who defend the character of global news flows argue that the international news organizations rightly pay more attention to the "major capitals" because that is where the important news is produced. The assumption beneath this explanation is that the production of news is a reflection of the various configurations of international power. The international ramifications of decisions made in these capitals—especially in the areas of economic and military relations—are seen as justifications for the structure of global news.

The logical extension to this line of thought is that the historical development of world political, technological, economic and military relations must be analyzed if we are to understand the character of global news flows. We also must examine changes in the global political economy in order to get a clearer understanding about the evolution of debate about global news and attempts at multilateral rule-making for news media and journalists. This is a core proposition of this book. The evolution of the global political economy and the concurrent technological revolution has profoundly affected the global media debate. This is why the foundation-building begun in this chapter is expanded in chapter 2, which explores the value of international news to the world political economy.

Chapter 2 is followed by successive chapters on the four individual planks of the primary argument of the book: chapter 3 examines international propaganda; chapter 4 is about inequality in global news flows; chapter 5 is on censorship; and chapter 6 explores the protection of journalists.

A word on the format of those four chapters is a useful road map for understanding my analytic approach. The four chapters are concerned with five dimensions of each of the problems. These are explained in turn below.

First, some time is spent clarifying definitions. This is a fundamental task of all good research. It turned out to be especially important in this book because attention to how issues were defined led to a better understanding of the ecology of those issues. For example, a bold assertion of the chapter on censorship is that the restricted definition of the concept is itself a barrier to progress on the problem. Likewise, by paying careful attention to definition, it was found that the literature on the "protection" of journalists sometimes includes protection from censorship. So a task of chapter 6 was making clear the importance of separating out the discussion of protecting the professional integrity of journalists (the work of chapter 5) from the discussion of the physical protection of journalists (the job of chapter 6).

Second, there is an analysis of the *international legal discourse* on the problem. All the chapters pay careful attention to the status of the issues under international law. The assumption is that international law is a form of discourse among the actors in international relations. When it exists concerning a particular issue it reflects particular values and norms, especially of the more powerful member-states of the international system. For example, in chapter 5 it is argued that censorship has appeared as a subdiscourse to the major discourse on *universal* human rights. International law guarantees freedom of information (the right to hold and impart ideas) through the Universal Declaration of Human Rights (UDHR) and the International Covenant on Civil and Political Rights (ICCPR). Approaching international law as a form of discourse means we regard the types of legal documents and their varying status as ways of making explicit and implicit statements. For example, the fact that the ICCPR, which recognizes permissible restrictions on freedom of information, has the more binding treaty status, and the less restrictive UDHR does not, is a statement on how states are protective of their sovereignty.

Third, *international political discourses* are examined. This feature refers to the rhetorical give-and-take of international politics. While international legal discourse is concerned with what is written down as international law regarding an issue, international political discourse is about what is actually said or done about the issue. In other words, it is about the de jure versus the de facto, or the rhetoric versus the reality. Political discourse and legal discourse intersect when legal discourse becomes a part of political discourse, reflecting and affecting the dynamic or power relations in international society. It is important to pay careful attention to political discourse because international law only gives a snapshot of what *should* happen. By looking at political interaction our understanding of a problem is made more complete, because politics tells us what actually *does* happen.[35]

A fourth dimension is the discussion of the role of *actors*. All the issues are examined to see the disposition of actors to them and the patterns of interactions among the actors involved. Actors in international relations are of five basic types: states; international organizations; business firms; non-governmental organizations (NGOs); and international non-governmental organizations (INGOs). Some outside the field of international relations might use the word *states* and *governments* interchangeably, but there can be a refined, elaborate discussion about what the term *state* actually means.[36] However, for the purpose of this book, states are merely those entities that are represented by governments and enjoy the privilege of formal sovereignty in international relations. Under this definition, factions in civil wars are not states even though they might run administrations in the territories they control. Such entities would be more correctly labeled NGOs—actors in international relations that are not governments but that represent specific interests. In contrast, INGOs are NGOs with briefs that are transnational in scope and which are comprised of members from diverse geographic locations. International organizations are actors in international relations formed by governments and represent interests that governments help to define. Chapter 4 shows how the attention to actors is critical by examining a case in which pressure from specific powerful states on an international organization (UNESCO) was found to have directly caused a shift in favor of "independent, pluralistic media" in the UN's mass media development activities.

Last, each chapter examines what kinds of *international cooperation* have been tried or actually established in the issue-area in question. In some cases, the forms of cooperation have been formal and at the level of states or their surrogate international organizations—such as the UN's unsuccessful attempt to create an international legal regime[37] to protect journalists. In others cooperation has been less formal and by NGOs or INGOs, such as the IFEX (International Freedom of Expression Exchange) system created by press freedom and human rights groups to deal with the same problem.

Chapter 7 is a comprehensive analysis of the similarities and differences between the four areas and a discussion of the implications the findings have for the study of international relations and global news flows.

THE ECONOMIC VALUE OF INTERNATIONAL NEWS

The international flow of news has always been directly related to transnational economic exchanges, especially international trade and investment. Therefore, when viewed in historical context, it is not surprising that the moves toward the establishment of a global capitalist order changed international debate about news flows from disagreement over a New World Information and Communication Order (NWICO) to a situation in the 1990s where there was a global gold rush for entry into the "information superhighway" that was being touted by the powerful. Communication, broadly defined (to include transportation) or tightly defined (referring specifically to telecommunications), has been the vital prerequisite and lubricant of international economic exchanges. There is a positive relationship between the expansion of some forms of international trade (especially services) and world financial markets, on the one hand, and the ability to communicate efficiently and rapidly, on the other. Therefore, by the mid-1990s the concept of economic globalization was being used to frame consideration of the role of communication and information in international relations.

The primary function of this chapter is to buttress the point that the character of multilateral decision-making about news and the treatment of journalists is influenced significantly by prevailing ideologies about international economic exchange. To do this, the chapter will explore the relationship between global news flows and the international structures of finance and production. The reason why news has value in the international economy and the concept of globalization will be examined. In addition, the case study of the evolution of Reuters will be presented as an illustration of how new communications technologies, changes in the world economy, and news organizations themselves interact in this policy-making environment.

VALUE

Global news flows are closely tied to the international structures of production and finance because news has some value in relation to them. A close look at the notion of value is important because all forms of decision making are determined by conscious or unconscious estimates of value. The more valuable a good or service is assumed to be, the more likely it is that those negotiating over it will try to protect it. Conversely, there will be no negotiation to protect something that is perceived as having little value.

Value can be defined as "[t]he material or monetary worth of a thing; the amount at which it may be estimated in terms of some medium of exchange or other standard of a similar nature."[1] A first approach to the concept of value is to view it as being either subjective (determined by the one individual it affects) or objective (determined by more than just one individual). But the definition of the term reveals that it is very difficult to produce a truly subjective approach to value. Value is most often objective. Even when it is found to be specific to a particular individual it is based on objective criteria, standards of worth set from outside, such as worth in relation to money. Value is determined by a comparison of the entity being assessed to something else.

On this premise that value is mainly objective, we can identify a number of ways in which objective value is determined.

1. Value is determined by the market—supply and demand.
2. Value is determined by those with power, such as economic classes and professional, political or cultural elites. For example, most people do not know how valuable a diamond is until it is appraised, giving those with the expertise in appraising diamonds a considerable amount of power.
3. Value is determined by a calculation of an entity's future utility or worth. Speculators use this approach to value in the futures markets.
4. Value is based on use. In the case of information, a key criterion in determining value is whether certain types of information can be combined with other entities to create wealth or some other benefit.

All of these four approaches to value are applied to communication and information in international relations. But it is important, before proceeding any further, to make the distinction between communication and information. The value of communication is not the value of information, and vice versa.

As I have argued before, communication is a process, involving set arrangements and media that must be in place for any relay of information to occur.[2] Seen in this way, a study of communication is not necessarily a study of information. In other words, the value of my being able to watch three television channels from three different countries at breakfast is different from the worth of the information carried by those channels. The fact that mere access to three channels can be considered valuable in and of itself is separate from whether the programs carried on Channel A are more valuable to me, because they are all about my profession, than those relayed by Channels B and C.

This separation of the value of communication from the value of information logically means that they have separate (although related) worth. The value of communication is different from the value of information.

Our concern here is with the value of a particular form of information: international news. The communication technologies—such as satellites, computers and modems—have their own value. This value is usually related to how efficiently they can transmit information, especially in an inexpensive and timely manner. However, the value of information is based on more than just its being available. Based on the evidence supplied in this chapter, our proposition is that the value of information can be represented by the formula:

Value of Information = Utility + Speed + Quality

[Components of Utility:
(a) the capacity to be combined with other information for greater value
(b) knowledge that informs decision making
(c) the ability to create competitive advantage
(d) symbolic worth, such as representing money]

[Definition of Quality: The capacity of the form the information is transmitted in to appeal to as many senses as possible. Therefore, information relayed in words via teleprinter is low quality information because it is sensed only by sight. But information coming in the form of a video transmission of a central bank official making an announcement is of much higher quality because the it is sensed by hearing in addition to sight. Moreover, the receiver of such information can glean much more based on the intonation of the speaker and her nonverbal communication.]

This description of the value of information helps us to understand better why international news flows have been allied to the international structures of production and finance. International news has served these exchanges not only by being useful in the four specific ways identified, but also by being timely. High speed in information flows is also a means to the end of eliminating the barriers of geographical space. Some writers argue[3] that "the compression of time annihilates space." In other words, the more new technologies enable rapid communication, the more irrelevant is the problem of distance. This is an important dimension of globalization because "space tends to be measured in time [as in the concept of 'light years' in astrophysics], to the extent that the time between geographical points shortens so space appears to shrink."[4]

Obviously, features that determine the value of communication (such as capacity, affordability, and speed) contribute to the value of information relayed. But high-quality communication can be used to relay information that is not valuable. Similarly, information loses its value the later it arrives, particularly in competitive situations.

THE CASE OF REUTERS

Speed was prominent in the origins and growth of international wire services. But speedy information was most important for the military (because it meant the difference between victory and defeat, life and death) and international traders (because it meant the difference between profit and loss). International news agencies grew because they served this demand for speedy information.

A look at the development of one of the world's oldest news agencies, Reuters, illustrates the value of international news in global economic relations. The Reuters story is also a case study of how the evolution of communications technology and the world economy are interlinked with the fortunes of international news agencies: sometimes technology and economic developments mold these services; other times these organizations develop technology and become players in the international economy in their own right. This interaction of technology, economy and news agency is the background for political decision making about global news flows and press freedom.

It was the need of the international economy for information that caused Paul Julius Reuter to found Reuters in 1850 when he used 40 carrier pigeons to fly stock market prices between Brussels and Aachen to compensate for the deficiencies of the European telegraph network. Over 145 years later, in the age of "globalization," Reuters has become one of the major financial information suppliers in the world. But, instead of using old technology to supplement new technology as was the case in 1850, Reuters has become a leader in developing new technologies. And instead of merely supplying stock markets with information, some of Reuters's business now involves facilitating actual trades. So the value of Reuters as a means of communication and the value of the information it supplies have both increased.

The official history of Reuters, attributes Reuter's success in establishing an international news agency to a combination of factors—the growth of technology, growth in demand for news, especially business and financial news, and Reuters's being fortunate to be based in London, a center of trade and the capital of a country where direct censorship had been eliminated.[5]

The unreliable telegraph technology that provided a pretext for Reuters to enter the information business in the first place soon became more extensive and reliable. Within 20 years of its invention by Samuel Morse in 1844, there were almost 150,000 miles of telegraph lines in the world, 15,000 miles in the British Isles, 80,000 on the European continent, 48,000 in North America.[6] The first transatlantic cable was laid in 1858 but it did not work. The first transatlantic cable to work was laid in 1866. This technology created nothing short of a revolution in its capability to speed up the relay of information. To illustrate the point, the news of Napoleon Bonaparte's death at St. Helena in 1821 took two months to reach England by sea.[7]

With the technology available, Reuters was poised to take advantage of developments in the commodity markets that created a demand for speedy information. The international markets for grain and cotton were illustrations of this.

The repeal of the British Corn Laws in 1846 gave Russia the opportunity to become Britain's chief source of grain imports in the third quarter of the 1800s. This international grain market then created a market for Reuters's news about grain markets in Russia and the Danube basin to Britain and other countries. "Grain supplies and prices were uncertain, at the mercy of climate or war; good weather and abundant supplies could be as disturbing to markets as bad weather and shortage," Donald Read, author of Reuters's official history, notes. "Reuter had spotted an important market for news, which he was glad to supply."[8]

In the other illustration, the American civil war caused cotton supplies from the Confederate states to the Lancashire cotton trade to be cut. But the Confederate states' loss was the gain of other suppliers. Reuters was a source of news about the civil war for the British press and business subscribers and the other European news agencies, Havas and Wolff, and to Reuters's agents and subscribers overseas. These non-European countries included India where cotton news carried by steamer was of great interest because merchants were poised to make fortunes by selling Indian cotton to Lancashire to compensate for the lack of supplies from North America.[9] Later Reuters added more services to businesses, in addition to financial information, such as telegrams, advertising and banking.[10]

Although Reuters originated as a supplier of financial information, that fact did not mean that such services remained the major area of business for the agency. As the mass media grew around the world in the late 1800s and early twentieth century, as Reuters contributed its part to an international news cartel with other European and American news agencies and as the demand for other types of news grew, financial information would not regain the central place it had in the company in the 1800s till the 1960s and 1970s. But the fortunes of financial information (or "commercial services") did not ebb and flow in the way general news did. Throughout the history of Reuters, its services dedicated to trade and business remained relatively stable. This is because the cost of financial information, relative to general news, is influenced by more than mere supply and demand. The two factors that set financial information apart are: (a) this information has a higher value-added component—e.g. analysis; and (b) it appeals to a specific segment of the population with a higher ability to pay for the specialized information. This made demand for commercial services relatively stable and accounted for its being a more reliable area of business activity for the company. During the interwar years the commercial service cushioned the losses on the editorial side. For example, in 1933 commercial subscriptions from the Far East alone were worth £59,900, £11,000 more than total United Kingdom newspaper subscriptions. In 1933 annual profits of the commercial service were £23,600.[11] In the 1940s and '50s Reuters's commercial services were considered secondary to the general news service and, according to Read, they were for "the sole purpose of subsidizing the news service." However, the profitability of commercial news steadily increased. The profits of Reuters's subsidiary Comtelburo (a company that reported commercial prices) went from £68,956 in 1950 to £143,197 in 1959, a year when its turnover was about one third of Reuters's total revenue. Comtelburo earned its revenue from the "sale of fast market information 'covering finance in every aspect, commodities of all sorts and freights and shipping.'"[12]

The two major factors accounting for the return of commercial services as the centerpiece of Reuters's news business since 1960 have been: (a) the revolution in communication technologies; and (b) the collapse of the Bretton Woods system and the consequent reorganization of the world economy.

The revolution in communication technologies in the 1960s and later meant that not only had the velocity of information relay increased again, but that the economics of communication had been transformed. For the first time in history the cost of transmitting information did not necessarily increase with the volume of information relayed nor the distance over which it was sent. The cost of sending information via leased channels, such as terrestrial

lines, microwave and satellites, was based on the time the channels were
occupied, not the wordage. And the real cost of sending information to locations within the same footprint of a satellite remained constant regardless of
how far away the remote location was.

With this boost from the communication revolution, Reuters was able to
exploit even more the two unique qualities of financial information mentioned above. In 1963 it set up the International Financial Printer (IFP), a
high-speed system for delivering general and commercial news to European
brokers and bankers. A year later Reuters introduced the Stockmaster service,
supplying stock price information. The service was credited with increasing
European investment in American stocks and thereby having a positive effect
on the U.S. balance of payments.[13]

By the late 1960s Reuters was moving away from distributing its news via
teleprinter to computers. The Reuter Ultronic Report (later to be called the
Reuter Financial Report)—a relay of U.S. prices and business news—was
introduced in 1968. It was the first Reuter product to be supplied on video display terminals.[14]

As the technology got better, Reuters became more than a mere financial
information provider and became a player in international markets that facilitated actual trading. If markets of all kinds are viewed as communication systems, where buyers connect with sellers, it should be no surprise that the same
technologies that Reuters used to transmit information were used as actual
extensions of the markets. That was the central idea behind the Reuter
Monitor Money Rates service that was started in 1973. The new product
was described in the official history of Reuters:

> With the break-up of the Bretton Woods system of fixed exchange
> rates, dealing in foreign exchange and money was about to expand
> rapidly. The problem for banks and dealers was how to receive quo-
> tations with sufficient speed. Dependence upon telephones and telex
> was unsatisfactory, since by the time an answer to a request for (say)
> a bank's dollar/sterling price had been given and transmitted, that
> price might well have changed. Seconds were important. [André]
> Villeneuve [of Reuters] had the idea of installing computing terminals
> in the offices of banks and other foreign-exchange markets. Reuters
> would in this way create an electronic marketplace. Market-makers
> (contributors) would be able to insert their foreign exchange and
> money rates into the system. At the press of a button, the rates would
> become available on a screen to interested parties (recipients) such as
> banks and international businesses. Reuters would charge both con-
> tributors and recipients for access to this interactive system.[15]

Reuters solidified its foothold as a player in the international money markets when it introduced in 1981 the Reuter Money Dealing service, a system that allowed dealers to "communicate with each other at high speed to buy, sell, or lend money through the same screen, taking hard copies of transactions from an associated printer."[16] By 1989 *The Wall Street Journal* was reporting that about one-third of all foreign exchange spot currency trades was being handled by Reuters terminals. Reuters had an edge in the field because in the global foreign exchange markets there was no competition from an established exchange.[17]

Looking back from the mid-1990s, Reuters's moving into commercial services in a determined way beginning in the early 1960s was an extremely shrewd strategy to ensure that the company would survive. At the turn of the 1960s, general international news was the company's main product. But such news was becoming less and less profitable. This was so for a combination of reasons, including the fact that television and radio were increased competition to wire services in the supply of breaking news. International news agencies have dealt with this problem by diversifying, supplying still photos, video, radio services, and financial information.[18] United Press International (UPI), the international news agency that was slow to diversify, became the one with the most financial problems and tottered on the verge of demise for a number of years.[19]

It is significant to note that, despite assertions to the contrary in its official history and the statistics supplied below, in 1995 a Reuters spokesman was reluctant to declare that financial news was more profitable than spot news. "What is it about financial news that has made it more profitable for a company like Reuters than spot news?" he was asked in an interview done by correspondence. His reply was:

> This question's premise is not necessarily accurate. The value of information, whether real-time news, real-time market data and prices, or historical information, and ultimately the revenues derived from these forms of information, depends entirely on the need of a given customer at a particular moment. In any event, Reuters rarely sells financial information without a news component as a significant feature of that information.[20]

But media products (the delivery of news in text, video, pictures, sound and graphics) accounted for only 6 percent of Reuters's £2,309 million annual revenue in fiscal year 1994. The other two-thirds of Reuters's business—transaction products and information products—accounted for 23 and 71 percent of revenue respectively. The fastest growing segment of Reuters's business was transaction products, the facilities that allowed traders to deal from their terminals in foreign exchange, futures, options, equities and securities. Reuters operated GLOBEX, the after-hours trading system for futures and options, on behalf of the Chicago Mercantile Exchange and the Marché à Terme International de France. Its trading service in equities was Instinet, while it provided two trading services for foreign exchange, Dealing 2000-1 and Dealing 2000-2. Reuters information products referred to the hardware and software used to deliver news and prices to customers.

The profitability of its services to financial institutions spurred the overall growth of the company. By 1994, Reuters had 40,000 customer locations in 149 countries and was producing its services in 19 languages. Its staff numbered 13,548, 1,639 of whom were journalists. Reuters had offices in 198 cities in 86 countries.[21]

As has been noted above, the value of information is based on not only utility and speed but also quality. So using Reuters as a case study for the value of international news in transnational economic relations, it is important to examine how Reuters sought to enhance the value of its financial services by increasing the quality of the information it sold.

By 1994, Reuters was following a competitor in the financial information services business, Bloomberg, in recognizing that information supplied in multimedia form on its computer terminals was the most adequate means of providing service that was of high quality and velocity. The company's computer multimedia service was Reuters Financial Television (RFTV), which was launched in Europe in 1994 and in the United States in 1995. Live television is the ultimate form of valuable information in terms of speed and quality. This point was emphasized by Reuters's top editor, Mark Wood, who described the new service in a company publication:

> RFTV is digital television for the PC window. It is NOT conventional television but information in video format. It is switched on only when there is information to relate and then turned off. This is much appreciated by its users who say they do not like being distracted by constant television. The principle is that we provide live coverage of events that might affect the financial markets. This means that customers are regularly in possession of important information 30-60 seconds before it appears in written news alert.[22]

The idea was summed up more succinctly by the press release announcing the start of the service in the United States: "You can't get faster than live."[23]

As will be discussed below, the variety of processes that are collectively labeled "globalization" have been facilitated by speedy, high-quality information

flows worldwide, but it is important to understand that key changes in the economic arena actually served to enhance the strategic role of communication
enterprises such as Reuters. For example, Reuters could not have become the
player in global money markets that it was by 1994 without the collapse of the
Bretton Woods system and the return of floating exchange rates. It was provided with even more opportunities by the liberalization and computerization
of stock markets in North America and Europe. Similarly, financial information was in greater demand as budget deficits got larger in the 1970s and
1980s and trading in government bonds increased. The expanding U.S. government securities market was especially rewarding for Reuters's competitor,
Dow-Jones Telerate. That company began in 1969 as Telerate Systems, Inc.,
the first company to distribute commercial paper rates electronically. In 1974
Telerate entered a partnership with Cantor Fitzgerald to disseminate U.S.
Treasury prices. In 1987 the company broadened its coverage to include the
equities markets, and it was acquired by the Dow Jones and Company Inc.,
another business information firm, in 1990.[24] By 1995 Telerate's interactive
terminals supplied statistical, graphic and textual information in a comprehensive range of global financial interactions, including foreign exchange
markets, corporate and government bonds, swaps and derivatives, international fixed-income, and U.S. government securities. It was also supplying an
automated trading system for U.S. Treasury securities in amounts of less than
$5 million. The service, the Daiwa Odd-Lot Machine, was developed in 1991
by Daiwa Securities America.

In turn, allowing actual trading via the computer screens of Reuter, Telerate
or another financial information company (a feature of liberalization) alters the
nature of markets significantly. One of the most glaring effects of trading by
computer, as opposed to on the floor, happened at the London Stock Exchange
after October 27, 1986, the day known as "The Big Bang." On that day restrictions that kept foreign firms out of London's financial markets were lifted, fixed
brokerage commissions were ended, and electronic stock trading was permitted. "The Big Bang" seemed like a fitting nomenclature because it was seemingly the beginning of a new global financial universe. Two years after "The Big
Bang," *The Wall Street Journal* reported how the change to electronic trading
caused members of the London Stock Exchange to lose money:

> Before computers, they would handle big orders—and make prof-
> its—by playing a delicate game of hints and winks on the exchange
> floor, taking pains not to reveal too much about their order's size.
> Suddenly all that information was laid out starkly on a computer
> screen. Knowing the size of orders to buy and sell enables traders to
> anticipate short-term price trends and price their orders accord-

ingly. But this also narrows the spread between bid and asked prices, eroding trading gains.[25]

According to George Hayter, the man who oversaw the automation of the London Stock Exchange, global financial information networks can, and have, displaced the communication function of traditional exchanges. This has meant that markets have become more transparent, brokers fees have gone down, brokers have even been eliminated, the volume of trading has increased and markets have got more volatile. Exchanges have had to reconsider their traditional functions, and (as in the case of GLOBEX) exchanges have even had to enter pacts with financial information networks.[26]

GLOBALIZATION

The case of Reuters is a useful illustration of how technology, market forces, and a communication and information company interact with one another. What should be clear by now is that what has produced the so-called global "information economy" is a combination of factors, working with and upon each other. To say that new communication technologies were the main cause would be to go the route of technological determinism, because specific changes in economic policy had to take place in order for the technology to be exploited by an actor such as Reuters. Similarly, economic liberalization in such a technological environment can often produce unforeseen consequences and uncertainty.

Because of this mixture of technological, economic and policy forces has been complex, producing a conceptual framework for understanding change in the global economic environment has been difficult. In the 1970s the concept of "post-industrial" society became a label for the new social environment in which new communication technologies enabled a majority of the workforce to be employed in service industries, in contrast to heavy industry or agriculture.[27] In the 1980s "globalization" became the popular term for such economic transformations on a transnational scale.

Before dealing with globalization, it is important for purposes of clarity to examine more carefully why technology has been so powerful a factor in economic change. In the 1970s the communication scholar, Colin Cherry,[28] accounted for this by explaining that the telecommunications technologies that are the foundation of post-industrial society have a special capacity to spawn increased capabilities and services. Unlike some other sectors of production, telecommunications is very *regenerative*—the more its quality improves, the more possibilities it creates for newer services, and this in turn enhances the demand for telecommunications.[29] This point can be illustrated by the example:

Telephone → Telematics → Databases → TBDF (Transborder Data Flow)

Here the basic invention of the telephone eventually leads to the technology of telematics, the merging of telecommunications and computers. Telematics came about because words, numbers and figures could be stored on digital computers instead of only on paper and this stored information can be relayed over telephone lines because the 1s and 0s of the computer can be converted to tones, which, after being sent by telephone, are converted back at the other end by another computer. This new capability allows information to be collected in a central place from many remote locations. Moreover, this information can be easily updated over time as well as tapped in parts (or combinations of its parts) to suit the needs of those having access to it. This is the essence of a database. These databases have led to TBDF (Trans-Border Data Flow), the processing and instantaneous relaying of large volumes of information of all kinds across international borders. Telematics technology is enhanced to create TBDF through the invention of satellites that facilitate telecommunication worldwide. What is very significant about satellites is that, unlike microwaves and cables, the cost of relays do not rise exponentially the longer the distance being covered. So communication between Ottawa and Jamaica, for example, would cost as much as communication between Ottawa and Caracas because the two foreign locations fall within the "footprint" of the same satellite.

At each stage of the example, telephone lines are being used. This technology is enhanced to create an entirely different service at each stage. And, because there are so many more uses for the telephone, the demand for this technology has increased.

This regenerative character of telecommunications is one of the most significant spurs of the rapid expansion of the service, or *tertiary*, sector in Western industrialized states in the 1960s, '70s and '80s. Media enterprises, such as the Associated Press and Rupert Murdoch's News Corporation, profited from computers and telematics because they enhanced the efficient collection and dissemination of news. Companies such as Dun & Bradstreet and Reuters collected and stored information on databases for customized sale to any client with the ability to pay. TBDF technology enabled American Express, for example, to not only make its credit card business global and more efficient but has facilitated its entry into a variety of other services such as international insurance and investment banking.

Services such as these have accounted for a steadily increasing proportion of trade, GNP and jobs in the OECD countries since the 1960s. The proportion of workers in the service sector in the Common Market area in 1960 was 39.5 percent, and this figure rose to 47.6 percent in 1973[30] and to about 59 percent in 1986[31]. Similarly, the OECD found that between 1960 and 1977 exports of information services alone rose annually by 25 percent from Japan, 19 percent for West Germany, 16 percent from Canada, 12 percent from France and the United States, and 11 percent from Britain.[32] By 1986 services were worth one quarter of the $2 trillion annual value of world trade.[33]

The idea of national and global "information superhighways" is where the notions of post-industrialism and globalization intersect. Both concepts are based on the idea that creation and use of communication technologies produce profound consequences for the ways societies organize work, business management, government, and other social activities, such as education. And, as noted above, in some ways globalization can be described as post-industrialism on a global scale. A similar straightforward definition of the concept is one that puts emphasis on the very transparent affects of new communication capabilities and calls globalization a term that merely "implies increasing volume and expanding scope of interactions among a broad range of actors in the international system, as well as a greater degree of interdependence resulting from this interconnectivity."[34] But a more thoughtful and better researched definition of globalization is that it is a "social process in which the constraints of geography on social and cultural arrangements recede and in which people become increasingly aware that they are receding."[35] Beyond the simplistic idea that globalization should be viewed as a good thing because it is the product of technological progress are questions about global inequality and power. Waters does a good job of articulating how globalization should be viewed in relation to these issues. He notes:

> The concept of globalization is an obvious object for ideological suspicion because, like modernization, a predecessor and related concept, it appears to justify the spread of Western culture and of capitalist society by suggesting that there are forces operating beyond human control that are transforming the world. . . . Globalization is the direct consequence of the expansion of European culture across the planet via settlement, colonization and cultural mimesis. It is also bound up intrinsically with the pattern of capitalist development as it has ramified through political and cultural arenas. However, it does not imply that every corner of the planet must become Westernized and capitalist but rather that every set of social arrangements must establish its position in relation to the capitalist West—to use [Roland] Robertson's term, it must relativize itself.[36]

Waters is very careful to emphasize that globalization refers to a more profound change than the internationalization of exchanges. It is about a sharing of symbolic meaning at the global level. Shared symbols are at the core of the concept of culture, therefore globalization involves a profound cultural shift, a change that can be called an "intensification of global consciousness." Evidence of this, according to Waters, is that "we redefine military-political issues in terms of a 'world order'; or economic issues in terms of an 'international recession'; or marketing issues in terms of 'world' products (e.g. the 'world car'); or religious issues in terms of ecumenism; or citizenship issues in terms of 'human rights'; or issues of pollution and purification in terms of 'saving the planet.'"[37]

This sharing of symbolic meaning is what I have referred to in another book as exercising the "power of information."[38] By having the "power of communication" (control of communication technologies) some state and non-state actors in the international system are able to exercise the power of information, strategically shaping the character of international relations in their own interest by controlling what others should think about and how they should think about them. An example of this at work is the propagation of the very technologically deterministic idea that the whole world should be connected to "information superhighways" that would be generators of wealth and intellectual enlightenment. Perhaps the most prominent promoter of a National Information Infrastructure (NII) and Global Information Infrastructure (GII) in the early 1990s was Vice-President Al Gore of the United States. In a speech before the International Telecommunication Union (ITU) in March 1994, Gore explained what global information superhighways would do.

> These highways—or more accurately, networks of distributed intelligence—will allow us to share information, to connect, and to communicate as a global community. From these connections we will derive robust and sustainable economic progress, strong democracies, better solutions to global and local environmental challenges, improved health care, and—ultimately—a greater sense of shared stewardship of our small planet.
>
> The Global Information Infrastructure will help educate our children and allow us to exchange ideas within a community and among nations. It will be a means by which families and friends will transcend the barriers of time and distance. It will make possible a global information marketplace, where consumers can buy or sell products. . . .[39]

Notice how the value of information, that we explored above, is subconsciously or consciously tied to speed through the metaphor that is invoked to describe the new national and international telematics technologies—"information Superhighway." It evokes images of many people traveling to many locations at very fast speeds.

But the World Bank researchers who quoted Vice-President Gore in complimentary terms pointed out elsewhere in their study that

> Most developing countries suffer from a dearth of readily available, reliable information—with adverse consequences for achieving their numerous developmental objectives. Worse still, the spread of information technology across all types of industries and services in industrialized countries is so fast and pervasive—with consequent improvements in price competitiveness, design, and quality of products—that developing countries find it increasingly difficult to compete internationally. . . . Researchers predict that the wave of technology sweeping the industrialized world will widen the gap between the rich and poor countries.[40]

These contradictions between the hopes of an Al Gore and international realities reinforce Ferguson's belief that the rhetoric of globalization "is as much concerned about what *should be* as what *is.*"[41]

The contradictions actually mean that globalization is actually a misnomer, the label is applied to intensified transnational exchanges not across the entire world necessarily, but in a few fractions of it. Some have yielded to this fact by calling the reality "uneven globalization."[42] Seen in this manner, the term *globalization* can also be viewed as an invocation to those parts of the world that are out of the loop to be like those that are. But, in terms of economic and technological change, the two decades between 1970 and 1990 have been remarkable in how the invocations of post-industrialism and globalization have not caused most of the deprived regions to catch up. As Reuters's service to business clients expanded in the 1970s, the major sources of its revenues became concentrated in a few capitalist regions at the core of the so-called expanding "global economy." In 1977, when the company's revenue exceeded £50 million for the first time, 16 countries, mostly in Europe and North America, each produced revenue exceeding £500,000. "In other words, although Reuters maintained a presence nearly everywhere, its prosperity depended upon the Westernized capitalist world," Donald Read, the writer of Reuters's official history, observed. "Its economic services were particularly designed to serve that world."[43]

What talk of globalization when no real globalization exists can serve to do is actually shift attention away from understanding the roots of division in the international system. The unequal distribution of technology and related services in the world not only means that many might be outside the post-industrial economy, but that they are at a strategic disadvantage when negotiating with those who are. At the beginning of the 1980s political economy scholars Rita Cruise O'Brien and G. K. Helleiner were noting that research on the role of information in international politics, in the wake of the information society, seemed to have been displaced. They pointed out that "the literature on international politics and relevant social science literature on information still examine the *effects* of increased communication and information flow as if they were simply accelerating the creation of global 'interdependence,' without considering the implication of unequal informational access—either for the efficiency and equity of international market functioning or for the creation of new forms of asymmetry in international bargaining capacity."[44] Focusing on the role of information in international negotiation, they said, "Differential access to information can . . . be a major element in the determination of the distribution of the world's income."[45] Strategic information—such as data collected by remote sensing satellites on the distribution of the world's resources, and data on markets—was all concentrated in computers, companies and institutions in the rich, industrialized countries.[46] Based on the observation of the World Bank researchers quoted above, not much had changed in 15 years.

CONCLUSIONS

What does all of the above say about how global news flows have appeared on the agenda of international politics? There are a number of propositions.

The first is that we get a more refined understanding of the nature of global news flows when we appreciate the fact that they mirror the contours of international economic exchanges. This chapter provides evidence that international news flows are antecedent to patterns of trade and investment. In turn, the character of international economic exchange has been shaped by historical occurrences, including colonialism and imperialism, wars, the cold war, the end of the Bretton Woods system of fixed exchange rates, the government debt crisis, the end of the cold war, the end of dictatorship, and the change to market economies in countries that were formerly communist.

The second proposition is that while the configuration of the international economy explains the broad outline of the global news system, it is of limited use in telling us about the evolution in content and value of international news over time. For such an explanation we must look at the forces that give international news its value. They are all the developments that enhance utility, speed, and quality. New technologies have done this, especially through making the flow of information quicker. Evolutions in the nature of domestic and international economies have also done this by enhancing the utility of certain types of information, especially financial information. The shift from industrial to post-industrial economies has meant that specific types of information with a high value-added component (e.g. currency rates and market analyses) are more valuable than others (e.g. mere spot news in text form).

Our third proposition is that in the context of post-industrialism and globalization, the international news system has been transformed to what is in reality an international *information* system. This is a more correct label for two reasons. The first is that (as we saw in the case study of Reuters) the changed international political economy has required an evolution in the character and service of all international news agencies that hope to survive. To enhance their utility in the changed international environment they have had to increasingly diversify their output into information services with higher value-added content than mere spot news. Second, the ability of new technologies to drastically enhance the quality and velocity of information and to personalize the distribution of such information has deposed the old concept of "news." News media have derived power from their ability to determine the definition of news (as we noted in Chapter 1). The new technological capabilities have undermined the news media's authority in this area.

In the United States news organizations responded to the challenge by questioning what non-news people have decided to call "news" (for example, on the "news" groups on the Internet) and have noted that newspapers' versions of news is purer than the new versions because their news is *edited* and compiled according to various journalistic standards, such as impartiality. "A lot of what's passed off as news on-line isn't really news at all, as most people have come to understand that term," declared a columnist in *The Wall Street Journal.* "One unfortunate side effect of the digital revolution, in fact, has been the distortion and debasement of the concept of news."[47] Such defensiveness reveals the extent to which online communication technologies—which give all who own them the chance to be mass communicators—threaten traditional bastions of power.[48]

These three propositions, therefore, are the key links between global news flows, post-industrialism and globalization. The fortunes of the international news system are tied to the ecology of the international economy. We get a clearer picture of what has happened in the four areas identified and examined in this book if we look at them within the context of these economic processes. The so-called "information revolution" is not merely a construct of technological development, therefore, but part of a more profound dynamic in which demands on the international information system change and transformations in the information system themselves act on the world political economy.

This relationship between the world political economy and the news media has profound implications for the ideological context of political discourse about mass media, information and journalists. All political economies embody certain assumptions about the role of the media. In the case of postindustrialism and uneven globalization it has been tempting for those with the *power of information* to invoke liberal-democratic ecumenism. Freedom of information is a hallmark of the *ideal type* of liberal democracy, and it is therefore understandable why it has been assumed that the new information environment created by postindustrialism would be inclined to be liberal-democratic. Indeed, the diffusion of technologies needed for post-industrial production has been linked to the spread of liberal-democratic civil society.

In this book the term "liberal-democratic" is applied to a theory that regards democracy as self-government through reasoned choice, whereby minority views have the potential of becoming those of the majority through rational persuasion. Prescription by autocracy is considered to be unhealthy. A cornerstone of this democratic theory is the quest for truth which is achieved by: the competition of facts and ideas in a free marketplace; the continuing entry of new ideas and facts; freedom of each individual or interest to express their point of view; the tolerance of bias and eccentricity; and consideration of minority views. The theory, therefore, allows a central role for the press in the quest for truth. The three major functions of the press that can be identified under the theory are: (a) a channel for information; (b) a watch dog on government to stem the abuse of power; and (c) a conduit for the two-way flow of views between citizens and the State. Therefore, liberal-democratic political systems are those which sustain Siebert, Peterson and Schramm's Libertarian theory of the press and its derivative, the Social Responsibility theory.[49]

UNESCO, the ITU and World Bank all placed emphasis on information technology diffusion as a means of making poor regions richer. A World Bank document circulated via the World Wide Web in 1995 began by succinctly stating the assumptions about the impact the diffusion of new technologies will have:

> Revolutionary advances in information technology reinforce economic and social changes that are transforming business and society. A new kind of economy—the information economy—is emerging where trade and investment are global and firms compete with knowledge, networking and agility on a global basis. A corresponding new society is also emerging with pervasive information capabilities that make it substantially different from an industrial society: much more competitive, more democratic, less centralized, less stable, more able to address individual needs, and friendlier to the environment.[50]

It should be noted that the idea of the new technologies helping to promote liberal democracy by empowering more people is a step beyond the approaches to technology diffusion that were voiced during the NWICO years. Back then technology diffusion was seen as a means of rectifying unequal communication capabilities and as a way to make international news flows more equal. Such thinking was at the genesis of such program's as UNESCO's IPDC (International Program for the Development of Communication) and the United States Telecommunications Training Institute (USTTI), and the various development initiatives of the ITU. The coming of personal computer technology and the end of the Cold War meant that technological diffusion could have even loftier ideals.

However, as the succeeding chapters will reveal, the role of the news media in international politics is not that simple. While UNESCO's new policies promoting "independent, plural" media systems can be viewed as a product of a shift to liberal democracy (as we will see in chapter 4), there are other major contradictions. For example, initial indications were that some of the world's fastest-growing economies and those very linked to the "information economy" were run by governments very hostile to liberal-democratic notions of press freedom (e.g. Singapore). The information age also did not automatically result in less harassment and fewer murders of journalists, nor in increased optimism by human rights and press freedom groups about the future prospects of protecting the physical safety of journalists. Let us explore the contradictions.

THE DEATH OF PROPAGANDA

A prominent dimension of the political discourse on the role of news in international relations has been about its strategic value. In other words, it has been a discussion about propaganda. The discussion has been very difficult because "propaganda" is an elusive concept at several levels. The first problem comes in reaching agreement about what should be defined as propaganda. As the cliché goes, one man's propaganda is another man's truth; but what most definitions of propaganda have in common is their focus on intent.

American mass media scholar L. John Martin defines propaganda as "a systematic attempt through mass communications to influence the thinking and thereby the behavior of people in the interest of some in-group."[1] However, such a definition that leaves room for the notion that propaganda can be worthwhile is rare. In international relations, propaganda is most often associated with malicious intent.

"When used as an invective, international propaganda has become identified with acts intended to change, destabilize, or subvert other countries' political, social, and economic systems by use of the mass media," says Jon T. Powell, communication professor at Northern Illinois University in the United States. "The information that comes to be categorized as propaganda depends upon the political and social philosophies or ideologies involved."[2]

Similarly, legal scholar Elizabeth Downey defines propaganda as "hostile communications," saying that "propaganda refers to communications about one state sent across international borders. . . . Note that even communications that are seemingly neutral may be objectionable to the subject of the communications or the receiving state, if it considers them dangerous, subversive, distorted or false."[3]

While both definitions acknowledge the very subjective, ideological nature of the term, they are problematical because they confine propaganda to interstate relations. What about propaganda use against and by political entities that are not states, such as national groups, non-governmental organizations and intergovernmental bodies? For example, this approach would be unhelpful in examining propaganda in relation to the Palestinians, a nation (at least by 1996) still without a state.

Other realities of world politics present different problems in defining propaganda. For example, propaganda has been defined by the UN Committee on the Peaceful Uses of Outer Space (COPUOS) as a hostile act, such as

1. Broadcasts making war propaganda which provoke the mentality of the people of receiver countries towards the initiation of war;
2. Broadcasts which incite subversive activities against the political institutions of receiver countries;
3. Broadcasts which slander receiver countries or their representative organs and injure the dignity and honour of receiver countries;
4. Broadcasts which interfere in the internal affairs of receiver countries by criticizing their policies and incite the people not to follow their policies;
5. Broadcasts which violate basic human rights, are offensive to the race, belief, religion etc., of the receiver countries' people.[4]

This approach is inadequate in accounting for the mass media activities of the South African apartheid regime. In response to international condemnation, the South African government embarked on a campaign to improve and maintain a good image. Among the themes of the South African campaign were the view that Blacks in South Africa were better off than Blacks in African countries where there was majority rule, and that economic sanctions against South Africa would hurt the very people they were supposed to help. The media and public relations campaigns of the apartheid regime were condemned as "propaganda" by the UN General Assembly in several resolutions. However, the behavior of the South Africans did not fit neatly into any of the definitions given above. This problem raises the question of whether the focus on intent directed against external actors does not severely restrict our approach to propaganda. As the South African case illustrated, the term can be given to the deceptive manipulation of information in cases where no malice against a clearly defined external target is involved. This is not to say that South Africa did not commit hostile acts against its neighbors, including activities that fit into the traditional definitions of propaganda, but there was also a system of information diffusion used to justify its system of apartheid at home, and such activities can also be described as propagandistic.

Because that focus on malicious intent against clearly defined targets is so limiting, the "structural" approach to propaganda is a welcomed contribution to the discussion of international propaganda. An example of this method of interpretation comes from legal scholar Adeno Addis. His definition of, and discourse on, propaganda is different from popular approaches in two key ways. First, he does not assume that there is deliberate intent, but states that certain communicative practices can have the "functional consequence" of being propagandistic. Second, he does not always link what he terms propaganda to specific hostile acts. Propaganda can be "structural," in the dynamic of communicative relations between states or nonstate entities.

> Propaganda is a structural or preconceived, systematic manipulation of symbols, aimed at promoting uniform behavior of social groups congruent with the specific interests of the communicator. This communication may be characterized by either of the following: (1) It is intentionally false, in which case it is called disinformation; or (2) It is selectively false, in which case one might refer to it as distorted or unbalanced information. In addition, the following desired outcomes or functional consequences distinguish propaganda from other forms of communication: (1) It might be intended to undermine the legitimacy of social and political institutions of a community or a nation, in which case one might refer to it as hostile or subversive; or (2) because of the selective (distorted) and one-sided nature of the communication, it might have the functional consequence of undermining the cultural and social structures of a community and hence undermine the community's capacity for self-determination.[5]

STRUCTURAL PROPAGANDA

A structural approach to propaganda shifts the discussion about propaganda from being attached to the discourse on peace and security to a link to the discourse on the right to self-determination. In order to make this shift there must be a considerable refinement of the definition of propaganda. The result is a rather new set of questions and debates. They make propaganda seem even more problematical in the context of international relations, but, at the same time, they can potentially remove the layers of rhetoric and hypocrisy that have masked consideration of the issue for so many years.

An example of such hypocrisy has been the tendency of powerful governments to scold less powerful ones for trying to restrict press freedom whenever those weaker countries criticize uneven global news flows. But from the days of the international news cartel, those same powerful governments have been aware of the strategic nature of news flows and the dominance of such relays by a few countries. For example, Roderick Jones of Reuters, in a speech at the Royal Institute of International Affairs in 1929, noted that

Americans and other people talk a great deal about the 'Reuter monopoly.' ... The Americans realize that the presentation of news from an American angle, not only American news but news of the world generally, is calculated to create a state of mind more favourable to American trade in the far east than the state of mind created or maintained if the people of the Far East are dependent in the main upon a service which either is British in its substance, or, in so far as the substance is foreign, British in direction.[6]

In comparison, the sentiments of Associated Press executive Kent Cooper illustrate an American perspective on this period of European dominance of cables and the European-dominated international news agency cartel.

In precluding the Associated Press from disseminating news abroad, Reuters and Havas served three purposes: (1) they kept out Associated Press competition; (2) they were free to present American news disparagingly to the United States if they presented it at all; (3) they could present news of their own countries most favorably and without it being contradicted [sic]. Their own countries always glorified [sic]. This was done by reporting great advances at home in English and French civilizations, the benefits of which would, of course, be bestowed on the world.[7]

Similarly, to the extent that international news from the North American and European elite press and international wire services is said to distort reality—by concentrating on negative news from poor, nonwhite countries—their operations can be described as propagandistic. Johan Galtung and Richard Vincent, two scholars from the University of Hawaii, Manoa, argue that an ideology called *occidental cosmology* determines why these media tend to concentrate on negative events in those countries, such as coups and earthquakes, and are reluctant to report about such negative occurrences in context. Their description reads like a description of a propaganda campaign:

... such reporting is detached from its context, generated by the news paradigm rather than by social reality, projected onto the periphery country as typical of such countries, and not seen in its structural context as partly created and constantly reproduced by strong forces in the relation to the industrialized world in general and to the First World in particular. This type of reporting is probably mainly serving one function: confirming to people in center countries what a miserable life people have in those periphery countries, and consequently how fortunate people in center countries really are for not being there or being members of periphery countries.[8]

The occidental cosmology is described as consisting of six themes that are expressed in this kind of faulty news coverage. These themes are:

1. A view of the world as being made up of only three parts—"Center, Periphery, and an outer periphery of Evil"
2. The belief that progress is normal and what comes from the outer periphery of evil is a deviance from such normality
3. "[A] tendency to present reality in a fragmented, scattered way, dividing it into small bits that can be understood and 'digested' one at a time"
4. A view that people are different from nature and should triumph over it
5. A view of people in two-dimensional terms of either winners or losers
6. A view of humans as subordinate to the supernatural—a Supreme Being (in religious terms) or "Supreme Value" (in secular terms).[9]

The reason why Galtung and Vincent's critique is worthy of consideration here is because it illustrates where ideology, global news flows and propaganda intersect as problems in international politics. Galtung and Vincent do not use the term "propaganda" to describe the consequences of such reporting and power relations, but Addis is concerned with the same questions and does. Because the news of the international, privately held and run media "is so selective, unbalanced, and one-sided that it produces a wholly inaccurate and incomplete understanding of the communities and situations at issue," Addis considers their work to be propagandistic, even though they enjoy the façade of being objective.

> Thus, Western media tends to cover developing countries from a point of view which sees the latter as culturally primitive, administratively chaotic, inefficient, and seriously backward. From such stereotypes flows a selection of information tending to reinforce those views. A developing country becomes of interest to the international media mainly when it offers personalities like Amin or Bokassa, or events like a natural disaster or a coup.[10]

The propagation of this type of information then has the political consequence of creating misinformed policies by the powerful countries, policies that can hurt the people from developing nations. Also, because the populations of small, poor countries get most international news from the transnational media, they stand to receive inaccurate portraits of themselves and others who are like them.

What is the solution to the problem of structural propaganda? While the political and legal decisions about international propaganda—as evidenced by League of Nations and UN resolutions and conventions (to be discussed below)—were based on trying to get offending nations to stop the practice, structural propaganda, because of its very nature, demands a different approach. It has been suggested that structural propaganda should be countered by arrangements giving developing nations more access to the powerful international media. Such access "would enable them to communicate their version of the events, to correct the error inherent in structural propaganda, and to supplement incomplete information."[11] Another suggested solution is an international right of correction and an international mass media council to investigate complaints.

The weaknesses of the proposed solutions illustrate the magnitude of propaganda's place as a problem in international relations. The very definition of structural propaganda suggests that it can never be reduced to specific incidents to which replies can be formulated. Also, given the intense hostility by the powerful transnational media to all proposals for regulating the work of reporters, it is very unlikely that any government-created body or rules would be taken seriously. However, as pointed out above, the concept of structural propaganda brings a degree of honesty to the international discourse about propaganda. The tussle and rhetoric between the Europeans and Americans earlier in the century over the control of news flows is evidence of how aware media and government officials in these countries were of how news could be strategic. So it is unfair and hypocritical to summarily dismiss claims by small countries for redress of the imbalance in global communication as all attempts to restrict press freedom.

Faced with the inability to change news practices in the powerful countries, all that is left for those who believe in the existence of structural propaganda is to argue for the powerless to have a place in the "international marketplace of ideas." But their getting such access would contradict their very position in the structure of global information flows. Is it not that the powerful are so described because they have control over the information and the weak are so because they do not?

Proving that all forms of propaganda are as damaging as their critics claim is problematical. But the burden of proof that should be the rational foundation of any effort to end propagandistic practices is especially difficult in the case of structural propaganda. While a specific government propaganda campaign can produce identifiable consequences over a short period of time, who can prove the consequences of structural propaganda? Who can prove in a systematic way that years of Western news media propagating stereotypes of Africans and Asians created specific damaging effects? Even if it is argued that racial prejudice in North America and Europe is the result of exposure to negative stereotypes, where is the proof that these stereotypes are solely the result of news-reporting practices?

So, although the emphasis on how mass media frame certain countries, issues and groups is a valuable contribution to the discourse about international propaganda, the discussion comes to a stop at the cul-de-sac of the international power structure. The new technology of the Internet, with its potential to expand the number of persons engaged in transnational conversations, offers some hope. But there must be healthy skepticism about such a "global village" occurring, because the wider access to new technologies in the rich countries and the unaffordability of such technologies in the poor ones can combine to ensure that the "global village" is still dominated by elite conversations, ideas and prejudices.

INTERNATIONAL POLITICAL AND LEGAL DISCOURSES ON PROPAGANDA

From its origins in the Congregation of the Propaganda, a committee of cardinals in charge of foreign missions, founded by Pope Gregory XV in 1622, right up to the time of the modern states system, "propaganda" was not a pejorative term. It got pejorative connotations with World Wars I and II. However, L. John Martin, who has written one of the most comprehensive histories of the international legal discourse on propaganda, identifies two international treaties in the pre–World War I period, at the bilateral level, that specifically proscribed behavior that could be described as propagandistic— an 1801 treaty between Russia and France and an 1881 treaty between Austria-Hungary and Serbia.[12] But in the twentieth century there has been considerable multilateral attention to propaganda and efforts to create international laws against it.

Two factors account for the appearance of propaganda on the agenda of international politics: (a) the end of secret diplomacy; and (b) the invention of mass media technologies.

The international political process was opened up by the end of secret diplomacy in the late 1800s. As public consent for policies became more critical, the more important it became to sway public opinion by means of persuasion. As the technologies for the transnational dissemination of news and other types of information improved, so did the potential effectiveness of propaganda as a tool for conducting international relations. The more senses to which a medium appealed, the more effective it was for propaganda purposes. For example, print only appealed to sight, and radio appealed only to hearing, but television was the most effective tool because it appealed to both sight and hearing.

Swedish international communication scholar Edward Ploman's seminal collection, *International Law Governing Communication and Information: A Collection of Basic Documents*,[13] does not identify international law regarding propaganda as a topic in its own right in either the table of contents or the index. It is subsumed under laws regarding "Security and Disarmament" and "Media Regulation." This is symbolic of how propaganda generally has appeared in international political and legal discourses—as a phenomenon subsidiary to larger problems, usually maintaining the peace, and often propaganda is considered a factor promoting international friction.

The "International Convention Concerning The Use of Broadcasting In The Cause Of Peace" was the closest the League of Nations got to creating a body of international law that attempted to specifically proscribe international propaganda. It was signed by 28 states on September 23, 1936, and went into force on April 2, 1938.[14] Article 1 stated that the signatory states "mutually undertake to prohibit and, if occasion arises, to stop without delay the broadcasting within their respective territories of any transmission which to the detriment of good international understanding is of such a character as to incite the population of any territory to acts incompatible with the internal order or the security of a territory of [another signatory state]." Article 2 further stated that the states would "ensure that transmissions from stations within their respective territories shall not constitute an incitement either to war against another [signatory] or to acts likely to lead thereto." The subsequent articles endorsed the principles of prior restraint and undertakings to correct errors, broadcast the truth, and collaborate in the exchange of positive information. The convention recognized that not all international broadcasters were state-run, and, in Article 6, the signatories agreed to put in place domestic policies that would ensure compliance to the obligations of the document by both state and nonstate broadcasters. Article 7 identified a number of means by which disputes arising from the convention could be settled, including through the Permanent Court of International Justice, an arbitral tribunal, and the International Committee on Intellectual Cooperation.

The shortcomings of the convention began with its inadequate definition of what actions would "incite the population of any territory to acts incompatible with the internal order or the security of a territory." Presumably that would be the task of the institutions arbitrating disputes. Another weakness was in the convention's not having any penalties for violators. Also, as Finland pointed out at the time of signing, it was likely that the document would not have a very practical impact on international relations because those signing and ratifying it would be those most likely to not violate its principles even if there were no convention.[15]

Indeed, Germany did not sign the convention, and it was Nazi propaganda use in World War II, under the direction of Hitler's propaganda minister Josef Goebbels, that solidified the pejorative connotations to the term "propaganda."[16] It is understandable, therefore, why there was some sentiment at the new United Nations to curb the practice.

The foundation for the UN's approach to propaganda was laid by General Assembly Resolution 110 (II), of November 3, 1947, which echoed the 1936 convention's prohibition of hostile propaganda—still without defining it, but at least using the explicit term "propaganda." The resolution condemned "all forms of propaganda, in whatsoever country conducted, which is either designed or likely to provoke or encourage any threat to the peace, breach of the peace, or act of aggression." But most significant is the resolution's espousing the idea that has been the most characteristic of post–World War II political and legal discourses on the subject—the recognition that some types of propaganda could actually help to preserve international order and they should be promoted. It requested

> the Government of each Member to take appropriate steps within its constitutional limits:
> (a) To promote, by all means of publicity and propaganda available to them, friendly relations among nations based upon the Purposes and Principles of the Charter;
> (b) To encourage the dissemination of all information designed to give expression to the undoubted desire of all people for peace. . . .

The resolution was passed with the explicit intention of its being communicated to the 1948 United Nations Conference on Freedom of Information. In its Final Act that historic conference not only specifically endorsed UN Resolution 110 (II), but also repeated verbatim the description of undesirable propaganda being information "either designed or likely to provoke or encourage any threat to the peace, breach of the peace, or act of aggression."

In the Final Act the discourse on propaganda was expanded in four ways. First, the labeling of undesirable propaganda was expanded to include false or distorted news and the idea of how such unwanted propaganda threatened the international order was made more explicit. So Resolution 2 of the Final Act condemned "all propaganda either designed or likely to provoke or encourage any threat to the peace, breach of the peace, or act of aggression, and all distortion and falsification of news through whatever channels, private or governmental, since such activities can only promote misunderstanding and mistrust between the peoples of the world and thereby endanger the lasting peace which the United Nations is consecrated to maintain."

Second, the discourse on propaganda was made more specific by the Final Act's identifying the news media—not just government-owned broadcasters or other media—as being the most important in the battle against unwanted propaganda. And Nazi and Fascist propaganda specifically were identified as being particularly offensive. So Resolution 2 stated that the conference

> Appeals vigorously to the personnel of the Press and other agencies of information of the countries of the world, and to those responsible for their activities, to serve the aims of friendship, understanding and peace by accomplishing their task in a spirit of accuracy, fairness and responsibility;

> Expresses its profound conviction that only organs of information in all countries of the world that are free to seek and to disseminate the truth, and thus to carry out their responsibility to the people, can greatly contribute to the counteracting of nazi, fascist or any other propaganda of aggression of racial, national and religious discrimination and to the prevention of recurrence of nazi, fascist, or any other aggression; and

> Therefore recommends that all countries take within their respective territories the measures which they consider necessary to give effect to this resolution.

The third point follows from the previous because it is about the Final Act's attention to propaganda instilling racial hatred. This theme would become a constant feature of United Nations political and legal discourse in later years, especially in the late 1970s and 1980s when the propaganda of the South African apartheid regime was condemned and the United Nations Department of Public Information was mobilized to counteract it.

Fourth, as did General Assembly Resolution 110 (II), the Final Act recognized a role for desirable propaganda. But the language of the Final Act made explicit the idea that such good propaganda fit into the liberal-democratic notion that a free and open flow of information fostered a marketplace of ideas in which the good would be accepted and bad rejected. Therefore, Resolution 4 stated that

> Considering that there are in some countries media of information which disseminate racial and national hatred,

> The United Nations Conference on Freedom of Information Recommends that the Governments of such countries should:

(a) Encourage the widest possible dissemination of free information through a diversity of sources as the best safeguard against the creation of racial and national hatred and prejudice;
(b) Encourage, in consultation with organizations or journalists, suitable and effective non-legislative measures against the dissemination of such hatred and prejudice; and
(c) Take, within their constitutional limits, appropriate measures to encourage the dissemination of information promoting friendly relations between races and nations based upon the purposes and principles of the United Nations Charter.

The four points identified above formed the kernel of ideas about propaganda at the United Nations and were not modified in the succeeding 50 years. All significant UN treaties, resolutions and other sources of international law either referred to General Assembly Resolution 110 (II) explicitly or repeated ideas about good and bad propaganda found in the 1948 Final Act. All that changed in the subsequent 50 years was that these ideas were directly applied to specific desiderata, such as the maintenance of human rights, ending apartheid in South Africa, and establishing rules governing transnational television broadcasting via satellite.

The International Covenant on Civil and Political Rights (1966) mentions propaganda in Article 20, stating that

1. Any propaganda for war shall be prohibited by law.
2. Any advocacy of national, racial or religious hatred that constitutes incitement to discrimination, hostility or violence shall be prohibited by law.

The 1967 Outer Space Treaty (officially called the "Treaty On Principles Governing The Activities Of States In The Exploration And Use Of Outer Space, Including The Moon And Other Celestial Bodies") mentions the 1947 resolution by name in its Preamble and says it is "applicable to outer space." This approach to propaganda also was implicit in the principles governing the operation of direct broadcast satellites set out by the General Assembly in 1982 because those principles were based on the Outer Space Treaty. Number four of the principles was that

Activities in the field of international direct television broadcasting by satellite should be conducted in accordance with international law, including the Charter of the United Nations, the Treaty on Principles Governing the Activities of States in the Exploration and Use of Outer Space, including the Moon and Other Celestial Bodies, of 27 January

1967, the relevant provisions of the International Telecommunication Convention and its Radio Regulations and of International instruments relating to friendly relations and co-operation among States and to human rights.[17]

The recognition of good propaganda is implicit in the second and third paragraphs of the list of principles, which state that Direct Broadcast Satellite (DBS) broadcasting

> should promote the free dissemination and mutual exchange of information and knowledge in cultural and scientific fields, assist in educational, social and economic development, particularly in the developing countries, enhance the qualities of life of all peoples and provide recreation with due respect to the political and cultural integrity of States.
>
> These activities should accordingly be carried out in a manner compatible with the development of mutual understanding and the strengthening of friendly relations and co-operation among all States and peoples in the interest of maintaining international peace and security.

UNESCO's Mass Media Declaration of 1978 (See Appendix 3) not only mentions Resolution 110 (II) by name, but identifies "racialism" and "apartheid" in its official title as evils to be countered by the media.[18] According to Article III,

> In countering aggressive war, racialism, apartheid and other violations of human rights which are inter alia spawned by prejudice and ignorance, the mass media by disseminating information on the aims, aspirations, cultures and needs of all peoples contribute to eliminate ignorance and misunderstanding between peoples, to make nations of a country sensitive to the needs and desires of others, to ensure the respect of the rights and dignity of all nations, all peoples and all individuals without distinction of race, sex, language, religion or nationality and to draw attention to the great evils which afflict humanity, such as poverty, malnutrition and diseases, thereby promoting the formulation by States of the policies best able to promote the reduction of international tension and the peaceful and equitable settlement of international disputes.

The prospect of regulating international propaganda by multilateral agreement was particularly contentious because it required a delicate balancing act between two significant principles of the post–World War II order—the free flow of information, and national sovereignty. A number of international instruments proclaimed freedom of information regardless of frontiers, such as Article 19 of the Universal Declaration of Human Rights, Article 10 of the European Convention on Human Rights, Article 4 of the American Declaration on the Rights and Duties of Man, and the Declaration of Principles in the Final Act of the Helsinki Conference on Security and Co-operation in Europe. But, as the United Kingdom pointed out during the deliberations of the Committee on the Peaceful Uses of Outer Space, the absolute right to freedom of information does not exist. In all countries the right is moderated by "rules and regulations, and these rules and regulations not only vary from country to country but sometimes also vary from province to province within the same State, because what is acceptable in a given community might not be acceptable in a neighbouring community, depending on variations in moral and cultural patterns."[19] These legal realities notwithstanding, the idea of regulating propaganda seemed more unviable as new technologies, such as satellites and the Internet, obviated territorial borders and national legislation.

GOOD PROPAGANDA

The idea that propaganda would become a standard means of conducting international relations was apparent within a few years after World War II. "Some weapons, such as poison gas, nations have managed to control; others have passed into their armories and become commonplace," L. John Martin concluded in 1958. "Propaganda is likely to develop into the latter type of weapon."[20] He was very right.

The early post–World War II period was the era when "public diplomacy"—or "international cultural relations"—became a standard means of conducting international relations for the states that could afford such expensive programs as the United States Information Agency (USIA), the British Council, and the Alliance Française. During the wars, the West European and North American states set up propaganda agencies only for the periods of conflict, after which time they were dismantled. Organizations devoted to "image promotion" (a euphemistic label for a subtle form of propagandistic behavior) were maintained permanently after World War II. Some were government agencies, such as the USIA, and others were funded from a mixture of government and non-government sources, such as the Alliance Française.[21]

In the early 1970s, the writer of one of the most widely used textbooks in the field of international relations, Hans Morgenthau, declared that propaganda was a major tool of states in the new age of "nationalistic universalism."[22] Morgenthau believed that modern means of mass communication (such as radio and satellites) were significant in two major ways: (a) as a means by which states tried to achieve their ends in the era of "nationalistic universalism" that characterized the post–World War II era; and (b) as a factor in the decline of diplomacy. According to Morgenthau, "While nationalism wants one nation in one state and nothing else, the nationalistic universalism of our age claims for one nation and one state the right to impose its own valuations and standards of action upon all the other nations."[23] He believed that propaganda, although not clearly understood in theory and practice, had become a major way in which states conducted relations with other states:

> Psychological warfare or propaganda joins diplomacy and military force as the third instrument by which foreign policy tries to achieve its aims. Regardless of the instrument employed, the ultimate aim of foreign policy is always the same: to promote one's interests by changing the mind of the opponent.[24]

Morgenthau also identified the efficient nature of modern international communication as one of a few factors—such as the end of secret diplomacy and the rise of "parliamentary diplomacy" (diplomacy via international conferences)—that account for the disintegration of traditional diplomacy.[25]

All international actors who enter the propaganda game do so from the belief that if they do not manage their images they can be hurt from misunderstandings of their policies and activities—or from others knowing the painful truth. For example, the UN General Assembly Information Committee's chairman, Miguel Albornoz of Ecuador, said in an address to the committee in 1982 that 80 percent of UN activities were in the economic and social field and that the other 20 percent were political; however, most information about the UN carried in the news media ignored its achievements in the field of development. This was an unfair way of portraying the UN's activities. He said he was not advocating propaganda, but a New World Information and Communication Order (NWICO), consistent with the mandate of the General Assembly.[26] At that time the UN was considering investing in means of international communication of its own. The committee considered a report that estimated the cost of a satellite system for the UN at $175 million. Another report before the committee examined the possibility of the UN having its own shortwave broadcasting system. It was estimated that it would cost about $28 million to build four regional production and transmission centers and about $12.5 million annually to operate the system. UN satellites and enhanced broadcasting capabilities would have been an unacceptable strain on the UN's budget. As an alternative, the committee recommended that the UN continue renting transmitters but that there should be daily broadcasts.[27]

South Africa's Propaganda War

The UN's propaganda war with South Africa, over the two main issues of the occupation of Namibia and minority apartheid rule, is a clear example of how the propaganda issue had evolved as a problem in international relations by the 1980s.[28] Propaganda had become more than merely one state broadcasting to another. It was a complex game involving persuasion through government agencies and the general mass media, it was overt and covert, it was financially intense, and it was a clear indication that the UN had reached the point where it realized that seeking prohibition of propagandistic behavior was futile and the best multilateral response was to enter the propaganda game on the other side.

In the so-called Muldergate scandal of 1978 it was revealed that the South African government maintained a slush fund of over $74 million to propagate its views, win friends and influence public opinion across the world, especially in the United States.[29] Included in this propaganda project were secret funds to a favorable newspaper in South Africa, *The Citizen,* and financial assistance for an unsuccessful attempt by an American publisher to buy the then-beleaguered *Washington Star* newspaper, the smaller of the two dailies published in Washington, D.C. The government also reportedly tried to buy into the international video news service UPITN.[30] The scandal got its name from the then information minister, Connie Mulder, whose Department of Information directed the campaign of covert and illegal activities that were reported to number in the range of between 150 and 200. Despite the revelations of financial impropriety, the National party government was not brought down and no person implicated in the scandal went to jail. The South African government's propaganda campaign also continued well up to the demise of the minority government in the early 1990s.[31] Journalists from other countries were given free trips to South Africa and expected to write favorable reports, lobbyists and public relations firms were hired in Washington, D.C. to maintain a good image of South Africa with the U.S. government and public, and the white racist government even recruited a black cricket team from the West Indies to break the international sporting ban and play a national South African team.

South Africa's illegal occupation of the territory it called South-West Africa (named Namibia by the UN) was one reason why the government needed to pay special attention to its international image. South Africa was defending its rule over the territory in the face of a guerrilla war from the South-West Africa People's Organization (SWAPO), which was fighting for Namibian independence. It also had been put on the defensive when the International Court of Justice ruled in 1971 that South Africa's occupation was illegal, and in 1978 the UN Security Council had called for Namibian independence in Resolution 435. The South African government insisted on the withdrawal of Cuban troops from neighboring Angola as a precondition to Namibian independence.

The details of the UN's counterpropaganda initiative concerning Namibia was nothing less than a frontal assault. General Assembly resolutions set out in great detail how the UN used every means available to counter South Africa's version of events in Namibia. The strategy was in the section titled "Dissemination of information and mobilization of international public opinion in support of the immediate independence of Namibia." That section of the resolutions passed by the 43rd (1988-1989), 42nd ('87-'88), and 41st ('86-'87) General Assemblies had almost the same language each year.[32] Each resolution only mentioned the word "propaganda" once and then only in reference to "the hostile propaganda and disinformation campaign of the racist regime of South Africa." They explained how the UN would use its Department of Public Information (DPI) to produce, inter alia, booklets, exhibitions, radio and television programs, advertising, news releases, posters, "media encounters," and even maps to counteract the South African government's propaganda. But never was the term "propaganda" used as a label for the UN's activities. (See Appendix 1.)

The years of military conflict in Namibia (which involved UN nonmilitary support for SWAPO) and the international propaganda war between South Africa and the UN culminated with a plan agreed to by SWAPO, Angola, Cuba and South Africa in 1988. It required the withdrawal of Cuban forces from Angola and black majority rule in Namibia. Namibia became independent on March 21, 1990.

The General Assembly resolutions on the "Policies Of Apartheid Of The Government of South Africa" all were passed between 1986 (the 40th General Assembly) and 1989.[33] That was the period during which events relating to the eventual demise of apartheid escalated. The resolutions condemned apartheid on human rights and security grounds, saying apartheid was "a crime against humanity and a threat to international peace and security." The subtle difference between the UN's rationale for the propaganda war in the case of apartheid and its reasons for counterpropaganda on the Namibian issue was that UN propaganda against apartheid was based more on a need to fill the information void caused by the censorship and other restrictions on the South African media. This is not to say that the propaganda machine of the South African government was not used to sell its apartheid policies as much as its occupation of Namibia, but the repression of the press in South Africa often made it difficult for South Africans at home and the wider world to get a true picture of the government's activities.

THE DEATH OF PROPAGANDA

In its official history of its work in relation to apartheid it is significant that the United Nations labeled its activities between 1967 and 1989 as the "international campaign against apartheid." It was a little short of saying the UN had conducted a propaganda campaign. The description suggests that activities against South Africa during the period had the demonstration effect of propaganda work. For example, in addition to recognizing and supporting anti-apartheid organizations (the African National Congress [ANC] being the most prominent), the UN promoted the plight of the imprisoned ANC leader, Nelson Mandela, as a symbol of South Africa's repressive system. The General Assembly's Special Committee against Apartheid (established in 1962) promoted the worldwide observance of Mandela's sixtieth birthday on July 18, 1978. Along with the other measures advanced by the UN—such as the oil and arms embargoes—Mandela's name was kept prominent as part of the strategy against the apartheid regime. According to the official history,

> While in prison, Mr. Mandela was accorded many prestigious awards and honorary degrees, and the freedom of many cities. Numerous institutions, buildings and streets around the world were named after him and he was elected an honorary member of many trade unions and other organizations. "Bicycle for Mandela" became an annual event in the United Kingdom on Mandela's birthday. In the Netherlands, the Holland Committee on Southern Africa issued a Mandela coin as part of its campaign against the krugerrand, and also as a means of fund-raising for the freedom movement. No political prisoner in history had been so honoured all over the world.[34]

The resolution passed at the 43rd General Assembly in 1989 included an entire section describing UN counterpropaganda against apartheid. Radio programs were a prominent part of the campaign because broadcasting into South Africa could be done from neighboring countries and radio could reach a very large audience by overcoming the problem of illiteracy. Beginning in 1978, the UN collaborated with neighboring countries and broadcast into South Africa daily in the main languages spoken by South Africans—English, Afrikaans, Sesotho, Setswana, Xhosa and Zulu. (See Appendix 2.)

The UN's Department of Public Information explained that

> The major theme of the programmes was the worldwide condemnation of apartheid, as well as the steady intensification of the international campaign against it. Within this framework, the programmes aimed at educating supporters of apartheid concerning their growing isolation, and at encouraging and reassuring the oppressed people and other opponents of apartheid about international solidarity

with their cause. Well over 1,000 programmes were produced annually and sent to interested broadcasting organizations in many countries for broadcast to South Africa, where they could be heard
throughout the country.[35]

The sign that the racist government was losing the propaganda war came
when its most famous and influential political prisoner, Nelson Mandela, the
de facto leader of the African National Congress (ANC), finally was released
from prison in 1990. Mandela was formally installed as president of South
Africa in early 1994 after he led the ANC to victory in nonracial elections.

Not only was the decision made to respond to propaganda by entering the
battle on the other side, but there also seemed to be a shift at the UN away from
the rhetoric of multilateral conventions against propaganda to the advocacy
of such prohibitions in domestic laws. An indication of this different attitude
is in the General Assembly resolutions condemning "Nazi, Fascist And Neo-
Fascist Activities And All Other Forms Of Totalitarian Ideologies And Practices
Based On Racial Intolerance, Hatred And Terror." Five of these resolutions
passed during the 1980s mentioned propaganda explicitly. The 1986 and
1987 resolutions stated that propaganda by such intolerant groups was to be
dealt with at the national level through national judicial systems. The resolutions invited member-states to "adopt, in accordance with their national
constitutional systems and with the provisions of the Universal Declaration of
Human Rights and the International Covenants on Human Rights, as a matter of high priority, measures declaring punishable by law any dissemination
of ideas based on racial superiority or hatred and of war propaganda, including Nazi, Fascist and neo-Fascist ideologies."[36]

THE PROPAGANDA OF INTERNATIONAL PUBLIC RELATIONS

The Gulf War quickly became a perfect example of a war fought as avidly in
the media as it was on the battle field. The tales of how both sides managed
their facts and their images by public relations, appearances on Cable News
Network (CNN), and restrictions on reporters spawned a small cottage industry of books.[37] And the most shocking revelation about how significant a role
public relations played in the war came, like the many books, after the fact. It
was the account of how one of the widely circulated stories about Iraqi atrocities in Kuwait actually was untrue. In the uncertain days before the war
began, a teenage Kuwaiti girl had testified before the U.S. Congress that Iraqi
soldiers in Kuwait were taking babies from incubators and leaving them to die
on the floor. But it was discovered after the war that the teenager was the

daughter of the Kuwaiti ambassador to the United States and she was not an eyewitness to the alleged atrocities. Her testimony was reported widely by the major media, and her claims were critical in getting support from some members of Congress and the general public for U.S. military action against Iraq. The story was promoted by Hill and Knowlton, the public relations firm hired by Citizens for a Free Kuwait, a front organization in the United States for the Kuwaiti government.[38]

It is tempting to believe that the use of public relations firms by governments to manipulate the media is a by-product of the growth of transnational electronic media, but it is by no means an innovation of the 1990s. According to Michael Kunczik, professor of mass communication at Johannes Gutenberg University in Germany, the American firm of Carl Byoir & Associates did public relations (PR) work in the United States for Czechoslovakia, Germany and Cuba in the 1930s, and another American firm, Sydney S. Baron, had a contract worth $500,000 to represent the Dominican dictator Rafael Trujillo.[39] Many small countries, such as the tourism-dependent islands of Barbados and Jamaica, also retain public relations firms to manage their images as a means of promoting their tourism. Indeed, the 1995 edition of *O'Dwyer's Directory of Public Relations Firms* listed 14 national governments[40] and one provincial government (British Columbia) as being the clients of public relations firms with offices in the United States.

Even in the seemingly benign case of promoting the image of a country so that tourists will visit, there are ethical questions to be resolved. Because many popular Caribbean and Asian destinations for rich American and European tourists are societies with severe income and racial disparities, poverty and political repression, a problem is whether public relations firms for some of these countries dishonestly try to portray images of social stability to mask the smoldering discontent.

Although the growth of transnational media did not start the practice of states using public relations firms, these new media enhance the global ripple effect of PR campaigns. All the available evidence suggests that states employ public relations firms most often with the goal of influencing the Western elite media and consequently manipulating public opinion in North America and Europe. The pattern of use of public relations firms therefore follows the contours of the international political power structure. But because the transnational media and most prestigious news organizations in the world are based in the capitals of the power centers, their news get the widest circulation. Therefore, the "Dead Kuwaiti Babies" story mobilized public opinion supportive of the war not only in the United States, but also in several other countries along the international news food chain. The lesson in this for the modern propagandist is that the use of state propaganda agencies is old-fashioned and unsophisticated; the most effective means of winning hearts and minds is to influence journalists for the powerful transnational media and have your angle on world events relayed as objective "news."

CONCLUSION

Based on the analysis in this chapter, we can make four conclusions about the evolution of the political discourse about international propaganda. First, no meaningful procedures regulating international propaganda ever have come into force, despite the several attempts. Second, image management and propaganda became an acceptable means of conducting international relations, particularly after World War II. Also, the establishment of permanent agencies for conducting international "cultural relations" (or "public diplomacy," as it is euphemistically called by Americans) is evidence of the recognition that using such information tools is tolerated in the game of international politics.

Third, the new international order that was constructed around the UN actually was based on the assumption that certain ideas would be propagated (good propaganda). This reached its most acute phase in the 1980s, when the United Nations devoted considerable resources to pursuing a propaganda war with South Africa.

Finally, the growth of transnational private electronic media networks (including the Internet and DBS television) increasingly puts state and non-state actors in international relations into the roles of lobbyists, competing for media time. The discourse about propaganda in international politics becomes less about rules to control government behavior (as was largely the case before World War II) and more about the ethics of international reporting. Among the more relevant questions, therefore, are: How truthful is the proposition that these transnational media are structural propagandists? And, How can these media ensure that they do not become the handmaidens of international PR firms that represent companies and governments alike?

INEQUALITY AND INJUSTICE IN GLOBAL NEWS

DISTRIBUTIVE JUSTICE AND INTERNATIONAL NEWS

The observation that the pattern of global news flows is inherently unjust because international news from the regions of the global South flows unequally in quantitative and qualitative terms is based on the concept of *distributive justice.* This term refers to "justice allocated by society as a whole to its members, according to some principle of distribution."[1] Distributive justice became prominent in the 1970s with the calls by poor states for reform of international society, especially the calls for a New International Economic Order (NIEO) (See below). One reason why the concept of distributive justice is so interesting is because the most prominent form of justice in modern international relations has been *reciprocal justice*—defined by Bull as "justice negotiated by the members of a society on the basis of an exchange of rights or benefits."[2]

The proposed "New World Information and Communication Order" (NWICO) of the 1970s, which sought to end such injustice in global news, grew out of the NIEO. Therefore, embedded in the international discourse over news flows are profound assumptions about what constitutes justice. The attempt to apply the principles of distributive justice to international news is a subversive development in international politics because (as we have seen in chapter 2) the structure of global news has historically mirrored the contours of international power, trade, production and finance, and (as explained in chapter 3) news has strategic value in international relations. To argue that anything other than power and technological capability should determine news flows is obviously upsetting to those with an advantage in the process. This is why the NWICO debate was one of the most bitter for the United Nations, and in particular for the UN agency responsible for communication matters, UNESCO. The conflict led to the United States, Britain and Singapore withdrawing from UNESCO, depriving it of dues that comprised more than a quarter of the organization's budget. However, the debate produced a sensitivity to the relationship between news flows and power and spurred the creation of a number of initiatives to improve journalism training and technologies for the dissemination of news in deprived areas.

THE PROBLEM

A major flaw in the character of international news has been its tendency to stereotype certain regions and people. The organizations that disseminate most of the world's news are based in North America and Europe, and their news traditionally has reflected the prejudices of those societies. News from certain areas, such as Black Africa, Latin America and some parts of Asia, is most often about crises and disasters, while more complete pictures of other regions are given because those regions are given more diverse coverage.

At the time the NWICO was introduced in the 1970s the international wire services—especially the "Big Four" of Reuters, the Associated Press (AP), United Press International (UPI) and Agence France-Presse (AFP)—were targets for the most criticism by NWICO advocates. But, as one writer has observed, the entrepreneurs who founded the international news agencies in the 1800s were guided by motives that

> were clear and businesslike: the Europeans were out to make money, the New Yorkers to cut news-gathering costs. High-minded thoughts of making the world a better-informed place in order to promote international understanding did not enter their calculations.[3]

And claims, such as the assertion that "private enterprise with a profit incentive is the best guarantee of objective coverage of world news,"[4] essentially were tagged on at a later date to justify the reality of news distribution being a business.

In tune with the tenor of imperial practices at the time, in the 1800s the European and American agencies divided the world into spheres of control. By the 1970s the patterns of coverage of the agencies still mirrored to some degree the delineations made by such agreements, even though the formal arrangements had long since ended. The first pact between the three European agencies[5] was the exchange agreement of 1856 in which they agreed to cut costs by exchanging news about each other's home countries and maintaining joint offices. Soon after the exchange agreement, Wolff entered a pact with a midwestern rival to the New York AP that got the German agency its news from across the Atlantic. This deal did not last long because the two APs soon achieved a truce. Then, in 1870, in what has been described as a "grandiose imperial gesture,"[6] the European agencies set up a global news cartel through their Cooperation Agreement. The deal demarcated the world into specific preserves in which each agency enjoyed a monopoly on sales of foreign news and provided coverage for the other two agencies.

The cartel was renewed in 1890. Although a number of new national news agencies were created in Europe during the late 1800s, none could expand beyond their national frontiers like Wolff, Reuters or Havas because the cartel monopolized the international market in news and all smaller agencies were dependent on the cartel for international coverage. The U.S. agencies, AP and United Press (the predecessor to UPI), were dependent on the cartel for international news as well. But AP ventured into foreign reporting when it sent reporters to cover the Spanish-American and Russo-Japanese wars. To this the cartel did not object because its domestic monopolies were not contravened. UP decided after 1912 that it did not want to be confined by the cartel and it would collect its own international news. UP's move proved a great success because it was helped largely by the Argentinean newspaper *La Prensa*, which was willing to pay up to half a million dollars annually for the agency's international news. This success threatened to make UP the major American agency at the expense of AP, and as a result AP gradually broke free from the cartel in order to be free to compete more effectively against UP. Between 1918 and 1919 AP assumed responsibility for Latin America from Havas. The de facto end of the cartel came in 1930 when the Japanese agency Rengo agreed to distribute the AP service in Japan and AP declared that it would end its agreement with the European cartel.

There were a total of 174 news agencies by 1980. These were in 93 countries, 60 of which were in the South. But, as *World Press Encyclopedia* editor George Kurian pointed out at that time, of the 174, "only some 20 may be described as major in the sense of possessing the capability to gather and transmit information across national borders."[7] Of the 20 international agencies the "Big Five"—Reuters, AP, UPI, AFP and TASS (the Telegraph Agency of the Soviet Union)—dominated the global circulation of news and no change of this situation was in sight for the near future because

> Despite UNESCO-led efforts to dilute the virtual monopoly of the Big Five, both technology and economics have tended to reinforce it. The spectacular technical developments in the collection and transmission of news, particularly via satellites, have favoured the larger news agencies with the know-how and the capital. The prohibitive cost of foreign operations also make it difficult for smaller agencies to compete with the Big Five or to establish new bureaus. It has been estimated that it costs AP an average of $300,000 per year to maintain one correspondent overseas. The very economies of news gathering seem to be working against UNESCO's New International Information Order.[8]

Evidence of how much a priority ending this dependence for news has been for developing nations can be gleaned from the single fact that the Non-Aligned Movement (NAM) established the Non-Aligned News Agencies Pool (NANAP) in 1975, early in the history of the NWICO debate.

INTERNATIONAL DIALOGUE ABOUT GLOBAL NEWS

Dialogue and decision-making regarding news flows was part of a much broader international discussion about world development. In the midst of decolonization it was realized within the UN system that political independence was not sufficient to bring improved standards of living to the global South. A model of what has come to be known as "dependent development" was advocated, based on the essential idea that "the industrial states continue to grow; that this growth translates itself into increased demand for imports from the developing countries; and that this, in turn, stimulates the industrial development of the latter."[9] The developing nations advocated a New International Economic Order and its derivative, a NWICO, in the early '70s after it became clear that this model had failed.[10] Dependent development was a failure because, the expected growth in the industrial economies did not come about, however, partly because the Bretton Woods system collapsed, bringing unpredictable exchange rates, hyperinflation and overall recession. Aid to the South, expressed as a percentage of GNP, also decreased. And it also was realized that the dependence encouraged by this model of development called for a new model that fostered individual and collective self-reliance in the developing countries. It is therefore quite significant that one of the 20 principles of the NIEO was "The strengthening, through individual and collective actions, of mutual economic, trade, financial and technical co-operation among the developing countries, mainly on a preferential basis."[11] This was in addition to the other principles of national sovereignty over raw materials and the need to regulate the activities of transnational corporations (TNCs).

The NWICO was considered vital to this new development strategy because communication and information undergirds the entire global system of production and consumption. News and advertising from affluent societies encourage the emulation of the wasteful habits of those societies in poorer areas. They create demands for imported consumer goods. Therefore, an information order dominated by the few wealthy countries fosters the cycle of dependence.[12]

The notion of self-reliance in development, and of a NIEO and NWICO in fostering these goals, was spawned by the nations of the global South who were successful in putting it on the UN agenda. For example, the economic program approved by the 1973 summit of the NAM in Algiers was the basis of the landmark resolutions adopted at the Sixth Special Session of the UN General Assembly (the "Declaration on the Establishment of a New International Economic Order" and the "Programme of Action on the Establishment of a New International Economic Order"). And the idea of a new international order in information was introduced to the diplomatic vocabulary at the NAM Symposium on Communications Policies in Tunis in March, 1976. But well into the new decade of the '80s, 90 percent of all patents still belonged to multinationals,[13] commodity prices were continuing to plunge, and the International Monetary Fund (IMF) and World Bank had effective control of many economies in the South as a consequence of the debt crisis. One explanation for the failure of the NIEO has been the fact that conservative administrations, not sympathetic to its principles, came to power in Britain, West Germany and the United States from 1979 onward. Another is based on a look at the coalition dynamics of the Group of 77 developing nations: this research found the coalition too weak to sustain the momentum of the lobby.[14]

However, the NWICO is a fascinating concept in the history of international relations because it was a clear attempt to apply the principle of distributive justice to international communication. That effort posed a number of questions that were a source of severe conflict. Can distributive justice be applied to the issue area of news in the way that it can be applied to material goods, such as water and food? Is the unevenness in global news flows necessarily unjust? Should parity and justice in the global flow of news take precedence over other values, such as liberal-democratic press freedoms?

Before exploring the international discourse over this attempt to apply distributive justice to international news, it is necessary to provide some evidence that distributive justice indeed was being invoked. To illustrate this we can look to some key documents of the NWICO debate: the Mass Media Declaration of 1978 (see Appendix 3); the extensively quoted call in 1979 for the new order made by Mustapha Masmoudi, the man regarded as the "father" of the NWICO;[15] and the MacBride Report of 1980.

The Mass Media Declaration sought to establish a set of principles, norms, rules and decision-making procedures governing the activities of journalists and the international circulation of news. Although resistance from the global North severely modified the original draft, the final 11 articles, though not managing to establish a regime, still proclaimed equality and justice in the operations of the mass media as the guiding principles. This was stated clearly in Article VI, which said that:

> For the establishment of a new equilibrium and greater reciprocity
> in the flow of information, which will be conducive to the institution

of a just and lasting peace and to the economic and political independence of the developing countries, it is necessary to correct the
inequalities in the flow of information to and from developing countries, and between those countries. To this end, it is essential that
their mass media should have conditions and resources enabling
them to gain strength and expand, and to co-operate both among
themselves and with the mass media in developed countries.[16]

Similarly, in his preamble to his itemization of the shortcomings of the
existing world information and communication order, Masmoudi stated that

The new world information order founded on democratic principles
seeks to establish relations of equality in the communications field
between developed and developing nations and aims at greater justice and greater balance. Far from calling in question the freedom of
information, it proposes to ensure that this principle is applied fairly
and equitably for all nations and not only in the case of the more
developed among them.[17]

Masmoudi's contribution and the views of others all helped to shape the
final recommendations of the MacBride Commission, which stated that the
"basic considerations which are developed at length in the body of our Report
are intended to provide a framework for the development of a new information and communication order."[18] In introducing its 82 recommendations, the
commission made it clear that equality and justice would be the principles
underlying the new order:

The whole human race is threatened by the arms race and by the
persistence of unacceptable global inequalities, both of which gen-
erate tensions and which jeopardize its future and even its survival.
The contemporary situation demands a better, more just and more
democratic social order, and the realization of fundamental human
rights. These goals can be achieved only through understanding
and tolerance, gained in large part by free, open and balanced
communications.[19]

To these ends, the MacBride Commission wanted the creation of a number
of international regimes. Among them would be one to regulate international
advertising and another governing the activities of TNCs in information and
communication, including limiting "the process of concentration and monop-
olization."[20] Of course, we must hasten to insert that although there is ample evidence that equality and justice were predominant goals, these were not the
only goals of the South. As was argued in chapter 2, the late twentieth century

has seen a shift to postindustrial production in the leading economies of the North, and any state hoping to be fully integrated into the global economy must possess an efficient communications infrastructure with such basics as working telephones and data relay capabilities conducive to data provision and other expanding service industries. So, by demanding increased aid for communications development, the South's goal was to also attain the basic resources needed for economic development in a changing global economy.

The NWICO and MacBride Commission of the 1970s became the best known examples of multilateral consideration of disparities in international communication capabilities because they were so controversial, but they were by no means the first examples of multinational attention to the subject. In 1926 the Press Congress of the World, founded in 1915, called for more journalism schools and increased international exchanges of journalists and technicians. Development was a topic considered at the UN Conference on Freedom of Information in 1948, and that meeting recommended, inter alia, more news agencies, newspapers and the production of inexpensive radio receivers.

In 1952 the UN General Assembly, recognizing these disparities in international communication, produced a scheme for the development of mass communication in the deprived regions. This attempt failed because it was realized that there needed to be more empirical data on international communication.[21] One questionnaire that was sent out by the UN to governments in the mid-'50s to compile such data found that many countries had common regional problems and needs, and this finding led to a series of regional conferences on journalism training for Southeast Asia, Latin America, Africa and the Middle East.[22] To provide more data, the UN Economic and Social Council decided in 1959 that UNESCO should undertake a global survey of mass media. In 1961 the survey's findings were considered by the Social and Economic Council and the Commission on Human Rights. Following from that, the UN General Assembly in 1962 said it was concerned over the fact that "70 percent of the population of the world lack adequate information facilities and are thus denied effective enjoyment of the right of information," and the assembly invited governments of the developed nations to "co-operate with less developed countries with a view to meeting the urgent needs of the less developed countries in connexion with this programme for the development of independent national information media, with due regard to the culture of each country."[23] In the early 1960s the Economic and Social Council also sponsored three regional conferences that explored the development of mass media: a conference for Southeast Asia, in Bangkok (January 1960); for Latin America, in Santiago, Chile (February 1962); and for Africa, in Paris (January-February 1962). However, it was not until the early '70s, by which time the developing countries were in a majority at the United Nations, that disparities in international communication were again prominent on the UN agenda. At the eighteenth session of UNESCO's General Conference in 1974 "communications" was identified as one of four "problem areas" to be addressed by the agency's medium-term plan, 1977–82.[24] But in the mid '70s it was again the problem of lack of empirical data on which to base informed policies that caused UNESCO to sponsor three intergovernmental conferences on communications policies[25] and convene the MacBride Commission.

GLOBAL NEWS AND THE UN SYSTEM

UNESCO

The reason why UNESCO[26] was the focal point for activity related to journalism and the mass media generally was its being designated the organ to handle such matters when the system of UN specialized agencies was set up after World War II. The newly independent countries were not wrong in venting their concerns about communication development through the forum the agency provided. However, the proposed NWICO created an uproar at UNESCO because the application of distributive justice to international communication was not in the vision of the North American and European founders of the agency. Simply put, they felt UNESCO would be a propaganda organization for peace.

UNESCO evolved out of the Conference of Allied Ministers of Education (CAME) that was organized by the British. CAME held a series of meetings in London between 1942 and 1945. From the start it was felt that UNESCO would be an independent actor, with strong policies of its own, even though it would be comprised of member-states. James P. Sewell, an international organization scholar at Princeton University[27] argues that an emphasis on education, culture and communications by the Allies was aimed at projecting a certain world view in those areas that had come under the influence of the Nazis or had not yet been converted to their outlook. For example,

> The French saw a Paris-based world organization as the logical successor to, or even as a strengthened continuation of, the Institut International de Coopération Intellectuelle (IICI). IICI was authorized by the League of Nations to serve as secretariat for the league's International Committee on Intellectual Cooperation. It was financed by the French government and located in the Palais Royal. The institute was, as UNESCO is, valued as an instrument of extending French culture to an elite in all corners of the globe.[28]

Peace was to be the functionalist ideology of UNESCO, and the norms by which peace could be achieved were Eurocentric versions of education, press freedom, and culture. Sometimes the expectations that the organization would be a de facto instrument of some governments' foreign policies were not that subtly expressed. For example, Sewell, in his study of UNESCO published in 1974, reported that

> The Korean War gave rise to such American newspaper headlines as "U.S. Looks to UNESCO to Tell Korea Truth"; "UNESCO May Assume New Duties in Korea after [Executive] Board Meeting"; and "UNESCO's Aid Sought Along Propaganda Front." The Continental Daily Mail observed on 29 July 1950 that UNESCO was becoming a veritable "psychological warfare organization for the Western Powers." On 14 August the News Chronicle (London) warned: "American insistence that UNESCO enter the cold war by spreading pro-Western, anti-Communist propaganda is producing a crisis which may almost wreck the Organisation."[29]

UN and UNESCO-sponsored studies and policies pursued within the UN system in the early years were committed to media development strategies in the former colonies based on Western European and American models. For example, at the time of the 1962 regional conference on communications in Africa, statistics compiled by UNESCO showed that, for every 100 people, on the continent there was an average of one copy of a daily newspaper, two radio receivers, and 0.5 seats in permanent cinemas. In contrast, based on the situation in the "developed" countries, UNESCO had devised a "minimum criteria" for the continent of 10 newspapers, five radio receivers, and two seats for every 100 people. Indeed, one UNESCO report urged African states to "immediately take action to develop the press, radio and film and . . . prepare for the introduction and effective use of television."[30] The assumption was that the acquisition in abundance of the means of communication was itself a positive move. Little or no attention was devoted to the fundamental questions of who would own and control these media and what impact foreign norms and values relayed through the mass media would have on the societies in the South. Scholarly works produced during this phase, such as Daniel Lerner's *The Passing of Traditional Society* (1958) and Wilbur Schramm's *Mass Media And National Development* (1964), were remarkable because of their inattention to these questions, issues that would provoke such debate in later years.

By 1980, when the MacBride Report was finished, UNESCO had developed critical, broader conceptions of the "development" of communication. The rise of TNCs, recognition of cultural relativism, and the realization that the means of communication can be used to promote class interests anathema to the equitable development of all of society, caused significant changes away from the Western-based models of mass media development. The new thinking at UNESCO about the role of communication in development stressed the importance of developing media systems along carefully planned national communication policies. Such policies would use the media to promote political and social reform, including the redistribution of national resources. Emphasis was placed on "communication"—the origin of which connotes sharing—instead of the old idea of media being used solely for "information," a term that suggests a vertical, one-way flow. The MacBride Report is the best example of this outlook. It noted that

> Communication policies and development strategies, considered as essential means of solving the major problems of our time, should be designed first and foremost to ensure that the "media of information" become the media of "communication". Because communication presupposes access, participation and exchange, different media should be involved in the process of democratizing communication.[31]

The NWICO

Although there was this clear link between the NWICO and the New International Economic Order (which was first mentioned in UN Resolution 3201 of May, 1974), the two attempts at global reform differed on the very significant point that the NIEO was more coherently defined than the NWICO. From the time the term "New World Information Order" was introduced into the diplomatic vocabulary in 1976 until the General Conference of UNESCO in 1987, when the director general of UNESCO was replaced and the NWICO lost much of its support in UNESCO's bureaucracy, the NWICO was largely an undefined, vague concept that embodied global change in as diverse an array of areas as (but not exclusive to) telecommunications, news flows, intellectual property rights, and international advertising.

There was a problem in finding a definition of the NWICO acceptable to all blocs of states. The Non-Aligned Intergovernmental Council For Co-ordination of Information passed a resolution on the "New International Information Order" in June 1980 that sought to define the order, including calls for the regulation of transnational corporations and the "right" of nations "to use" their means of information.[32] The ideas in that document were reflected later in the year by UNESCO Resolution 4/19, passed at the twenty-first General Conference in Belgrade, which listed 11 objectives of the "new world information and communication order":

(i)   elimination of the imbalances and inequalities which charac-
       terize the present situation;
(ii)   elimination of the negative effects of certain monopolies, pub-
       lic or private, and excessive concentrations;
(iii) removal of internal and external obstacles to a free flow and
       wider and better balanced dissemination of information and
       ideas;
(iv)   plurality of sources and channels of information;
(v)   freedom of the press and information;
(vi)   freedom of journalists and all professionals in the communi-
       cation media, a freedom inseparable from responsibility;
(vii) the capacity of developing countries to achieve improvement of
       their own situations, notably by providing their own equipment,
       by training their personnel, by improving their infrastructure
       and by making their information and communication media
       suitable to their needs and aspirations;
(viii) the sincere will of developed countries to help them attain
       these objectives;
(ix)   respect for each people's cultural identity and for the right of
       each nation to inform the world public about its interests, its
       aspirations and its social and cultural values;
(x)   respect for the right of all peoples to participate in interna-
       tional exchanges of information on the basis of equality, justice
       and mutual benefit;
(xi)   respect for the right of the public, of ethnic and social groups
       and of individuals to have access to information sources and to
       participate actively in the communication process[33]

The resolution's assertion that UNESCO's activities in the future should
"contribute to the clarification, elaboration and application of the concept of a
new world information and communication order" was an indication of remain-
ing uncertainty about the order's finer points as much as it was an allowance
for Western reservations about wholehearted adoption of the order. Five years
later at the UNESCO General Assembly in Sofia there still was no common agreement upon definition of the NWICO except that it was an "evolving and continuous process," a compromise definition that was adopted to diffuse Western
worries that the NWICO was too prescriptive and endangered press freedom.

But, despite its conceptual vagueness, the quest for the NWICO did produce three significant actions at UNESCO: the 1978 Mass Media Declaration;
the MacBride Report; and the creation of the International Program for the
Development of Communication (IPDC) in 1980.

The Mass Media Declaration took six years to draft before it was adopted by
the UNESCO General Conference in 1978. Western media interests preferred

that there be no declaration on the media at all; and categorical opposition to it came from the International Press Institute, Freedom House, the World Press Freedom Committee, the Inter-American Association of Broadcasters, Reuters and *The Times* of London. In its final form the declaration was a slim document of only 11 articles called the *Declaration on Fundamental Principles concerning the Contribution of the Mass Media to Strengthening Peace and International Understanding, to the Promotion of Human Rights and to Countering Racialism, Apartheid and Incitement to War.* These principles were meant to guide journalists the world over in the conduct of their profession. Although the passage of the Mass Media Declaration can be regarded as a defeat to the West, Western opposition still had succeeded in moderating its content so that it was very descriptive in character instead of being a normative document.

The declaration clearly articulated the major demands of the developing countries regarding international information and communication, especially in its assertion that correction of "the inequalities in the flow of information to and from developing countries, and between those countries" is a prerequisite for "just and lasting peace" and "economic and political independence of the developing countries."[34] But evidence of the uncertainty about its effectiveness almost 10 years after it was passed by UNESCO was the discussion at the 1987 General Conference about the need for an assessment of how widely the principles were being heeded.

In contrast, the MacBride Report produced clearer results. With the passage of Resolution 4/19 (which recognized the usefulness of the MacBride Commission's work) and Resolution 4/21 (which set up the IPDC) UNESCO moved from a stage of reflection about information and communication problems (and of attempting to establish normative principles, such as the Media Declaration) to one of action. However, the evidence does indicate that the practical suggestions of the report did serve to fuel Western media hostility to UNESCO and lead down the path to the withdrawals of the United States and the United Kingdom.

The task of UNESCO's MacBride Commission on international "communication problems" was to analyze such criticisms of the structure of global news institutions and news flows (and other issues of contention) and suggest solutions. But although the report was criticized as hostile to a free press (see below), in its text there are no proposals for regulating the "Big Four" wire services (AP, AFP, Reuters, and UPI) or censoring their news. The MacBride Report reflected the same liberal-democratic assumptions about the role of the mass media as was held by Western media interests. This perspective was explicitly articulated on page 233, which said that

> Freedom of the press in its widest sense represents the collective enlargement of each citizen's freedom of expression which is accepted as a human right. Democratic societies are based on the concept of sovereignty of the people, whose general will is determined by an informed public opinion. It is this right of the public to know that is the essence of media freedom of which the professional journalist, writer and producer are only custodians. Deprivation of this freedom diminishes all others.
>
> The press has been described as the fourth estate because full and accurate information on matters of public interest is the means by which governments, institutions, organizations and all others in authority, at whatever level are held accountable to and by the public.[35]

In other words, each individual is free to choose for him or herself and the only way an individual can make a rational choice is by having access to unadulterated information about his or her environment; the "public opinion" formed by the collective choices of all these individuals is what should guide government action and determine the future of those placed in authority over the people. The report stated that restrictions on journalists not only damaged this social process but also hurt the profession of journalism itself because they could produce "a situation in which honest journalists abandon the profession, and young people of talent decide not to enter it."[36]

Only two of the report's recommendations were addressed directly to the operations of the news agencies. Recommendation 6 advocated the creation of alternative news agencies as a means of fostering independence and ending the dominance of news from the few international wire services:

> Strong national news agencies are vital for improving each country's national and international reporting. Where viable, regional networks should be set up to increase news flows and serve all the major language groups in the area. Nationally, the agencies should buttress the growth of both urban and rural newspapers to serve as the core of a country's news collection and distribution system.[37]

Recommendation 70 urged that the cooperation started by the Non-Aligned countries, as an alternative to the existing order, should be encouraged:

> Joint activities in the field of communication, which are under way between developing countries, should be developed further in the light of the overall analysis and recommendations of this report. In particular, attention should be given to co-operation among national news agencies, to the further development of the [Non-Aligned] News Agencies Pool and broadcasting organisations of the non-aligned

countries as well as to the general exchange on a regular basis of
radio, TV programmes and films.[38]

The report also reflected another assumption about the press that is popular in the Western democracies. This is the idea that press freedom is a two-
dimensional right: the right to communicate news, information and views;
and the right to receive news, information and views. Directly linked to this
idea is the view that, although the press has rights, it also has responsibilities,
a proviso that has been given the status of international law in a number of
agreements that have been signed by nation-states of various ideological
hues. For example, Article 29 of the Universal Declaration of Human Rights
states that while exercising their rights and freedoms persons are subject to
"such limitations as are determined by law solely for the purpose of securing
due recognition and respect for the rights and freedoms of others and of meeting the just requirements of morality, public order and the general welfare in
a democratic society." Article 19 of the International Covenant on Civil and
Political Rights guarantees "freedom of expression" but it also states that
such rights are conditioned by "duties and responsibilities." The covenant says
legal restrictions can be made

(a) For respect of the rights or reputations of others; [and]
(b) For the protection of national security or of public order (ordre
    public), or of public health or morals.[39]

Article 20 prohibits "propaganda for war" and "advocacy of national, racial
or religious hatred."[40]

Apart from the recommendations on news agencies, and on the protection
of journalists (see chapter 6), there were two other sets of proposals in the
MacBride Report that dealt directly with the profession of journalism: recommendations 39-43 on the "Responsibility of Journalists" and recommendations 44-49 on "International Reporting".

Recommendations 39-43 urged that journalism be acknowledged as a
profession and that this professionalism be promoted through improved training and mechanisms to assure accountability such as media councils, press
ombudsmen and codes of ethics.

Among the suggestions regarding international reporting was that foreign correspondents be given free access to news sources. But the commission
also saw a need for improvements in the standards of foreign reporting. Said recommendation 45, "Higher professional standards are needed for journalists to
be able to illuminate the diverse cultures and beliefs of the modern world,
without their presuming to judge the ultimate validity of any foreign nation's

experience and traditions."[41] Recommendation 46 went on to suggest that "reporters being assigned to foreign posts should have the benefit of language training and acquaintance with the history, institutions, politics, economics and cultural environment of the country or region in which they will be serving."[42] The commission recommended that the media in the industrialized countries carry more news about other countries in general and about developing nations in particular. Recommendation 48 endorsed the idea of an international "right of reply and correction."[43] But such measures should be adopted voluntarily by media houses. Recommendation 49 was that governments should "refrain from using journalists for purposes of espionage."[44]

"Statist" is the adjective often used to describe the MacBride Report. This was so because the document's 82 recommendations were directly addressed to governments, and when the private sector was mentioned in these proposals it was in relation to government policy. The report's seemingly built-in suspicion of TNCs and other commercial interests was most manifest in the three recommendations (31-33) that were subtitled "Reducing the Commercialization of Communication." They recommended that:

[31] In expanding communication systems, preference should be given to non-commercial forms of mass communication
[32] While acknowledging the need of the media for revenues, ways and means should be considered to reduce the negative effects that the influence of market and commercial considerations have in the organization and content of national and international communication flows.
[33] . . . consideration be given to changing existing funding patterns of commercial mass media. In this connection, reviews could be made of the way in which the relative role of advertising volume and costs pricing policies, voluntary contributions, subsidies, taxes, financial incentives and supports could be modified to enhance the social function of mass media and improve their service to the community.[45]

The suspicion of TNCs also was evident in recommendation 38, which said that TNCs "should supply to the authorities of the countries in which they operate, upon request and on a regular basis as specified by local laws and regulations, all information required for legislative and administrative purposes relevant to their activities and specifically needed to assess the performance of such entities."[46]

Recommendation 78 of the MacBride Report, which called for the setting up at UNESCO of an "International Centre for the Study and Planning of

Information and Communication," led to the founding of the IPDC. But it failed to mention an explicit role for the private sector in the new program. According to the report, the new program "may be guided by a tripartite coordinating council composed of representatives of developing and developed countries and of interested international organizations."[47]

The IPDC is the only one of the three major developments that generated a degree of enthusiasm from North, South and East. However, its effectiveness soon was hampered by a shortage of funds that has made the program inadequate to deal with all the requests for aid from developing nations. The IPDC was another source of the funding for UNESCO's communication aid activities—added to those of funds-in-trust donors, assistance from the UN Development Program (UNDP) and direct funds from the UNESCO budget. For example, during the 1979-1980 biennium the UNESCO communications program provided aid by way of consultants, training and equipment for the following news agency–related activities: developing the new Caribbean News Agency (CANA) and a national news agency for Mongolia; news agency training in West Africa; and journalism training in the Seychelles, Costa Rica and Surinam.[48] By 1983 UNESCO had upgraded its communications subsection to a full division of the organization and the expansion of its aid activities in the South is revealed by the figures provided by the director-general. According to his report,

> The 1981-1983 triennium was marked by an increase in activities for the development of communication infrastructures and training, made possible by the increase in extra-budgetary resources, the diversification of financing sources being accompanied by a proportional increase in contributions from sources other than UNDP (funds-in-trust and IPDC in particular). The funds thus available for extra-budgetary projects which had amounted to some U.S.$4,600,000 during the 1979-1980 biennium, totaled U.S.$18,247,500 in the 1981-1983 triennium.
>
> The total extra-budgetary funds available to the Organisation increased by 20 percent in 1982 and by 38 percent in 1983. The decrease in UNDP funding (20 per cent in 1982 and 25 per cent in 1983) was compensated in large measure by the increase in funds-in-trust (17 per cent in 1982 and 50 per cent in 1983). The amounts paid into the IPDC Special Account rose by 110 per cent in 1983 as against 1982.[49]

The increasing pressures on UNESCO caused a qualitative shift in its activities in 1984-1985. The director-general's report explained that "On account of the divergence of views regarding the concept of a new world information and communication order, seen as an evolving and continuing process, work focused upon consolidating knowledge in this area."[50] However 1984-85 still was a period of expansion of UNESCO's aid to new alternative news agencies, training and improving communications infrastructure in the South. Money for projects financed by extra-budgetary resources, which totaled U.S.$18,500,000 in 1981-83, rose to U.S.$19,454,309 in 1984-85, representing an annual increase of about 30 percent. U.S.$2,953,312 was pledged to the IPDC in 1984-85, and the program approved 32 projects costing U.S.$2,200,000. Three hundred and eighteen people benefited from training programs under the auspices of the IPDC.[51] Significantly, 30 percent of UNESCO resources for communication development was devoted to improving communication exchanges in the developing nations (i.e. "news agencies and information networks, exchanges of radio and television programmes and other communication systems designed to strengthen co-operation among developing countries and to boost the international circulation of messages and programmes").[52] In addition to CANA, the Pan-African News Agency (PANA), the Latin American Features Agency (ALASEI), the Asia-Pacific News Network (ANN) and the Federation of Arab News Agencies (FANA) were among the new alternative news agencies that got UNESCO aid through the IPDC.

In 1985 over half of UNESCO's communications aid was going to Africa (53.6 percent), followed by Asia and the Pacific (18.32 percent), Latin America and the Caribbean (13.59 percent), the Arab states (5.15 percent), Europe (0.10 percent) and the "regional and world programme" (9.22 percent).[53]

By 1987 total contributions made to the IPDC's Special Account amounted to U.S.$12.6 million. In its seven years of existence it had contributed to the financing of 227 communication projects in developing countries and had allocated 470 scholarships. But (significantly) only 11 out of 34 industrialized countries had contributed to the IPDC Special Account.[54] The argument was not about whether the South deserved aid and technical assistance, but about the political economy of such aid. Should it be primarily the responsibility of the state or the economic market (private sector)? Should the various international organizations have aid programs of their own or should aid be funneled through the UN's general aid conduit of the United Nations Conference on Trade and Development (UNCTAD)? Should the functional ideologies of states regarding information and communication be criteria for denying states aid? According to Leslie Milk, of Georgetown University's Center for Strategic and International Studies, who coauthored a study for the State Department of the United States's options before the International Telecommunication Union (ITU), the United States refused to contribute to the

IPDC "on the grounds that it supports the kind of news organizations that we oppose because they are not free organizations."[55]

HOSTILITY FROM ELITE MEDIA

Although the NWICO was an umbrella term used for a number of proposals—the revision of telecommunications tariffs and reform of aspects of the ITU, the World Intellectual Property Organization (WIPO) and the Universal Postal Union (UPU)—more often than not the proposed order was identified solely by its implications for the mass media. Indeed, for many the issue of news *was* the NWICO. For example, Indonesian journalist Mochtar Lubis, who was on the MacBride Commission, said that

> During the Unesco commission's deliberations, I got the definite impression that some of the spokesmen from Third World countries demand a new world information order with the main purpose of being able to prevent what they consider "negative reporting" around the world about their undemocratic governments.[56]

An essay in *Time* magazine said that the "new information order" "directly threatens press freedom as Americans and Europeans conceive it."[57] And in 1986 *Newsweek* reported that the NWICO "seemed a direct attack on freedom of the press."[58]

From early in the life of the concept, therefore, it was the object of attack from press freedom groups and the media in Europe and North America. Whereas books written about AFP, UPI, Reuters and AP before the NWICO debate were largely descriptive of the agencies' achievements and individual efforts to secure worldwide markets,[59] works produced in the 1970s and afterward devoted considerable attention to assessing whether the criticisms from the South of the "Big Four" really were justified. The three writers on the international news agencies—Oliver Boyd-Barrett, Jeremy Tunstall and Jonathan Fenby[60]—all defended the Western "Big Four" using the same or very similar arguments. The essence of their argument was that an examination of the history and organization of the four dominant Western agencies reveals that any imbalances in their coverage of the world is a product of their trying to survive in a marketplace where news is a commodity for sale and where the greatest demand is for news about the North. The very competitive nature of the international news market and the fact that none of the agencies have a long history of amassing great profits (especially UPI) was evidence enough, they argued, that the "Big Four" really did not have the power attributed to them by their detractors.

It is worth quoting Fenby not only because his book (a study underwritten by the Twentieth Century Fund) was the most defensive but also because he was a top executive of one of the "Big Four," having been the editor of Reuters's World Service of two years and later a member of Reuters's Executive Committee. He noted that:

> The four agencies exist to serve markets, whether it is the global market for news of an event of international interest or the restricted market for coverage of a story of local or national significance. Their international operations are conducted on a commercial basis, although—paradoxically—they frequently operate in ways not calculated to maximize profits. Their prime concern is with the rich media markets of the United States, Western Europe, and Japan, and increasingly with the business community, which requires fast information services that can be used to make money. . . . The result of this application of the commercial market approach to news is that an agency may well have more staff reporters in a single major European country than in the whole of black Africa.[61]

Fenby backed up his argument by quoting statistics, compiled by Denis Mcquail for the Royal Commission on the Press and published in 1977, which indicated the two best-selling British dailies devoted in excess of 90 percent of their news columns to domestic news. He also explained that from the 1960s onward the number of foreign correspondents employed by U.S. media has steadily declined. Full-time staff employed by American publications overseas numbered 919 in 1963. That number was down to 676 in the mid-1970s.[62]

The MacBride Report was the last straw in tension that had been accumulating between the Western mass media interests and NWICO proponents since UNESCO began considering the Mass Media Declaration in the early 1970s. The Western media confronted the NWICO in four ways. An international press freedom lobby, spearheaded by United States media, was formed. They supplied extensive (sometimes quite faulty) coverage of UNESCO, especially of meetings where mass communications was a prominent topic, and this coverage was not only in the form of "straight news" reports but also editorials that usually were hostile to the agency in general and its communications program in particular. The concept was openly attacked in speeches by prominent journalists and in the well-publicized Declaration of Talloires (See Appendix 6). And advertising interests portrayed the NWICO as anathema to them.

The World Press Freedom Committee

The World Press Freedom Committee (WPFC) was the vehicle press interests created to resist the media initiatives of UNESCO and respond to the demands of the South by providing aid of their own. According to its own literature, the WPFC was "activated in May 1976 by a group of international journalists to unify the free world media for major threats that develop."[63] By 1980 the WPFC was comprised of 32 journalistic organizations that provided the WPFC with "a strong global voice against those who advocate state-controlled media; those who seek to deny truth in news; and those who abuse newsmen."[64] But although its membership included the Caribbean Publishers and Broadcasters Association, the Japan Publishers and Editors Association, and the Asia-Pacific Institute for Broadcast Training, the majority of the organizations were from the United States, and that country's private media supplied most of its funding and leadership.

Press Coverage

Because the proposed NWICO directly related to the role of the mass media, the Western press devoted an unprecedented amount of resources to covering the deliberations about communications at UNESCO. At the Twentieth General Conference of UNESCO in 1978 in Paris, when the final draft of the Mass Media Declaration was considered, there were 350 reporters, 10 times more than those at the previous General Conference in Nairobi. *Newsweek* of November 6, 1978, reported that "as many as 26 countries could walk out of UNESCO" in the confrontation over the declaration. But Thomas McPhail, a Canadian mass communication professor who attended the General Conference, noted that "This walkout threat was a creation of the media, not of the Western delegations. And it appeared in much of the copy under the guise of factual, objective reporting."[65]

After the adoption of the Mass Media Declaration the next flurry of media attention occurred two years later with the release and adoption of the MacBride Report and the founding of the International Program for the Development of Communication (IPDC) at the Twenty-first General Conference of UNESCO in Belgrade. In light of the fact that the media was at the center of the issues, and was the main source of information about them, by then a diverse group of scholars had started to study media coverage of UNESCO to determine bias.[66]

A National News Council study of U.S. newspaper coverage of UNESCO's 1980 Belgrade General Conference found that the coverage concentrated excessively on the communications debate at the expense of deliberations over the many other activities of UNESCO. The study embraced over 650 news stories and editorials from newspapers in all parts of the country. The report stated that

> analysis of news coverage in the United States indicates a strong correspondence between the judgment of editors on what constitute news about UNESCO and the fears that their papers express so unanimously on their editorial pages about the possible adverse impact on freedom of the press of UNESCO's attempts to achieve a global consensus on problems of international communication.[67]

Research for this book revealed that between September 30 and November 2, 1980, the *International Herald Tribune, The New York Times, The Times, The Sunday Times, The Daily Telegraph* and *The Observer* published between them no fewer than 12 editorials and op-ed articles critical of the proposed changes and suggesting different solutions.[68] An example of the tone and content of many of the editorials was that which appeared in the *International Herald Tribune* of January 13, 1981. It said the MacBride Report "encourages government control of international news organisations." The *International Herald Tribune* supported the idea of a "louder voice" for the Third World, but argued that the NWICO was being used by authoritarian governments to justify press control and that the only way the Western media could counteract such hypocrisy was to "demonstrate, by their practices, why their system is essential."[69]

In his study, American scholar C. Anthony Giffard argued that the U.S. media presented a coordinated strategy to oppose the NWICO. The first step was the establishment of the World Press Freedom Committee, and the second was the publication of news stories and editorials aimed at influencing the U.S. political establishment. His investigation of U.S. media coverage of the withdrawal from UNESCO in 1984 shows that the U.S. media was very hostile to UNESCO and did play a role in the United States deciding to quit. He explained:

> The most common complaint was that the agency is politicized. The second largest cluster of criticisms centered on allegations of mismanagement. Then came press issues. Here UNESCO was accused of supporting the New World Information Order, of favouring state control of media systems, and of wanting to license journalists and impose codes of conduct on the press. It is clear from the coverage that UNESCO's communications policies were a major factor in the decision to withdraw.[70]

The allegations listed by Giffard were among those given by the United States and the United Kingdom as reasons for withdrawing, and it does seem curious that Western concerns about these problems were raised in the months following UNESCO and the UN's endorsement of the MacBride Report.

But Western media coverage of UNESCO was not consistently high. After the United States withdrew and the wings of the NWICO appeared to have been clipped, the media presence at the Twenty-third General Conference in Sofia declined sharply compared to the previous meetings. McPhail, in his study of the history of the NWICO, noted that AP and UPI carried "little copy," and AFP and Reuters did not even send full-time reporters to the conference.[71] Indeed, the Royal Institute of International Affairs's (Chatham House) clip file on UNESCO for the years 1985-1987 (based on whatever stories appeared in *Le Monde, The Guardian, The Times, The Daily Telegraph,* the *Financial Times, Frankfurter Allgemeine Zeitung,* the *International Herald Tribune* and the *Christian Science Monitor*) was found to be relatively free of reports relating to communication and information issues compared to the barrage of stories that appeared every year between 1979 and 1985. The Chatham House clip file on the Non-Aligned Movement for 1985-1987 also contains few reports on the subject. This lack of interest by the international media was due largely to the fact that the NWICO and UNESCO seemed less of a threat to press freedom following: (a) the emasculation of UNESCO with the withdrawal of the United States and the consequent cut of 25 percent of its budget; (b) the compromise reached at the 1985 General Conference, where it was agreed the NWICO would be regarded as an "evolving and continuing process"; and (c) the move to satisfy demands from the South through the work of the International Program for the Development of Communication.

However, media scrutiny was again high in 1987. Indeed, my review (for this study) of Western press coverage of UNESCO from 1979 to 1987 in the clip files of the Royal Institute of International Affairs, London, shows that by the time of the 1987 UNESCO General Conference all the alleged failings of UNESCO were being attributed in the prominent English-language Western dailies to one man—UNESCO director-general Amadou Mahtar M'Bow. M'Bow made his enthusiasm for the NWICO no secret. He got the support of the West in 1974 for his election and again in 1980 for a second term, but articles and editorials in the *International Herald Tribune, The Times, The Guardian* and the *Daily Telegraph* were all urging that he not be reelected to a third term in 1987.

Speeches and Talloires

Criticisms of the MacBride Report from media interests started in the document itself. They came from Sergei Losev, the director-general of TASS—the only head of an international news agency on the commission. In a separate comment in the appendix, Losev said that although the report contributed to "peace and international understanding" it compromised the "New International Information Order." It did this because the commission had not got its definitions clear, the terms used were "too westernized," and it presented an incomplete picture because it did not adequately consider threats to the Third World from Western information and culture. Nor did it note the contribution to self-reliance in the field made by the Eastern Bloc. According to Losev, the commission did not give adequate consideration to the difficulty of formulating international law to govern information and information exchange.[72]

Within the body of the report, Losev also registered his objection to Recommendation 56, which stated that "Censorship or arbitrary control of information should be abolished."[73] His alternative was that "This whole problem of censorship or arbitrary control of information is within the national legislation of each country and is to be solved within the national, legal framework taking in due consideration the national interests of each country."[74]

This latter objection is a good illustration of the ideological differences that separated TASS from the other major international news agencies. Whereas the director-general of TASS, an information arm of the Soviet government, condoned censorship, the Western news agencies opposed the MacBride Report on the grounds that it promoted censorship.

Among officials of the Western "Big Four," the most vociferous critics of the MacBride Report were Mort Rosenblum of AP and Gerald Long, managing director of Reuters. In the same month that the report was submitted to UNESCO, Rosenblum attacked Recommendation 58(b), which said that "Effective legal measures should be designed to . . . circumscribe the action of transnationals by requiring them to comply with specific criteria and conditions defined by national legislation and development policies."[75] In defense of the Big Four, Rosenblum argued that

> Most Third World proponents say their only source of international news is the large agencies, and they are right. But these agencies compete fiercely among themselves. If together they constitute a monopoly, it is because no alternative Third World agency has been organised. All major Western news agencies are on record as supporting such a venture, and each has offered to help with equipment, training and organisation.
>
> None of the major Western news agencies make a profit. In fact greater coverage of remote areas makes it harder for them to operate without considering the sort of government subsidy that could render them vulnerable to the influence which critics decry.[76]

Later Rosenblum said that if the report was not "soundly rejected" it would lend "international sanction to any government which seeks to ban correspondents, muzzle sources" and hamper legitimate reporting in a number of ways.[77]

The same month the report was submitted, Gerald Long of Reuters, in an address to the National Press Club in Canberra, Australia, also voiced his criticisms. He said that the members of the commission who were journalists had managed to temper the report but that the document still contained "dangerous" elements. With regard to the recommendation that an international center be set up at UNESCO for the study and planning of information and communication, he said such a center would be used as a permanent body for promoting ideas hostile to practicing journalists.[78] In March, Long, speaking at the Foreign Correspondents' Club, Hong Kong, said that the MacBride report was "a monster, a hybrid, full of irreconcilable contradictions, but with negative stance [sic], and, I am afraid, hatred of free information always prevailing."[79]

Later in the year, Long suggested that the UNESCO General Conference's first step in devising a "practical programme of media development" should be "throwing away the MacBride Report." His argument was that—despite the declarations at UNESCO and elsewhere—the poorer states had received no assistance to develop their media, and this was due to a basic clash between Western and Soviet ideology on the media. In his view, the means toward correcting the structural imbalance in the flow was improvement of the flow of information at the domestic level in the Third World, a task that should be completed with the help of the West. He added that "the new countries will then have to face for themselves the realisation that you cannot control information at home and then convince the world that your country tells the truth about itself."[80]

A response from UPI came in October at a meeting of its newly formed Advisory Board for Europe, Africa and the Middle East at which the board expressed concern about the role that UNESCO was playing in the coverage of world news. It promised to look at trying to improve the flow of news among nations. However, the board asserted that there was a growing trend, especially at UNESCO, to use the justified appeal for better coverage of the developing world to increase government control of the media.[81]

Rejection of the MacBride Report by the wider Western media interests was likewise not slow in coming. In 1979 the American Newspaper Publishers Association (ANPA) was highly critical of the commission's Interim Report, and in May, 1980, chairman of the ANPA executive committee and president of the Gannett newspaper group, Allen Neuharth, attacked the report in an address to the thirty-third congress of the International Newspaper Publishers Association in Tel Aviv. He said he was against the report because it was:

(a) proposing that the press promote goals set by governments; (b) calling for the UN to set up a broadcast arm with satellite capability; (c) biased against private ownership of news and communication facilities; (d) biased against "transnational" corporations, including international news agencies; and (e) against advertising as a means of supporting the press.[82]

After UNESCO and the UN embraced the proposals for reform of global news flows another act of protest from the Western media was the Declaration of Talloires, a product of the World Press Freedom Committee's (WPFC) Voices of Freedom Conference held in Talloires, France, from May 15 to 17, 1981.[83] Over 75 journalists and news executives from 24 countries in Asia, Africa, Europe and North and South America attended. Their declaration (See Appendix 6) said, inter alia, that:

> the free flow of information and ideas is essential for mutual under-
> standing and world peace. We consider restraints on the movement
> of news and information to be contrary to the interests of interna-
> tional understanding, in violation of the Universal Declaration of
> Human Rights, the Constitution of UNESCO, and the Final Act of the
> Conference on Security and Co-operation in Europe; and inconsis-
> tent with the Charter of the United Nations.

The declaration also called for "UNESCO and other intergovernmental bodies to abandon attempts to regulate the content of news and to formulate rules for the press." Instead, the declaration urged that:

> Effort should be directed instead to finding practical solutions to the
> problems before us, such as improving technological training,
> increasing professional interchanges and equipment transfers, reduc-
> ing communications tariffs, producing cheaper newsprint and elim-
> inating other barriers to the development of news media capabilities.

The Declaration of Talloires was in the same vein as the criticisms of the NWICO and MacBride Report voiced by some Big Four executives, and it represented Western ideals about the operations of the media. It was not surprising therefore that TASS held a different point of view on the matter. TASS analyst Yuri Kornilov said the campaign by the Western press in the name of protecting press freedom amounted to "psychological war against sovereign states." He singled out the Big Four, saying, "A handful of corporations are known to have firmly monopolised the mass media in the non-Socialist part of the world."[84]

The WPFC continued its battle to win over the media interests of the South in 1983 with its "Talloires II" conference, held from September 30 to

October 2, three weeks before the UNESCO General Conference in Paris. The 90 delegates who attended came from 25 countries, including 15 developing nations.[85] They drew up "The List of Talloires"—"a cross-indexed listing of more than 300 programs in 70 countries designed to equip journalists in developing countries with more professional skills."[86]

In 1987 the WPFC organized another "Voices of Freedom" conference on censorship problems. It was held in London, January 16-18, in collaboration with the International Federation of Newspaper Publishers (FIEJ), the International Press Institute (IPI), the Inter-American Press Association (IAPA), the North American National Broadcasters Association, and the International Federation of the Periodical Press. The journalists from 34 countries attending the meeting approved the "Charter for a Free Press," a set of principles they felt should be in place to ensure free, independent news media. (See Appendix 4.)

OPPOSITION FROM ADVERTISING INTERESTS

Opposition to the NWICO from the advertising industry, though not as elaborate as that of the mass media, was just as hostile. Shortly after the MacBride Report was released, the president of the American Association of Advertising Agencies, Leonard Matthews, in an article in *Business Week,* claimed the report was part of "a calculated attempt to set the stage for a nightmarish system of trade barriers, of propaganda agencies, of managed news, and of advertising bans, all aimed at uplifting the masses by depriving them of their right to see, hear, discuss, and buy whatever that want."[87] Months later, in 1982, at UNESCO's world conference on cultural policies in Mexico City, the advertising industry organized to show its opposition to what it feared might be the MacBride Commission's consequences. The industry's journal, *Advertising Age,* reported that

> International officers at U.S. ad agencies are fearful this is the next step in the battle to impose the commission's recommended restrictions on advertising and press freedom on Third World governments. A coalition of ad agency associations is meeting with the U.S. delegation to brief them on the issues; Mexican agencies and advertisers are standing by to air their views against it.[88]

That coalition included the American Association of Advertising Agencies, the European Advertising Agency Association and the International Advertising Association. They got support from the World Press Freedom Committee.

AID INITIATIVES

It is important to understand that the attempt to apply distributive justice to global news flows did not elicit denial from powerful transnational media interests that inequalities existed. The core problem was with the assumptions by NWICO proponents and the MacBride Report that government action was the best way to redress these imbalances. The attention at the two Talloires conferences to training and other forms of development assistance was symbolic of the belief that the preferred strategy in correcting imbalances was for non-governmental press bodies to help themselves and their colleagues in other parts of the world.

A number of media organizations and private foundations in North America and Europe had media development programs. Some of the more prominent were the Reuter Foundation and the Thomson Foundation in Britain, and the Friedrich Ebert Stiftung of Germany. The threats the NWICO seemed to pose were an incentive for these organizations to redouble their efforts.

By 1980 Gannett, the largest newspaper chain in the United States, had provided the biggest donation to the World Press Freedom Committee (U.S.$100,000). The WPFC used its funds for training projects in the South (its spending included $2,000 on journalism textbooks in Kenya and $10,000 on a seminar for business writers in Malaysia), publications that propagated the committee's line on UNESCO's activities concerning communications,[89] and conferences such as those at Talloires. By 1995, the WPFC had completed 150 projects under its George Beebe Fund to assist news media and journalism schools in Central and Eastern Europe, Africa, Asia, Latin America and the Caribbean.[90]

During the 1980s and early 1990s other organizations started, or enhanced, their journalism training programs, especially directed toward the "new democracies" of Central and Eastern Europe following the collapse of communism. Most prominent among these was the Freedom Forum of the United States, which set up offices in Asia and Europe to handle regional concerns.

For some, training programs by North American and European interests actually did not resolve the concerns of global news flows that the NWICO symbolized. As has been noted in chapter 3, it is the very way in which the powerful American and European media define and frame the "news" that is at the heart of the problem. With these media creating the training programs, it seems as though the problem will be reproduced rather than confronted.

On this point it is also important to note the reaction of the world organization representing journalists of the left, the International Organization of Journalists (IOJ), to 1981's Declaration of Talloires. IOJ president Kaarle Nordenstreng, a Finnish writer and intellectual, regarded the declaration as nothing more than another version of the "Marshall Plan" strategy that was used by the United States in the late 70s to neutralize the NWICO. The declaration's call "to abandon attempts to regulate global information and strive instead for practical solutions to Third World media advancement" received this characterization from Nordenstreng:

> Seen in the perspective of the media debate of the 1970s, this means, first, to turn attention away from a normative consideration of the content of communication and socio-political objectives which the media are supposed to serve and, second, to invite the media of the developing countries to co-operate with the private sector of the industrialized West in setting up, training, and maintaining their media infrastructure and personnel; in other words, "trading ideology against cooperation."[91]

THE IMPACT OF POLITICAL AND TECHNOLOGICAL REVOLUTIONS

The NWICO debate is a case study of how the media can act to protect their own interests when threatened. Such a scenario has serious consequences for observers on the periphery of such a confrontation who rely on the media to carry an accurate account of the facts. The press coverage of UNESCO not only was sometimes erroneous or negative, but also, to anyone not very familiar with UNESCO, gave the impression that most of the agency's work was in communication.[92] Partly because of the nature of the issue and the posture of the powerful Western media interests toward it, the NWICO did not have the image of a positive innovation for international relations and was not an easy idea to sell to the various publics.

The numerical majority of the South at the UN General Assembly and UNESCO ensured that symbolic gestures such as resolutions in support of the NWICO gained passage, even though (as the example of the Mass Media Declaration proved) much negotiation often was expended to ensure wording acceptable to all sides. However, UNESCO and the UN were noticeably restricted in translating all of these symbolic items into concrete action on their own terms because of the power of the rich countries, which was manifested most visibly by their financial support of the UN system.[93] Also, the collapse of communism abruptly undermined whatever support there was in the UN system for "statist" mass media policies.

When the debate reached its climax in about 1985 a compromise was reached on the NWICO at UNESCO when (at the Twenty-third General Conference in Sofia) it was decided that it should be seen as an "evolving and continuous process." This compromise remained in place at the Twenty-fourth General Conference in Paris in 1987. There Commission IV, which discussed UNESCO's communication activities, did consider the NWICO again, but, significantly

> the debate generally reflected the consensus reached at the twenty-third session of the General Conference, and again emphasized by the 126th session of the Executive Board . . . whereby such activities would be directed mainly towards the evaluation of previous work and the dissemination of earlier findings. However, several pleas were made in the course of the debate for a departure from the controversies of the past, and an attempt to find common platforms for concerted, practical action.[94]

By 1987, therefore, within UNESCO the emphasis was on trying to avoid controversies regarding the concept of the NWICO and concentrate on concrete action. That translated into the organization abandoning normative, "statist" proposals for changing the international communication structure for the idea that the wider diffusion of new technologies would be the solution.

The policy turnaround was articulated at UNESCO's Twenty-fifth General Conference in 1989, which approved a new communication policy for the organization. It was called "Communication in the service of humanity."[95] Prior to the General Conference, the UNESCO policy-making body, the Executive Board, had admitted that UNESCO's promotion of the NWICO was perceived by "professional communicators" as "a more or less avowed ambition on the part of the Organization to undermine freedom of information and impede the free flow of messages, individuals and ideas; this resulted in a misunderstanding that was used to tarnish the Organization's image."[96] The new policy would "dispel the misunderstandings." The board said

> That strategy, while recognizing the legitimacy of the call for a new world information and communication order [,] seen as an evolving and continuous process, consists in developing, in countries requesting such assistance, the training of communication professionals and the facilities for a media education that would lay emphasis on the development of critical acumen among users and the capacity of individuals and communities to react to any kind of manipulation and would at the same time promote a better understanding of the means available to users to defend their rights.[97]

The prevailing communication policies of UNESCO and the UN are reflected in the resolution on "Questions Relating to Information" passed annually at the UN General Assembly. The reports and the suggestions from the General Assembly's Information Committee were debated in the Special Political Committee of the General Assembly before resolutions were passed embodying the consensus reached. In contrast to the resolution of 1981 that mentioned the NWICO several times and made the explicit link between the NWICO and the proposed New International Economic Order,[98] the resolution of 1989 made only one reference to the NWICO,[99] the best indication of the toned-down rhetoric that marked the late 1980s and early 1990s. The UN General Assembly, reflecting the changed policies at UNESCO, passed basically the same resolution each year for 1990, '91, '92 and '93.[100] These resolutions contained four basic themes: (a) the need for technical assistance to improve mass media in poor countries; (b) promotion of cooperation in communication at the South-South level; (c) protection of journalists doing their work; and (d) "reducing existing disparities in information flows at all levels by increasing assistance for the development of communication infrastructures and capabilities in developing countries."

The articulation of the last theme included the allowance for national sovereignty by emphasizing "due regard for their needs and priorities" and recognizing the importance of developing countries' needing to "develop their own information and communication policies." However, the resolution said that the goal should be a "free flow of information at all levels." A major reason for the dispute over the NWICO was the perceived shortcomings of the so-called free flow doctrine, which many at UNESCO said should be replaced by a doctrine of "free and balanced flow." A free flow was not necessarily going to become a balanced flow because countries differ in their abilities to take advantage of such freedom.

These policies were reflected in the actual programs of UNESCO in the communication field. UNESCO helped establish the Central and East European Media Center in Warsaw, Poland (opened March, 1991) "to serve as a regional mechanism to respond to the urgent needs in Eastern European countries to train journalists, to exchange information and documentation, and to introduce to the Eastern European news media the principles and practices prevailing in societies with independent and pluralistic media."[101] Activities by UNESCO to promote liberal-democratic journalistic practices in Eastern Europe simply would not have occurred during the Cold War.

In Africa, the Pan-African News Agency (PANA), an organization notorious for its government control, was being restructured with UNESCO's help in 1992 as "a commercial enterprise with mixed government and private-sector shares, maintaining an independent editorial stance."[102] Similarly, following the recommendation from a UNESCO-sponsored seminar of 60 African publishers and journalists in Windhoek, Namibia, the International Program for the Development of Communication (IPDC) modified its rules in February 1992 to include projects from non-government media. (See Appendix 7, "Declaration of Windhoek on Promoting An Independent and Pluralistic African Press.")

By mid-1993 three prominent international press freedom groups—the Index on Censorship, the International Press Institute and the Commonwealth Press Union—were so impressed that UNESCO had become "a leading international force in the campaign to promote independent and pluralistic media" that they called on the British government to rejoin the organization.[103] But the surest indication that UNESCO was pursuing communication policies more amenable to its detractors came in late 1994 with the decision by the United States to contribute, through UNESCO, $10,000 to the Central and Eastern European Media Center and $35,000 to the IPDC for its project titled "Development of the Independent Press in Africa."[104]

CONCLUSIONS

With decolonization, it is understandable that there eventually was an effort to apply the principle of distributive justice to global news flows, especially as the technologies of international communication exploded. But the lesson learnt was that distributive justice could not be applied to news flows in the same way it was applied to physical resources, such as minerals, food and water. Because distributive justice, in order to be feasible, requires some institution to set and enforce the principles of distribution, it seems very threatening to press freedom. An international media system that is totally or mainly composed of government-owned and controlled mass media is more amenable to the application of distributive justice for the obvious reason that international government negotiations about news flows are more transferable into actual policy and practice by the press. However, the reality has been a plural international media system, consisting of many different approaches to media ownership and journalistic freedom. After the collapse of the European Communist Bloc and the end of Latin American dictatorships in the late 1980s, that international media system became more liberal-democratic in character, making it even more unlikely that distributive justice would be applied to global news flows. The revolutions in trade, finance, and technology discussed in chapter 2 were forces that served only to reinforce the power of this particular press ideology.

By the early 1990s the activities by UNESCO, private foundations and media companies to upgrade the technologies and training of journalists of

news media in poor countries represented an effort to apply distributive justice. But it was applied only to a certain point. The principle that all media
should be equal in terms of *capabilities* clearly was endorsed and acted upon.
But the principle that there should be equality in the *coverage* of regions had
been shelved. At UNESCO, the abandonment of this principle was inevitable
in light of UNESCO's embracing the notion that the less government control
of the media there was, the freer the media would be.[105] This distinctly
American brand of the liberal-democratic approach to press freedom scoffs at
any suggestion that forces outside the media should dictate what news the
press should cover and how journalists should cover news. It has provoked
arguments that press freedom under such conditions is still compromised by
advertisers and the tendency of journalists to build their reports from sources
that are ideologically similar.[106]

Distributive justice applied to international news coverage, and liberal-
democratic press theory and ideology, are fundamentally incompatible. The
more liberal-democratic the world press system is, the more unlikely it is that
claims for equal coverage of regions will be realized.

CENSORSHIP: THE IRONY OF AN INFORMATION AGE

It is common to think of censorship as an activity of governments. *The Compact Edition of the Oxford English Dictionary* defines it as the office or function of a censor, whom it in turn defines as "an official in some countries whose duty it is to inspect all books, journals, dramatic pieces, etc., before publication, to secure that they shall contain nothing immoral, heretical, or offensive to the government."[1] However, the industrialization of the news media and the growing concentration of them under the control of conglomerates and other large corporations has forced a broader approach to the discourse on censorship in liberal-democratic societies. And in other places, formal censorship is a practice of religious authorities. Therefore, in 1993, Ursula Owen, in her first editorial as editor and chief executive of the *Index on Censorship*, noted that

> Silencing takes many forms, the ultimate of which is assassination. Classic censorship—the thought policeman with his thick pencil— survives; other voices are suppressed by the rise of fundamentalism, the epidemic spread of authoritarian nationalism; concentration of media ownership, restricted access to technology and other hazards of the unmediated market economy have their own censoring effects. The old scourges of war, famine, poverty and illiteracy flourish; the arguments—over "hate speech," obscenity laws, rights of minorities—are, as yet, undecided.[2]

Similarly, in her book-length study of censorship, Sue Curry Jansen defined censorship as "all socially structured proscriptions or prescriptions which inhibit or prohibit dissemination of ideas, information, images, or other messages through a society's channels of communication whether these obstructions are secured by political, economic, religious, or other systems of authority."[3]

The idea that illiteracy is a form of censorship means that not just the particular circumstances of news media are relevant to the discussion of censorship. Private citizens can be censored merely through their material circumstances, which inhibit their abilities to express themselves. However, our concern in this book is with the news media in particular. And for journalists, any practice or situation that curbs their free expression is a threat to their earning a living. So, while everyone can be victimized by restrictions on freedom of expression, not all persons are directly denied a livelihood because of such practices as is the case with journalists, writers, publishers and those working for the mass media.

The concern of the news media with censorship goes deeper than merely the ability of media workers to earn a living. All modern political systems are constructed around assumptions about the role to be played by mass media. In liberal democracies it is assumed the media will perform the triple function of being: a watchdog for the public on the activities of government; a conduit for information and ideas on matters of public interest; and a communication link between the people and their government. Therefore, censorship is anathema to the efficient functioning of a liberal-democratic political system. Because the countries that control most of the content of international mass media systems are liberal-democratic states, the assumptions of liberal democracy are often made the reference point for discourse on censorship.

CENSORSHIP AND LIBERAL DEMOCRACY

European and North American writers on the subject of censorship have been smugly ethnocentric. It is often assumed among them that censorship is a practice that was given a pejorative meaning with the coming of the European "Enlightenment" and that societies still practicing government censorship are primitive, not modern.

In providing a history of censorship in its first issue of 1993, *The Economist* suggested that the practice has no place in modernity. The earliest and most glaring examples of it are religious censorship based on, for example, the prohibitions on idolatry found in the Bible and Holy Koran. Religious censorship declined in Europe following the "Enlightenment" and the yielding of power by religious authorities to secular governments, the magazine noted. The idea that blatant censorship is from another era when religious authorities were powerful and the habit is, therefore, not modern, came out in the way the periodical wrote about the practice. "The world's great religions have also gone through censorious phases, and some have not yet grown out of them," it declared, for example. Similarly, it noted that

> China's crackdown on artistic expression since Tiananmen Square
> is reminiscent of the worst excesses of Stalinism. China's greatest film
> directors have become non-people. Their works simply failed to

appear at the 1992 international film festival in Hong Kong. Some
African and Arab countries are just as primitive.[4]

But, the information supplied by *The Economist* about the history of censorship was evidence that censorship in Europe and North America was still
quite systematic for several years after World War II, and even after restrictions
had officially ceased, there was still a very real risk that some censors would
return. The British government's banning of *Spycatcher* in the late 1980s (see
below) was a clear illustration of this.

A number of secular practices in Britain and the United States restricted
expression until very recently.[5] Between 1737 and 1968 (when the Theater
Act was passed) the British office of the lord chamberlain censored and
licensed plays. The US Postal Service was empowered to censor printed material that was deemed to be obscene. And Hollywood studios abided by "The
Code," a list of restrictions that prevented them from running afoul of government censors. In the United States, the power of censors was reduced by
legislative and court action in the 1950s and 1960s, particularly the US
Supreme Court's rulings in the 1957 Roth case and the 1964 "Tropic of
Cancer" case. In Britain, the 1959 Obscene Publications Act made "literary
merit" a possible defense against censorship, and one of the most famous
publications to be permitted publication after this milestone was D. H.
Lawrence's *Lady Chatterly's Lover.*

Legal scholar Pnina Lahav emphasizes the recent nature of freer expression in North America and Western Europe by noting that free expression has
grown as a result of two largely twentieth century phenomena: (1) the solid-
ification of the liberal-democratic state; and (2) the increasing importance of
mass media to the political process in those states.[6] However, she notes that
press laws in liberal-democratic societies are deceptive because they are
authoritarian in nature while giving the semblance of still serving liberalism.
According to this view, governments still do not respect the "societal value of
freedom of the Press":

> In modern democracies, the tension between the authoritarian/
> instrumental and libertarian/constitutional conceptions reappears,
> in the form of the tension between the nation state and universal lib-
> eral values. The state, typically invoking arguments of national secu-
> rity or public peace and order, seeks to gain more discretionary power
> to regulate speech. The press resists by appealing to universal values.[7]

The temptation to assume that all major arguments over the credibility
of censorship ended with the European Enlightenment even predates the

twentieth century. When John Stuart Mill wrote the classic treatise on liberal-democratic theory, *On Liberty*, in 1859, he refused to discuss press freedom on the grounds that he felt these assumptions were so widely held that "[t]his aspect of the question, besides, has been so often and so triumphantly enforced by preceding writers, that it needs not be specially insisted on in this place."[8]

John Milton was perhaps the most celebrated of those "preceding writers" who "triumphantly" argued the case for press freedom. His *Areopagitica*, a speech, was a passionate plea for an end to the censorship caused by the Order of Parliament of 1643. The Order made it illegal to set up a printing press or publish anything without a license from the government. The authorities were also given the power to destroy unlicensed presses, confiscate illegal literature and arrest violators of the law.

Milton gave a number of reasons why licensing and censorship were counter-productive. For example:

- They were not in the tradition of free speech established by the ancient Greeks and early Roman emperors. The government of Athens only censored blasphemy and libel. Censorship was not even imposed on heretics by the later Christian Roman emperors, and they only had books destroyed after hearings in the councils.
- People should be considered mature enough to discern good from evil.
- If the rationale for the censorship was taken to its logical conclusion, even the Bible would have to be censored because that book contained tales of both good and evil.
- Objective truth is that which is tested by contrary points of view.
- In becoming the final judge on whom should be censored the government was assuming infallibility.
- To get the specified aims, a number of restrictions must be imposed across the board, not only on censorship.
- Because of the increasing volume of published material, a more elaborate order and bureaucracy will be needed to meet the required aims.
- Countries that had imposed censorship, Italy and Spain, did not reap any benefits from it.
- Whomever were selected to be censors would have to be very well read, and they would have the laborious task of reading all the literature that was submitted for license.
- England would lose its reputation for intellectual freedom, long revered by thinkers in other parts of Europe, including no less a person than Galileo who had been imprisoned in Italy for his views on astronomy.
- The people might not be as enthusiastic to defend their government in times of foreign attack.[9]

The *Areopagitica* has been held up as the classic liberal-democratic argument against censorship. But, for Curry Jansen, the contradictions in this argument begin with the contradictions in Milton himself. Milton served as Censor in Oliver Cromwell's government. Also, in his "Of True Religion, Heresie, Schism, and Toleration" (1673), he argued in favor of the use of Latin among the learned because the common people did not understand it. Therefore, in the context of Milton's life, the *Areopagitica* can be read, alternatively, as "an elitist apology for intellectual privilege."[10]

Curry Jansen's critique of Milton is part of her larger argument that "Enlightened discourse can say nothing new about censorship." The preoccupation of liberal democrats with government restrictions is seen as too limited. She believes censorship is intrinsic to the struggle to get and maintain power that is a feature of all human societies.

> My historical and semantic digs convince me that censorship is an enduring feature of all human communities. They indicate that knowledge and power are still bound together in an inextricable knot. Moreover they suggest that no amount of human ingenuity, scientific rigor, or political will can sever this knot. These digs force me to reject the claim that the Enlightenment abolished censorship. They lead me to conclude that Enlightenment merely transferred the office of Censor from a civic to a private trust. So that Liberalism's "Good Lie"—its claim to have abolished censorship—merely replaced church and state censorships with market censorship. And that as a consequence the discontinuity that separates pre- and post-Enlightenment censorships is largely semantic.[11]

The "market censorship" to which Jansen refers includes the supervisory power of private industry gained from market research, electronic databases storing vast amounts of personal information about private citizens and credit reporting agencies.

Curry Jansen is not the only one to view censorship as an existential phenomenon, protecting the power and privilege of various social groups. For example, some other writers argue that censorship is a practice that protects racial superiority.[12] An existential conception of censorship rids our consideration of it of the ethnocentrism inherent in the view that Europeans eliminated censorship as an acceptable government practice back in the Enlightenment. With such ethnocentrism gone, we are better able to understand fully the ways in which freedom of expression is compromised. In other words, the question shifts from being "Why are others not as advanced as us?" to "What can all societies do to ensure fuller participation in public dialog?"

CENSORSHIP IN INTERNATIONAL RELATIONS

Censorship rarely appears on its own as an issue in international politics. It is usually subsumed in the international discourse on human rights. So in many ways the discussion of censorship is a sub-discourse, subject to the various controversies that have hounded attempts by the United Nations' founding powers to create a universal human rights regime. Among these controversies has been the charge that the powers have been selective, and therefore hypocritical, in their invocation of universal human rights. Pariahs, such have Cuba's Fidel Castro, have been singled out for condemnation, while lackeys who abuse human rights, such as Zaire's Mobutu Sese Seko, have been patted on the wrist. There is also the argument that the declaring of some rights "universal" is part of a project of domination because it disdains cultural relativism.

Because it comes with the baggage of human rights, censorship has not been able to escape the debates mentioned above or other controversies. But we can isolate six ways in which censorship in particular has become a problem in international politics.

1. *When particular cases of censorship are the focus of international condemnation either due to the type of censorship or the person or institution censored.* Such international public relations and isolation was used by the United Nations and other groups against the South African apartheid regime. But often the leaders of such campaigns are non-governmental organizations (NGOs) or media companies concerned with promoting freedom of expression in particular. These groups and media are almost always based in the liberal-democratic states of Western Europe and North America and have the access to financial resources and global media needed to conduct international PR. Among the most prominent of these NGOs are Article 19, International PEN (both based in London), the Committee to Protect Journalists, Freedom House, Human Rights Watch Free Expression Project (all headquartered in New York City), and the International Federation of Journalists (based in Brussels). (See Appendix 10.)

The plight of Salman Rushdie became the most prominent illustration of how censorship could be a problem in international politics in this way. It was such a problem not only because it involved a number of countries, but also because it showed how decision-making about censorship is compromised by the contradictions in the international policies of states and the subordination of free speech rights in international politics to other imperatives.

Rushdie was sent into hiding in 1989 after Iran's Ayatollah Khomeini declared Rushdie's novel, *The Satanic Verses,* blasphemous and offered a bounty for his murder. Although Rushdie was a citizen of the United Kingdom, he was born in India where the book was also banned by the government for fear it would inflame Muslim sentiments. The international ramifications of the book's content and the Ayatollah's *fatwa* were even broader. Riots against the book in Pakistan in 1989 killed seven and injured many. In 1991 the book's Italian translator was wounded in a stabbing in Milan, and in Tokyo its Japanese translator was stabbed to death. The book's Norwegian publisher was shot and wounded in 1993. Diplomatic relations between Britain and Iran were broken for a short period of time soon after the death sentence was declared.

The *fatwa* was condemned by writers, intellectuals and publishers in a number of countries as an attack on free speech. That international non-governmental community created by Rushdie's cause organized a number of activities aimed at mobilizing public opinion behind Rushdie and getting the death sentence lifted. An International Rushdie Defense Committee was formed. Among the activities were the circulation in the United States of thousands of flyers on Rushdie's predicament, and the organization of meetings between Rushdie and government officials in Europe and the United States.

But despite Rushdie's being able to have conferences with British Prime Minister John Major and U. S. President Bill Clinton, six years after the *fatwa* was declared, there was no success in getting Iran to formally lift the death sentence and open the way for Rushdie to live a normal life again.[13] One reason for the stunning unwillingness or inability of the powerful countries to put pressure on Iran was fear of terrorist reprisal. That seemed to be the case when President Clinton seemed cautious and even apologetic about his meeting with Rushdie in late 1993. President Clinton did not allow the conference to be photographed, and was even quoted as saying he "meant no disrespect" to the Muslim world when he had the meeting. In contrast, Rushdie reportedly said afterwards that the President had "a passion" for his cause and his situation would be made a priority in the United States' future dealings with Iran. But, although the encounter did not immediately yield a lifting of the *fatwa*, by early 1996 Rushdie had realized one benefit from it. "There was a point at which it would have been uncool to meet me, and suddenly it became cool," he said on American television. "Suddenly they were queuing up to meet me. And since then the European Union's policy in this matter has toughened considerably and they have engaged in a campaign of pressurizing Iran into coming to a solution of the matter. And that has happened in the wake of the meeting I have had in the White House not only with the President, but also with [Secretary of State] Warren Christopher and [National Security Adviser] Anthony Lake."[14] Although the President's apparent waffling on the encounter with Rushdie was criticized in some sections of the

American media,[15] the changed attitudes that Rushdie noticed subsequently might have been evidence of the American government strategy for resolving the problem. It could be that the government realized that the high emotions inspired by the Rushdie case could be best resolved through quiet diplomacy. Open confrontation with Iran over the religious matter might add insult to injury and inspire terrorist attacks.

The lesson learnt from the Rushdie case is that international conflicts over censorship are, by their very nature, public, and this can constrain efforts to solve them. The reason why there was censorship in the first place was because one party did not want the other's ideas or information to get attention. But the more publicity the problem gets, the more attention the offending information and ideas are likely to get, and, as a result, the censor is likely to become more offended. This is especially the case with a government, like Iran, that, due to its oil resources and strategic location, has a great degree of power in international politics. Pointing out this vicious cycle is of little comfort to the censored and their allies because their major concern is for the censorship to end as immediately as possible, and publicizing their plight to embarrass the censor is a popular strategy to bring this about.

2. When it is an impediment to achieving international consensus of some sort. The most common manifestation of this is the attempt to establish and maintain an international system of liberal-democratic states. Censorship impedes liberal democracy because it kills press freedom, and the libertarian or social responsibility approach to press freedom is fundamental to the identities of liberal democracies.

Censorship of the news media is worthy of careful attention because it is an important part of the attempt to build consensus around the idea that the spread of democracies will mean a more peaceful international system. Research has shown that democracies do not go to war with each other. Because press freedom is one of the most prominent hallmarks of liberal-democracies, censorship is logically an impediment to the creation and maintenance of such democratic systems.[16]

The principle of freedom of information (the right to hold and impart ideas) is just one of the principles that have been codified and propagated by the United Nations as international law, beginning with 1948's Universal Declaration of Human Rights. But the fact that states continued to exercise censorship in some of the most blatant ways is testimony to the ability of political imperatives to supersede international law. In his overview of the United Nation's legal order, Oscar Schachter repeatedly felt a need to refer to how international law is shaped by the contours of political power. For example, he noted that

On the one hand, the concepts of international law provide a necessary code of communication, and therefore greatly facilitate the
institutionalization of international society. On the other hand, international law is often relied upon by states to resist the transfer of their
power to international authority. We have to look beyond international law itself to evaluate the likely consequences.[17]

Similarly, arguing that press law in modern democracies reflects the tensions
between the imperatives of the nation state (with its authoritarian inclina-
tions) and "universal liberal values" (founded in the European
Enlightenment), Pnina Lahav declares that political discourse is, therefore, the
key to understanding press law. "The search for understanding the law of the
press cannot focus exclusively on forms of regulation," she notes. "It must
transcend the form and inquire into the political theories that underpin the
systems of regulation."[18]

With regards to the specific question of complying with, and enforcing, international human rights law, Schachter noted that governments were gradually
forced to take their obligations more seriously because of the pressure of public
opinion.[19] However, Salman Rushdie's situation was evidence that even though
human rights was taken more seriously in the 50 years following the founding
of the UN system, even powerful governments would still be unable to act at times
to promote compliance if it is not in their strategic or economic interests. It
seemed that what was needed to get the Western European and US governments
to pressure Iran to lift the fatwa was wider support for Rushdie's cause. But, seven
years into the fatwa, Rushdie was still a *cause célèbre* for a prominent, but not very
powerful, lobby of elite journalists, writers and intellectuals. "Though he's the
toast of talk shows today, how many Americans will be preoccupied with Mr.
Rushdie's fate after the book tour ends?" American journalist Frank Rich asked
in an article in *The New York Times*. "The media party is fun while it lasts, but as
always in this restless culture, all too quickly moves on."[20]

**3. When censorship practices are subject to judicial arbitration by
international courts or by domestic courts whose rulings have extra-
territorial impact.** This was the case when the British government
attempted to enforce an international ban on the book *Spycatcher.*

In the late 1980s the British government pursued a two-year court battle
to have Peter Wright's *Spycatcher* banned. It went to the highest courts in
Australia, the country where Wright lived, and in Britain, where the book's
publisher was based. The government argued that Wright's revelations about
the running of Britain's intelligence service seriously compromised the United
Kingdom's national security. It also argued that Wright, a retired British

intelligence officer who had sworn to maintain secrecy, had committed a serious breach of ethics.

Among the revelations in the book were that: the British spy service bugged foreign embassies in London and carried out investigations into left-wing groups in Britain; the British intelligence services plotted to destabilize the Labour government of Harold Wilson between 1974 and 1976; the British government had planned to assassinate Egyptian President General Nasser while he was in office; and the British security service was compromised because either Sir Roger Hollis, MI5's Director General from 1956 to 1965, or Graham Mitchell, Hollis's deputy, were agents of the Soviet Union.

Some of the specific allegations in Wright's book had been made before in *Their Trade Is Treachery*, a book by Chapman Pincher which was published in the early 1980s, and the British government did not seek a ban then. Indeed, Peter Wright had given a lot of the information to Pincher.

When the British government was defeated in Australia's federal High Court it meant that the United Kingdom and Hong Kong were the only countries where *Spycatcher* could not be sold legally. The publicity surrounding the government's attempts to ban the book made *Spycatcher* a best-seller in the United States. The British newspapers also thumbed their noses at the government with their reports about how the ban was still meaningless because people were buying the book overseas and bringing it to Britain, and British public libraries were putting it on display.[21] The book and newspaper extracts from it were banned for a total of 29 months until the House of Lords ruled that further censorship was pointless.

The censorship of *Spycatcher* was only one of a number of attempts by the government of Prime Minister Margaret Thatcher to curb press freedom on the grounds of the actions being in the national security interest. For example, in early 1988, after a mob murdered two military officers at an IRA (Irish Republican Army) funeral in Northern Ireland, the government forced the television services into handing over video tapes made at the funeral for use in the investigation. Later, in 1988, when television journalists attempted to give the public more information about what happened in Gibraltar when a branch of the British armed services (the SAS) gunned down three suspected terrorists, the government launched a vain attempt to stop the program from being aired. The report contradicted the official version of events, which said that the three were shot in self defense. It suggested that they might have been shot without being given the chance to surrender peacefully.

In January 1988 the International Press Institute's annual survey of press freedom in the world featured the declining situation in Britain prominently, along with better-known violators of press freedom, such as South Africa.[22]

Even if the British government was successful in getting the courts to censor *Spycatcher*, it would have still lost the battle to keep the book's information from the public. The government's behavior also had the opposite effect of what it intended. The court cases gave the book the oxygen of publicity.

4. *When censorship is circumvented by technological innovation.* In the *Spycatcher* case the British government lost to the technological innovation of jet travel that rendered the efficient banning of a book published internationally almost pointless. Similarly, a reinterpretation of the Holy Koran which was banned in some states where Islam was a major religion, sold over 30,000 copies in Syria, Lebanon, Jordan and the Gulf. The book was by a Syrian, Muhammad Shahrur, and was titled *Al Kitab Wal Koran* (The Book and The Koran). The bans in Saudi Arabia, Qatar, the United Arab Emirates, and Egypt were circumvented by the photocopier.[23]

The telematic technology (the linking of computers and telecommunications) employed by the Internet and commercial information services providers was at first seen as the last nail in the coffin of censors. But such optimism was proved premature with the acquiescence of the US-headquartered on-line services company, CompuServe, to an order by the German government. CompuServe suspended access by its members to 200 Internet newsgroups that the Germans considered pornographic. The censorship affected all of CompuServe's users worldwide because it was not then technically possible to restrict access to only its German subscribers.[24] After taking the measure in December 1995, CompuServe reinstated access to all but five of the newsgroups in February 1996 after it appeased the German government by enhancing parents' abilities to use software to restrict their children's access to the service.[25] The move was one way market forces could produce censorship. Eager as they are to expand internationally, it seemed the on-line services companies might be willing to tolerate some censorship, and in exhange gain access to foreign markets, rather than have no censorship and lose some markets.

5. *In international agreements, when governments undertake to not practice nor tolerate censorship.* In these cases censorship is a practice that is considered subversive to the higher goal of promoting "universal human rights." Therefore, the non-governmental organizations that are the watchdogs against censorship invoke Article 19 of the 1948 Universal Declaration of Human Rights. "Any such declaration of principles that any government signs off on legitimizes the issue," explained William Orme, Executive Director of the Committee to Protect Journalists.[26] When governments want to disobey international conventions they have signed they must do it clandestinely and with denials.

Article 19 of the Universal Declaration of Human Rights says

> Everyone has the right of freedom of opinion and expression; this right includes freedom to hold opinions without interference and to seek, receive and impart information and ideas through any media and regardless of frontiers.

The Declaration is of a non-binding character. Another UN document, the International Covenant on Civil and Political Rights (1966), is a codification of the Declaration's principles in international law and is binding on states which sign it. The Covenant makes freedom of information less cut and dry. It mentions that communicators have responsibilities as well as rights. Article 19 of the covenant (in contrast to the Declaration) says

1. Everyone shall have the right to hold opinions without interference.
2. Everyone shall have the right to freedom of expression; this right shall include freedom to seek, receive and impart information and ideas of all kinds, regardless of frontiers, either orally, in writing or in print, in the form of art, or through any other media of his choice.
3. The exercise of the rights provided for in paragraph 2 of this article carries with it special duties and responsibilities. It may therefore be subject to certain restrictions, but these shall only be such as are provided by law and are necessary:
   (a) For respect of the rights or reputations of others;
   (b) For the protection of national security or of public order (*ordre public*), or of public health or morals.

Article 20 goes on to identify other specific grounds for restrictions:

1. Any propaganda for war shall be prohibited by law.
2. Any advocacy of national, racial or religious hatred that constitutes incitement to discrimination, hostility or violence shall be prohibited by law.

It is understandable that press freedom activists, in their international rhetoric, are more likely to cite Article 19 of the Universal declaration than Articles 19 and 20 of the International Covenant. Similarly, it is understandable why governments are more willing to sign on to the covenant which by no means regards press freedom as absolute.[27] Suppression of expression, according to the Covenant, is allowed as long as it can be justified for one or all of the reasons permitted.

This feature of the Covenant that stresses responsibilities and allows for justifiable restrictions is also in another widely quoted document in the international discourse on press freedom, the European Convention for the Protection of Human Rights and Fundamental Freedoms (also known as the European Convention on Human Rights). The relevant section is Article 10 which says

1. Everyone has the right to freedom of expression. This right shall include freedom to hold opinions and to receive and impart information and ideas without interference by public authority and regardless of frontiers. This Article shall not prevent States from requiring licensing of broadcasting, television or cinema enterprises.
2. The exercise of these freedoms, since it carries with it duties and responsibilities, may be subject to such formalities, conditions, restrictions or penalties as are prescribed by law and are necessary in a democratic society, in the interests of national security, territorial integrity or public safety, for the prevention of disorder or crime, for the protection of health or morals, for the protection of the reputation or rights of others, for preventing the disclosure of information received in confidence, or for maintaining the authority and impartiality of the judiciary.

The European Convention has a relatively sophisticated system of surveillance and arbitration through the European Commission of Human Rights, the European Court of Human Rights, and the Committee of Ministers of the Council of Europe.

The provisos allowing censorship in the International Covenant and the European Convention have been sources of disagreement between American and Western European activists. The Americans tend to prefer no press law at all, and, if there are such documents, they should be as liberal as possible, such as the First Amendment of the US Constitution and Article 19 of the Universal Declaration. According to Dana Bullen, Executive Director of the World Press Freedom Committee, it is "quite astonishing" the degree to which some groups rely on Articles 19 and 20 of the International Covenant. Said Bullen, "The restrictions set out in it provide more than enough excuses for any restrictions one might desire."[28]

Invoking absolute rights is as much a dogmatic preoccupation as it is a rhetorical strategy by press freedom groups to deal with political power. Saying press freedom should not be restricted under any conditions is a means of trying to ensure as minimal interference as possible. But the fact is that even the most liberal-democratic countries have laws restricting racist speech and other incitements of hatred towards groups based on race, religion, skin color, national or ethnic origin, and sexual orientation. Many countries also restrict publication of information deemed pornographic or offensive to "public morality." Some types of advertising are restricted on the grounds of protecting public health. For example, tobacco advertising was banned on broadcast media in the United States from 1971.

6. During international military conflict, when military authorities practice censorship. In times of war or occupation the news media are censored by military authorities usually on the grounds that absolute press freedom might compromise strategic planning or the safety of everyone. The news media counter by arguing that the publics they serve should have a right to know, especially the families of soldiers or those concerned about vague war aims and the committing of atrocities. The news media are also conscious that their reports serve posterity as a historical record for others to see.

As the technological capability of the news media to transmit reports as widely and as rapidly as possible has increased, the news media have become more significant players in the conduct of war. Censorship takes the form less of outright restriction and more of careful manipulation of what reporters can cover. In a media-saturated environment crude censorship yields bad public relations. Manipulation is a better strategy because it satisfies the curiosity of reporters and maintains a good image.

THE INTERNATIONAL JOURNALISM SURVEY

By the mid 1990s the demise of the European communist bloc and the technological revolution symbolized by the global diffusion of the Internet made it tempting to be optimistic about prospects of censorship being less of a problem in international politics. However, a survey for this book of nongovernmental organizations that promote press freedom and human rights revealed more pessimism than optimism. (See Appendix 9.) Representatives from six of the 10 groups that responded said they were not optimistic that there would be less government censorship in the years to come. Only three were optimistic, and one indicated that optimism or pessimism varied according to the region of the world being discussed.

The focus on the power of states in the replies of those who explained their pessimism goes contrary to the trend of focusing on the demise of state power in the wake of transnational forces. "The officials of most governments—70 percent by our reckoning—regard news and information media as essential to the maintenance of their political and economic power," the representative of Freedom House asserted bluntly.

"I think governments are about control, but their tactics might become less violent, and that would be something we would all hope for," said the official of PEN American Center. "But I think there always would be subtle means of trying to control the flow of information. And I think we are a long way away from seeing a planet earth where there is no such thing as oppression and intolerance, and all of those things feed censorship."

Those who are optimistic tend to emphasize the impact of new technologies, such as facsimile and telematics that are no respecters of territorial borders. "There is certainly much less censorship today than there was 10 years ago, and there was less 10 years ago than there was 20 years before," the head of the New York–based Committee to Protect Journalists (CPJ) noted. "The technological revolution is an unflappable reality that governments cannot control, China can't control."

What the International Journalism Survey also revealed was the ideological division that exists between the international press freedom groups based in the United States and those based in Europe. The Americans are more likely than the Europeans to view freedom from censorship as an absolute right, with no tolerance of restrictions. The member of the World Press Freedom Committee (WPFC) said that "The effort of Western European nations to codify 'permissible restrictions' on the press is a major unreported threat, especially as they promote this at the UN Human Rights Commission, Council of Europe, etc." The representative of Freedom House expressed his concern about the efforts to create press laws in Eastern and Central Europe and the former Soviet states:

> These laws and others in draft stage include wide loopholes through which censorious officials can control the content and the practice of journalism. We are also disappointed to see the Council of Europe recommending a similar course, and the new Rapporteur of the UN Human Rights Commission justifying "permissible limitation" on press freedom—far beyond allowance for laws on libel, pornography and strictly defined national security. We express our disagreement with such proposals through our own publications, by direct statements to the principals (heads of state, ambassadors, etc.), and by joining with other groups of like mind. On occasion, we also express our view to American diplomats and urge counter-action.

A recent effort by American press freedom groups to promote such an absolutist ideology concerning press freedom was the Inter American Press

Association's Declaration of Chapultepec (Appendix 5). Interestingly, that document (which the IAPA managed to get a number of heads of state to sign, including the US President) made no reference to the fact that some areas of mass media content are censored, even in the United States (content such as child pornography).

A partial explanation for the ideological difference might be the fact that the European media industry has historically had a much less suspicious attitude to government involvement in the media. Governments have not only owned and controlled major European broadcasters (such as the British Broadcasting Corporation), but have even subsidized print and other media (such as the French government's relationship with Agence France-Presse). In stark contrast, the US mass media model is based on the idea that government ownership of media is a threat to freedom of speech, and what little direct government ties exist are confined to the regulation of broadcasting and subsidies to the public broadcasting system.

Another explanation of the difference is the recent history of regional and world wars being caused by European ethnic and ideological differences. The Europeans, as evidenced by the presence of laws in some countries proscribing fascist and racist propaganda, seem much more attuned to the possibility of media agitation being sources of social disorder and conflict.

CONCLUSION

International disputes over censorship are all over the rank ordering of priorities. For example, in theocracies authorities invoke religious values to justify censorship. The Rushdie case was an example of how such beliefs were ranked higher than freedom of information. In liberal democracies, governments use "national security" or other values said to be in the interest of wider society to justify restrictions.

Understanding how priorities are ranked and valued is the first step to understanding why censorship has remained a problem in international relations. The attention to this ranking by no means disputes Curry Jansen's profound notion that censorship is about power, a knot that binds power and knowledge. It actually compliments this idea by taking the discussion further, for the purposes of the study of international relations, to ask such questions as "Who determines the ranking of priorities?" and "How are these rankings embedded in the legal and political foundations of international society?"

Asking such questions bring us back to the rationales for the abhorrence of censorship that should be at the core of the discussion. In this chapter we have seen that censorship is largely a preoccupation in the discourse on

European "Enlightenment" and the growth of liberal democracies. In such discourses, censorship is considered evil because it is seen as a means of disenfranchising some members of civil society and a tool by which minority or majority tyrannies can be imposed. In other words, all means by which expression is thwarted are as threatening to liberal democracy as government censorship and prior restraint. Therefore, confining the discussion to government censorship is short-sighted and will not bring progress towards the creation of a liberal-democratic order.

Ways in which many are excluded from public dialog are often hard to identify. For example, a study by Article 19 of laws affecting press freedom in 11 democracies[29] found that some of the ways in which expression was curbed included interference by media owners, import restrictions, and broad scope of legal liability in libel and slander suits. Article 19 found that a majority of the countries had legal systems with positive features for a free press, such as no licensing requirement to publish newspapers, recognition of the right of journalists to protect confidential sources, and no export restrictions on publications.[30] But these features are only one dimension of the status of free expression in societies. Other factors include: whether ownership of mass media are restricted to a privileged few who can afford the investment; differential access to quality education due to socio-economic class, gender, race, or all of those categories; and institutionalized discrimination that systematically restricts certain social groups from being heard in the mass media.

Often the rank ordering of social groups determines the censorship of their expression. This ordering is done through structures for granting public and private funding, the financial structure of media markets, popular prejudice, and even the news values of the mass media. United States–based Ethiopian film-maker, Haile Gerima, explained his predicament in trying to make a film about slavery:

> In America, slavery is a very sensitive topic. The moment I wanted to make *Sankofa* (1993) my credentials in the USA vanished, because I was venturing into forbidden territory. The resource centres were closed to me: I couldn't get funding. Censorship became a reality; the funding agencies for cultural development shut their doors. They'd talk about timing: 'This year's budget is nearly spent. You're too late—or too early.' Nobody comes out with it straight and says that the subject matter is wrong. The press is much the same; they wouldn't touch *Sankofa* at Berlin, though it was in competition with big budget movies. They censor you by making you non-existent. We went to Montreal and Toronto: they skipped us, didn't even talk to us. They thought we were finished.[31]

So the examination of censorship in relation to the news media must begin and end with a critical understanding of what a democratic society truly is. Unfortunately, the preoccupation with legal and government restrictions alone misses the point. And the logical extension to this view is that even if the International Covenant on Civil and Political Rights was free of the provisos that allow government censorship, the news media would not be necessarily nearer to performing their ideal roles as institutions of democratic societies.

KILLING THE MESSENGER

THE PROBLEM

One televised incident in 1979 illustrated to the world just how dangerous work as a foreign correspondent could be. On June 20 of that year, Nicaraguan government soldiers shot and killed 37-year-old ABC-TV reporter Bill Stewart and his interpreter. The two were killed in Managua, the Nicaraguan capital, when they attempted to talk with the national guardsmen who were manning a roadblock near the scene of fighting with Sandinista rebels. The shooting of Stewart was recorded on videotape by Stewart's television crew and shown around the world in newscasts soon afterward. The footage was shot from a distance of 15 to 20 yards away.

The executions were condemned by the heads of both the governments involved. Nicaragua's president, Anastasio Somoza Debayle, expressed his "most deep condolences." He termed the murder an "unforgivable and isolated incident" and said "I never wanted it to happen in Nicaragua." Those responsible would be punished under the "full weight of the law," he promised.[1] U.S. president Jimmy Carter stated that the executions were "an act of barbarism that all civilized people condemn." "Journalists seeking to report the news and inform the public are soldiers in no nation's army," Carter said. "When they are made innocent victims of violence and war, all people who cherish the truth and believe in free debate pay a terrible price."[2]

Hostility between the foreign news media covering the war and the Nicaraguan government was the context of the killings. According to a *Washington Post* report at the time,

> The government has repeatedly accused the foreign press, including reporters from the United States, Europe and other Latin American countries, of distorting the situation here in its description of strong public support for the anti-Somoza insurrection led by Sandinista National Liberation Front guerrillas.

Tuesday [the day before the murders] the government radio network began broadcasting charges that foreign reporters were part
of an "international Communist conspiracy" to topple Somoza and
install a Marxist government. An article in the Somoza owned newspaper[,] Novedades[,] Tuesday accused the international press of
"criminal silence" about what it called Sandinista Communists.[3]

In a statement of protest to Somoza against the murders, foreign correspondents said that general antagonism against them "foments hostility
toward us and makes our work even more dangerous than it is already."[4]

The immediate effect of Stewart's killing was to reduce the numbers of
foreign journalists covering the Nicaraguan civil war. A day after he died, 32
journalists, including most of the American network TV crews, fled the country in protest and fear.[5] The incident added to the stream of negative publicity against the Somoza government that eventually produced its demise.

Despite the graphic murder on TV of an American foreign correspondent
and all of the attention it brought because of the power of the U.S. media over
the world's mass communication systems, the years following the Nicaraguan
incident did not see the world becoming a safer place for journalists. According
to Table 6.1, the situation actually deteriorated. In all the categories, the situation was worse in 1994 than it was in 1982.

The figures must be read with a few caveats in mind. First, it is unclear to
what extent the increases were due to better reporting of such incidents—a
result of heightened sensitivity—rather than actual increases. The practice of
compiling statistics on physical harm to, and restrictions on, journalists only
started in the 1970s. So the international human rights and press freedom
groups have been honing their skills in compiling such data.

Second, there is some variation on the numbers according to source.
Freedom House, the organization that compiled the numbers listed in Table
6.1, got its information from its own sources and three other organizations.
The numbers compiled by the Committee to Protect Journalists (CPJ) and
Reporters Sans Frontieres (RSF), two of those additional sources, were different from each other and from the tally of Freedom House. There is no question that 126 journalists were killed around the world in 1994. But the
organizations had varying degrees of reluctance to list some murders as due
to journalistic work, or they took longer periods investigating the circumstances of the deaths.

What Freedom House, the CPJ and RSF did not disagree on, however, was
that more journalists were murdered in the line of duty in 1994 than in any
previous year since they started compiling such figures. In its annual report
on press freedom worldwide, RSF gave the tally of journalists killed because of

TABLE 6.1
PRESS FREEDOM VIOLATIONS — 1982–1994*
(Numbers of journalists killed, kidnapped, disappeared, arrested, detained, expelled)

	1994	'93	'92	'91	'90	'89	'88	'87	'86	'85	'84	'83	'82
Killed	126ª[27]	74ᵇ[27]	107ᶜ[27]	62[19]	45[19]	73[24]	46	32	19	31	21	14	9
Kidnapped/ Disappeared	38[17]	47[17]	34[9]	20[7]	16[8]	38[8]	14	10	13	13	5	4	11
Arrested/ Detained	345+[58]	368[48]	225[52]	298[42]	168[45]	354[33]	225	188	178	109	72	80	145
Expelled	43[17]	12[9]	24[13]	22[12]	31[14]	75[14]	24	51	40	9	22	19	23

Bracketed numbers [ ] are number of countries in which events occurred.

ᵃAfghanistan-1; Algeria-24; Armenia-1; Belarus-2; Bosnia-8; Brazil-1; Burundi-1; Cambodia-3; Colombia-5; Egypt-2; Georgia-2; Guatemala-2; India-2; Iraq-1; Madagascar-1; Mexico-3; Nepal-1; Pakistan-2; Palestinian Territory-1; Philippines-1; Russia-11; Rwanda-37; Somalia-3; South Africa-3; Tajikistan-5; Turkey-1; Zaire-2.

ᵇAfghanistan-2; Algeria-9; Angola-3; Argentina-1; Bosnia-9; Colombia-5; Congo-1; Croatia-2; El Salvador-1; Georgia-4; Guatemala-2; Honduras-1; India-2; Italy-1; Lebanon-1; Lithuania-1; Mexico-3; Peru-1; Philippines-1; Russia-8; Rwanda-1; Somalia-1; South Africa-1; Tajikistan-3; Turkey-4; United States-1; Venezuela-1.

ᶜAngola-2; Azerbaijan-2; Bosnia-25; Chad-3; Colombia-5; Croatia-4; Egypt-1; Ethiopia-1; Georgia-1; Guatemala-2; Haiti-1; Hong Kong-1; India-5; Lebanon-2; Liberia-1; Mexico-1; Papua New Guinea-1; Peru-10; Philippines-5; Russia-1; Rwanda-2; South Africa-1; Sudan-1; Tajikistan-7; Turkey-15; Ukraine-1; United States-1; Venezuela-5.

*SOURCE: Freedom House – based on reports from Freedom House correspondents, the Committee to Protect Journalists, Reporters Sans Frontières, and IFEX (International Freedom of Expression Exchange).

their profession as 103 (77 in Africa, 15 in Europe, 8 in Asia, 2 in the Middle East, and 1 in Latin America).[6] The comparative number given by the CPJ in its annual report was 72, but the CPJ pointed out that "the real number" was definitely larger. "In 1993, 64 journalists were killed on the job; 10 of these cases, however, were not confirmed until 1994," explained the CPJ. "Reports of journalists killed in the line of duty are investigated by CPJ staff researchers, who verify that the victims were employed in news-gathering and were killed as a direct consequence of their work."[7]

RSF identified seven trends related to press freedom in the world that were evident in 1994. (Some of these trends also were identified by respondents to our International Journalism Survey, the findings of which are given in a later section of this chapter.) The first is the deliberate targeting of journalists as a form of military strategy in armed conflicts. This has happened in the former Yugoslavia and in Algeria, Rwanda, Russia and Egypt. Second is the tendency of killers to get away with their crimes. "How many of the people who ordered the murder of journalists were arrested last year?" RSF asked rhetorically. "Maybe three or four."[8] Similarly, the CPJ noted that no one had been arrested in any of the 18 countries where it found such political assassinations to have taken place.[9] A third trend has been the emergence of hate media that fanned the fires of ethnic hostility. The most well known case was Radio Libre des Mille Collines (RTLM) that was used by the Hutu in Rwanda against the Tutsi. According to RSF, that radio, operated by some of Rwanda's top journalists, broadcast that war against the Tutsis was inevitable and directed soldiers and militia to genocide victims. There were also examples of such media in Burundi, Bosnia, Crimea, Romania, Tajikistan, Nagorno-Karabakh, and Georgia (of the former Soviet Union). "The use of propaganda by the state or by political, military or religious pressure groups to stir up their supporters is not new," RSF said. "What is astonishing is that in some countries it is hard-won liberal press legislation, adopted after long struggles by human rights militants, that has made it easier for private media to broadcast extremist propaganda, often with discreet support in high places. Such laws also enable dictators to subcontract atrocities that international pressure would not let them perform themselves, with impunity."[10] Fourth, the number of disputed territory, or "twilight zones," around the world makes it difficult for journalists to get into some areas. Journalists can be kicked out of places despite having the required passes (as happened in East Timor), or they can be denied access completely (as with Israel's "closed military zones"). Fifth has been the growing influence of organized crime. Sixth is the systems of de facto licensing of journalists, known as "institutes." For example, only Indonesian journalists who were members of the state-run Association of Indonesian Journalists were accredited to cover the Asia-Pacific Economic Council summit in October 1994. The seventh is a trend common in the rapidly industrializing economies of Asia, such as Singapore and Malaysia. RSF called it "development blackmail"—restricting the press on the grounds that such action was in the interest of the economic development of the country.

The harassment of journalists in these many ways is particularly disturbing because of the important role reporters and other news media workers play in the development and maintenance of international society. A free press can be viewed as contributing to international peace in two ways. The first is directly, through the surveillance function the media plays, in such activities as covering wars and reporting atrocities, seeking out multiple sources of facts, and publicizing civil abuses that are often the cause of wars. The second is indirectly, by being the required institution of liberal democracies. A powerful argument, supported by historical evidence, has been that democracies are less likely to go to war with each other.

DEFINING A JOURNALIST

We must make clear our definitions of who actually qualifies to be called a "journalist" before plunging into any discussion of the physical protection of journalists as a problem in international relations. In journalism, as with other professions, having others outside the occupation define who is a journalist is a serious threat to the freedoms that are necessary for media professionals to perform their work with integrity.

One reason why consistency in the definition of who is a journalist is important is because the organizations that collect statistics on the harassment of journalists (e.g. the CPJ, Freedom House, the IFJ, and the IAPA) have subtle differences between them in how they define a journalist. Are personnel of government information services journalists? Are interpreters killed while working for reporters to be classified as journalists killed? Is a journalist who also is a political activist to be classified as a journalist killed in the line of duty if the reasons for her murder are not clear?[11]

There often are great variations in how journalists are defined. For example, the UN's Draft Articles of the International Convention on the Protection of Journalists Engaged in Dangerous Professional Missions in Areas of Armed Conflict (1972) characterize a journalist as

> any correspondent, reporter, photographer, film cameraman or press technician who is ordinarily engaged in any of these activities as his principal occupation and who, in countries where such activities are assigned their particular status by virtue of laws or regulations, have that status (by virtue of the said laws or regulations).[12]

The "Casework Manual" of the Committee to Protect Journalists (CPJ) says that

> We define a journalist as someone who contributes news or commentary to one or more news organs that appear regularly. Editors, publishers and directors of news organs are also considered journalists, as are broadcasting crews (camera operators, sound recordists, etc.). In some instances, a documentary filmmaker or freelance writer may be considered a journalist when he or she is working on a journalistic project. Although newspaper vendors and

distributors are not journalists per se, we do view attacks on them as violations of press freedom and document such attacks in our annual report. Notable cases of this sort have occurred in Algeria (the killing of newspaper vendors) and India (attacks and raids on trucks delivering newspapers).

In some countries, such as China, a samizdat journal may appear very irregularly and have limited distribution. In Vietnam, contributors to an unofficial newsletter that was circulated by cassette were arrested and sentenced to long prison terms. Because of the constraints on the press in these countries, CPJ considers people engaged in such activity as journalists.[13]

For the purposes of this book, the definition used by Amit Mukherjee, a researcher on the international protection of journalists, is preferable. Mukherjee says that

> a "journalist" is (a) a person who, on a regular or on a temporary basis, creates media news coverage, i.e., a correspondent, a photographer, a cameraperson, or a media technician, whose job consists of working with words, images, or sound destined for the printed press, radio, film, or television; or (b) a person whose regular occupation is the professional assistance of persons belonging to category (a) above.[14]

This definition is preferred because it is inclusive. The more inclusive definitions are, the more likely it will be that many "support" staff for foreign correspondents will be included in the tallies of those persecuted and killed. For example, the murder of Bill Stewart's interpreter got much less attention or no publicity at all in some news coverage of the 1979 murders in Nicaragua. Indeed, some U.S. media reports did not carry his name, and some found it difficult even to get his name correct when they did. *The New York Times* and *The Washington Post*'s initial reports called him "Juan Espinosa," but a report in *The Washington Post* some days later said he was "Francisco Espinoza." In contrast, there were no contradictions in the name and spelling of Bill Stewart. Also, the Nicaraguan remained faceless in the newspaper coverage, in contrast to the pictures of Stewart that were relayed.[15] A problem in the global discourse on the physical protection of journalists has been the tendency of the global media to pay more attention to the plight of North American and European journalists. Often, African, Latin American and Asian journalists who get killed in the line of duty get scant attention or are totally ignored. Such disparities were mirrored in the Salman Rushdie case.[16] Writers in Latin America, Asia and Africa were victimized before and after the *fatwa* on Rushdie, but the plight of the British writer Rushdie got the international press coverage that those other persecuted writers did not receive.

HISTORICAL CONTEXT

Three distinctions can be made in the discussion of protecting journalists: (a) physical versus professional protection; (b) protection in times of peace versus protection in time of war; and (c) national versus international measures to protect journalists.[17]

Physical protection refers to safeguards against physical harm. Professional protection works against all the problems that prevent journalists from pursuing their profession, including censorship, laws of defamation, and restrictions on freedom of movement. Some actors are primarily concerned with the physical protection of journalists (e.g. the Red Cross and Amnesty International) while others refer to both types when they speak of "protection" (e.g. the Committee to Protect Journalists, and the International Federation of Journalists).

According to Mukherjee, organizations representing mainly working journalists (e.g. the IFJ, CPJ, IOJ and RSF) "are at least as concerned with physical safety and security of their colleagues at home and abroad as they are with the issue of press freedom." In contrast, groups made up primarily of publishers and senior editors (e.g. the IAPA, WPFC, and FIEJ), "tend to put more emphasis on press freedom issues vis-à-vis issues relating to physical safety of journalists."[18]

The distinction between protection during peace and war is important because codified international law to physically protect journalists is more developed for circumstances of international armed conflict than during peace.

International and national measures must be distinguished because it has been found that they work in tandem to protect journalists. Historically, it has been the non-governmental press freedom groups that have been behind international initiatives to protect (broadly defined) journalists. This fact largely accounts for why there has been a failure to establish and maintain multilateral systems for ensuring the professional and physical protection of journalists.

Beginning in the nineteenth century, there has been more discussion of protecting journalists than action. Journalistic protection was a topic at the international press congresses of the professional journalists' organizations in Chicago in May 1893 and in Anvers, Belgium, in July 1894. It was also considered at the Conference of Press Experts sponsored by the League of Nations in Geneva in 1927. After World War II, the four Geneva Conventions of 1949[19] provided for the humane treatment of war correspondents but that is as far as the states system has got with international law on the problem.

According to international legal scholar Melissa A. Young, it was recognition that the Geneva Conventions were not enough that produced the effort to establish a specific legal international regime for the protection of journalists, beginning at the 1957 Lisbon Congress of the International Federation of Editors-in-Chief.[20] At that conference there was discussion of the protection of journalists on dangerous missions. The federation had become concerned about the topic after a number of war correspondents had disappeared in Korea, Vietnam, Africa and Latin America. It eventually referred the problem to the International Commission of Jurists, which produced a 1968 draft convention for the protection of journalists on dangerous missions. The Montecatini Draft Convention (as it came to be called) was adopted by the International Federation of Editors-in-Chief in May 1968, but nothing became of its recommendations, such as its call for the setting up of an International Committee for the Protection of Journalists on Dangerous Missions. Similarly, nothing became of the International Press Institute's proposal in the early 1970s to establish an International Professional Committee for the Safety of Journalists that would issue safety cards to correspondents on dangerous missions and maintain records on such journalists.

Various organs of the UN's Commission on Human Rights (CHR) considered the topic over a period spanning more than 30 years with little concrete result. These initiatives began with the Sub-Commission on Freedom of Information and of the Press of the CHR during the late 1940s and early 1950s. In 1971 the CHR produced a Preliminary Draft International Convention on the Protection of Journalists Engaged in Dangerous Missions. The draft was revised twice before essentially being shelved. The Preliminary Draft International Convention (transmitted to the General Assembly by the Economic and Social Council in its Resolution 1597 [L], 1971) provided for journalists working in dangerous missions to have "safe-conduct" cards. The cards—bearing name, date and place of birth, habitual residence and nationality—would be a form of identification certifying that the carriers were professional journalists. Parties to the convention were to extend to holders of such cards "the same protection of their persons as to their own journalists." Such a convention, granting governments the power to certify the professional status of journalists, was a departure from the liberal ideology regarding the press that prevailed in the early days of the UN. The NWICO debate was to reveal that there were powerful interests, with money and access to sources of publicity, who quickly mobilized to defeat any initiative that proposed government control of the press. Also safe-conduct cards would be a two-edged sword, identifying journalists for harassment as well as protection.

The CHR's Sub-Commission on Prevention of Discrimination and Protection of Minorities produced a final report on freedom of opinion and expression in 1992 that was written by Louis Joinet and Danilo Turk, two of its members. Although the report said that there was an absolute right to hold opinions, the right to freedom of expression was not absolute and some restrictions were permissible. These restrictions had to meet the criteria of legitimacy, legality and democratic necessity.[21] Responses to the sub-commission's report revealed again the ideological divisions that separate the Americans and Europeans on the issue of press freedom. The World Press Freedom Committee (WPFC) and the U.S. government's observer criticized the notion of permissible restrictions. In contrast, Article 19 endorsed Turk and Joinet's conclusions and recommendations.

Two major documents from the ill-fated NWICO debate at UNESCO—the 1978 Mass Media Declaration and the 1980 MacBride Report—also covered the protection of journalists. However, they also did not produce an international regime. (See the discussion in a later section of this chapter.)

In contrast to the paucity of attention to international press freedom matters in the political science and international relations literature, there is some attention to the issues by international legal specialists. This is because international law relating to journalists' rights presents some interesting dilemmas. For example, the right of physical protection is within the range of two kinds of human rights: the right to life; and the prohibition of torture and cruel, inhuman or degrading treatment or punishment. The various regional and international human rights instruments have loopholes. While there is language prohibiting murder, torture, and inhuman or degrading punishment, a death sentence by an official court or tribunal is not always a violation of international law. Similarly, the UN Convention against Torture has a loophole that might allow journalists and others to be tortured if the acts are not officially sanctioned but are done with the secret compliance of government officials.[22]

THE MACBRIDE REPORT

Despite the long history of non-governmental press freedom organizations' lobbying for better protection of journalists, the attempt by UNESCO to discuss and act on the matter in the 1970s provoked hostile reactions from the World Press Freedom Committee, the International Press Institute (IPI), other such organizations, and the international elite media.

The MacBride Commission quoted statistics from Amnesty International concluding that over 104 correspondents were imprisoned or missing in 25 countries in 1977. The IPI figures for 15 months (1976-1978) indicated that 24 journalists were murdered, 57 journalists were wounded, tortured or kidnapped, and 13 newspapers were bombed.[23] In a working paper prepared for the commission, Sean MacBride stated that "there seems to be a general consensus among the various organizations of journalists, broadcasters and publishers that some effective measures should be adopted to ensure the better protection of journalists in the exercise of their profession in dangerous situations whether such situations arise in international or non-international armed conflicts."[24] But that assertion seems remarkable in light of the fact that after the report was released MacBride seemed isolated from the commission and Western press organizations with his views on "protection."

A view voiced by two North American members of the commission, Elie Abel (of the United States) and Betty Zimmerman (of Canada), was that proposals to "protect" journalists would only evolve into ploys by governments to control them. The report made an allowance to this perspective by discussing the issue of "protection" gingerly. It noted that "Licensing schemes might well lead to restrictive regulations governing the conduct of journalists; in effect, protection would be granted only to those journalists who had earned official approval."[25]

The report made two recommendations on the thorny question of protecting journalists. One (Recommendation 51) was that UNESCO should periodically convene round tables for interested parties to "review problems related to the protection of journalists and propose additional appropriate measures to this end."[26] The other (Recommendation 50) was that the professional integrity and independence of journalists should be respected but that the best guarantee of journalists' rights was the safeguarding of all human rights. The report explained:

> Far from constituting a special category, journalists are citizens of their respective countries, entitled to the same range of human rights as other citizens. One exception is provided in the Additional Protocol to the Geneva Convention of 12 August 1949, which applies only to journalists on perilous missions, such as in areas of armed conflict. To propose additional measures would invite the dangers entailed in a licensing system since it would require some body to stipulate who should be entitled to claim such protection.[27]

To that suggestion, MacBride responded that "Because of the importance of the role of journalists and others who provide or control the flow of news to the media, I urge that they should be granted a special status and protection."[28]

Because of the party and state's control of the media in the USSR it was easy for critics of the NWICO to suggest that the Eastern Bloc supported the idea of "protection" for journalists as a cover for increased control, so it is worth noting that the USSR's representative on the commission, Sergei Losev, did not support MacBride's call for such special status and protection. Instead Losev said, "A historical analysis of the attempts to set up a statute is not in favor of statutes, since statutes existed in Mussolini's Italy and sanctified fascist regulations on journalists."[29]

THE INTERNATIONAL JOURNALISM SURVEY

A majority of the organizations that responded to the International Journalism Survey conducted for this book during the last three months of 1995 were not optimistic that there "will be less physical harm and murders of journalists" in the coming years. Seven out of the ten groups that responded were not optimistic. There were a number of reasons for the pessimism.

First, a growth in the political democracy does not necessarily mean that there is more respect for the professional integrity and physical safety of journalists. Latin America, where there was a shift from military dictatorships to civilian rule in the 1980s, was an illustration of this point. The threat from the military and death squads there merely was replaced by hostility from drug traffickers and other non-governmental sources of violence. Of the combined total of 307 journalists murdered in 1992, 1993 and 1994, according to Table 6.1, 32 (10 percent) were in Latin America. "While there is a better relationship between the government and the press, democracy did not generally show a decrease in the murders of journalists in Latin America," the IAPA respondent explained. "Now groups such as narco-traffickers and radical terrorists groups are involved in the killings, rather than the governments."

Second, the end of the Cold War did not create a less violent, war-plagued world. Indeed, in the case of Yugoslavia, it seemed to release old ethnic hostilities that had merely been kept in check during the Communist years. In 1992, twenty-five journalists were killed in Bosnia, nine were killed the following year, and eight in 1994. "Journalists are jailed, expelled, beaten, killed for one of two reasons," the World Press Freedom Committee's respondent declared. "First, because they are journalists. Two, because they go to dangerous places. None of this is likely to change. Only realization (based on performance) that journalists are impartial observers could help." The list of countries that were embroiled in outright civil wars or other kinds of internal conflict in the years following the demise of the Cold War was long and diverse. It included Haiti, Bosnia, the former Soviet Union, Liberia, Burundi, Guatemala, Somalia, Algeria, Rwanda and Papua New Guinea.

Third, parties in civil conflicts began to change their policies toward the protection of journalists, from courting them as a part of good public relations to killing them as a form of military strategy. This was poignantly illustrated in Algeria, Tajikistan, Bosnia, and Somalia. The Committee to Protect Journalists' representative explained that in El Salvador's civil war of the early 1980s, "Neither the FMLN [Farabundo Marti National Liberation Front] rebels nor the Salvadoran army saw it in its interests to harass and murder foreign correspondents, instead they wanted to get them to relate their side of the story as it was being played out before the theater of international public opinion." In contrast, in Bosnia, journalists, especially the more powerful Western journalists, were shot as a matter of military strategy. According to the CPJ, this did keep stories of atrocities from being covered by the influential Western media.

Fourth, the growth of democratic government can be viewed as a double-edged sword, because a more independent, aggressive press makes it more likely that journalists will discover information that others want to suppress. The rise of organized crime in Russia is a case in point.

"There are very few societies that have functioning criminal justice systems just as a basic starting point," said the CPJ's spokesman. "There are more countries than not where you can still—if you are reasonably professional at it—kill people with impunity. And I think you will see more criminal violence against journalists especially."

In contrast, in explaining why she was optimistic, the International Freedom of Information Exchange's (IFEX) representative pointed to the "strong NGOs working in the field," and the "possible trend towards more subtle forms of harassment and censorship of journalists." These would mean that there would be less inclination to take harsher measures against reporters.

In seeking out views on the best strategies for ensuring the physical safety of journalists, the survey found that the international discourse on press freedom was in an ironic bind. While international press freedom and human rights groups abhor government censorship and other controls on journalists, they must rely on government action to ensure the physical protection of journalists. This government action can be direct—in the case of armed escorts in war zones—or indirect, as in governments' ensuring that the physical violence against journalists is not condoned or left unpunished.

The question of the best ways to ensure the protection of journalists has been a very controversial issue, as the deliberations on the MacBride Commission revealed. This largely results from the ironic dilemma identified above. Journalists are skeptical about the ability of governments to be sincere in protecting them, even though it is often governments that are charged with this responsibility. Also, international ID cards for journalists have been seen as contradictory—possibly identifying journalists for either protection as noncombatants or for murder. The contradictions surrounding this proposal have extended beyond the United Nations to the policies of international press freedom groups themselves. For example, while the CPJ's respondent dismissed the idea of ID cards as a means of protection, he did acknowledge that the CPJ issued membership cards to journalists around the world because such cards often help reporters gain access from low-level government officials, who give journalists more respect if they think journalists are linked to a foreign organization. This response is in effect an acknowledgment of the elitism and inequality that is a significant part of the global news flow process. Journalists from the North American and European media often get more respect than do journalists from other places, and local journalists who can prove they have links to the states at the top of the power structure of international politics seem more likely to have their professional integrity and physical safety respected.

The survey revealed that there is no one preferred means to protecting journalists' physical safety. Based on preliminary research, the questionnaire listed eight choices (in addition to "Other strategies not listed above") and asked respondents to identify as many as they found necessary. The options were:

1. "UN resolutions and declarations"
2. "national laws"
3. "identification cards for journalists in war zones"
4. "declarations by organizations such as yours"
5. "public education about the role of journalists"
6. "an end to international wars"
7. "an end to civil wars"
8. "no solution because threat of death is a hazard of the profession."

UN resolutions and declarations were only mentioned by three of the organizations in their combinations of options. This was interesting because so much time and effort was spent over the years in diplomatic negotiation over such instruments and by writers on the subject of press freedom analyzing their importance. Similarly, identification cards for journalists were only mentioned by three groups.

It was clear from the responses that the organizations felt action at the local, rather than multilateral, level would be more useful. The most favored strategies were securing national laws and public education about the role of journalists. Six organizations mentioned national laws in their combinations. Six also mentioned public education.

The International Federation of Journalists' respondent felt that UN resolutions and declarations would only be effective if they were "incorporated in national law." She also pointed out the need for education of the police and army, in particular, on the role of journalists.

"The primary concern, in addition to stressing that journalists have an important job to do, is to avoid all manner of ideas (such as licensing) that

pretend to help but actually mask efforts to control," the WPFC's representative explained.

The preference among the groups for securing national laws made the
comments of the CPJ's respondent concerning such laws seem the more interesting. He argued that there was little correlation between the body of national
press law in a country and the actual state of press freedom. In his view, the
press gets freedom by fighting for it. He compared and contrasted press freedom in countries with liberal press laws (such as the United States and Latin
America) and those with more repressive legal systems (such as the United
Kingdom and the Commonwealth countries). In Latin America, many of the
countries had, ironically, first amendment rights that were copied from the U.S.
constitution, but still had in the 1970s and 1980s some of the most serious
violations of press freedom in the world. Therefore, Jamaica, with more repressive press laws, had a freer press system than Argentina which had laws that
were more accommodating of the press. "The law is a living breathing thing,"
Bill Orme, the CPJ's executive director explained. "The law is whatever the
people in power say it is at a given point."

The national and international press freedom organizations were considered important for some groups because such groups promote public education about the role of journalists. For example, the International Federation
of Journalists' (IFJ) respondent felt that declarations by organizations such as
the IFJ were important in securing physical protection "only as a means to
raise awareness." The representative of PEN American Center said that journalists in Algeria would have received more protection from the government
there if there was a local organization in that country lobbying for journalists' rights.

Because of the IAPA's recent success in getting several heads of state to sign
its Declaration of Chaputlepec, it was understandable that the IAPA's officer
felt that declarations by professional organizations were important. But he said
such a strategy must be combined with other initiatives. He explained that
"The best way to protect journalists against such threats is through declarations by specific organizations (such as the IAPA), public education on the role
of journalists and special missions to the countries to press the authorities to
investigate and resolve the crimes against journalists." The IAPA included with
its questionnaire documentation on its missions during a period spanning
from late 1992 to late 1995. For example, between December 16, 1994, and
August 4, 1995, the IAPA undertook nine missions to a total of seven countries. The missions to Mexico and Guatemala were to investigate the murder
and harassment of journalists.

CENSORSHIP AND PROTECTION COMPARED

Censorship and threats to journalists' safety are two sides of the same coin. Journalists often are physically harmed in attempts to censor their work or in retribution for what they report and write. So multilateral rules against censorship are also in effect rules to protect journalists. However, not all rules to protect journalists are made to protect them from censorship. For example, the proposal for ID cards was based on the idea that they would be a tool in helping to make clearer the distinction between journalists and combatants on battlefields. The explicit protection of journalists against censorship is the group of rules to uphold the doctrine of freedom of information.[30]

Because of the assumption that uncensored mass media are the hallmarks of a liberal democracy, and because of the recent finding in international relations that democracies (broadly defined) do not go to war with each other,[31] it follows logically that the expanding number of states embracing various forms of democracy might provide fertile ground for finally getting a multilateral regime against censorship. Even if such a regime cannot be created, it would seem that at best the arguments over censorship and protection of journalists also might be neutralized because a majority of all states would be democracies. However, the problem is more complex. Although transformations of the world political economy and the communications revolution have accounted for the neutralization of attempts to create global rules against propaganda and promoting even global news flows, these changes will not have the same impact on the international discourses on censorship and the protection of journalists.

Regardless of political rhetoric, no state has permitted absolute freedom of information. What has existed globally and will continue despite the technological and political transformations are relative levels of journalistic freedom. This is so because all states, at various times, put other values ahead of freedom of information and notions of journalists' rights. For example, although countries such as Britain and the United States now lecture African, Asian and other states on the need to end censorship and promote media freedom, these European and North American states have been notorious for not respecting such values in regions under their colonial or neocolonial control.[32] However, in the first half of the 1990s the cases of censorship and threats of physical harm that have been the most publicized around the world have been in Islamic societies. The best known examples have been the case of Salman Rushdie, the British writer forced into hiding in 1988 after the Ayatollah Khomeini imposed a *fatwa* (death sentence) on him, and that of Bangladeshi author Taslima Nasrin, who had to leave Bangladesh to protect her life after Muslim mobs called for her death following the publication of her writings promoting women's liberation.[33] These examples serve to show that in many societies religious and other values supersede liberal-democratic ones.

This pessimistic outlook on prospects for the propagation of liberal-democratic press freedoms is the first similarity between the two related topics in international relations of censorship and the physical protection of journalists. It is a pessimism that was shared by the majority of the press freedom and human rights lobbyists who responded to the International Journalism Survey. They were pessimistic because they saw firsthand that the displacement of military or Communist governments by elected executives and legislatures did not necessarily bring the expected press freedoms. Religious and ethnic strife, and other causes of civil wars, were some of the factors killing such hopes. Organized crime and drug cartels were others. Also, disagreements among democracies about the meaning and nature of press freedom and press law—exemplified by the disagreement between the Americans and Western Europeans over the International Covenant on Civil and Political Rights' permissible restrictions—was another.

The second similarity between the treatment of the two topics is that the same body of international law is used as the rhetorical point of reference in the international discourses on censorship and on the protection of journalists. The UDHR and the ICCPR are the most widely quoted documents. But they derive their very existence and maintenance from states, while the most active lobbyists for press freedom are the nonstate actors, the international NGOs. So, on the one hand they satisfy the rhetorical and psychological need for lip service to press freedom, but, on the other, they do not threaten the prerogatives of states in imposing restrictions on the grounds of protecting "national security" or "public order" (as is explicitly stated in Article 19 of the ICCPR).

There are significant differences between censorship and the protection of journalists as international problems, however. These differences are why it is important to not consider them as a single topic.

The first difference is that the physical threat to journalists is easier to quantify than the threat from censorship. Our discussion in chapter 5 showed that, from the perspective of democratic necessity, there is a serious flaw in the way censorship is usually discussed. Conceiving of censorship as merely the presence of government controls removes an array of other restrictions from the discussion. But the reason why censorship is believed to be so dangerous in the first place is the idea that any curbs on participation are bad for liberal democracy. So monopolies, oligopolies, racism and unequal access to education also are fair game in the discussion of censorship. These factors are more difficult to define and quantify than are murders and cases of journalists being kidnapped or imprisoned.

The second difference springs from the first. Because there has been better quantification of murders, arrests and other threats to the physical safety of journalists, there is the impression that the outlook concerning the protection of journalists is bleaker. Because of the technological revolution and the declining number of military and Communist governments, the outlook for censorship, in contrast, has appeared relatively brighter. The international NGOs have spent more time collecting information about, and analyzing, laws, murders, disappearances, arrests and expulsions than on the forms of censorship outside government activities. So there is less of a clear picture about the relationship between freedom of expression and differential access to education, or concentration of media ownership, for example.

Third, there is no question that technological innovation has a greater impact on obviating censorship than it does in the efforts to protect journalists. The Internet and other telematic services allow the exchange of information across the world, circumventing the barriers of customs agents, police and military surveillance and official censors. But by the mid-1990s these technologies still are not evenly diffused around the globe and so are of limited or no benefit in sending or retrieving information from many areas. Also, the so-called information revolution can be seen as a doubled-edged sword. It has made censorship more tedious, but it has enhanced the panoptic capabilities of government and industry.[34] In other words, there seems to be a trade-off between more freedom of information and less privacy.

POLITICAL AND ECONOMIC DECISIONS ABOUT GLOBAL INFORMATION

In this final chapter it is time to assess what objective lessons are gained from the primary argument of the book and the other arguments derived from it. The primary argument is that the news media have been problematical in international relations in the four ways examined successively in chapters 3, 4, 5, and 6. The analysis of each of those issue-areas provided a set of deeper insights into the international politics of news. For example, in chapter 3 it was noted that despite international law prohibiting various kinds of propaganda, the practice became an institutionalized means of conducting international relations after World War II, so the evolutions in international politics and technology essentially have neutralized the debate on propaganda.

In taking stock, it is necessary to begin by looking back at enquiry so far into the subject of the news media and international relations. How have others written about the matter? What is new about the approach taken in this book?

WRITING ON THE POLITICS OF INTERNATIONAL NEWS

Until the 1970s, when the NWICO controversy at UNESCO spurred much interest in debates over the global news system, there was scant attention to the character of international cooperation and decision-making about news. Indeed, in addition to the occasional League of Nations and UN official documents,[1] there were only individual histories of the major international wire services, usually written by retired executives of those companies.[2] There probably was little attention to the international politics of news because there hardly was a global news system. In addition to the obvious fact that there were no technologies to create such a system (satellites and transnational telematics such as the Internet), the patterns of international news exchanges mirrored the patterns of international trade and imperialism.

That inattention to international news changed in the late 1970s and early 1980s. Three books in particular—Rosemary Righter's *Whose News? Politics, the Press and the Third World* (1978), Oliver Boyd-Barrett's *The International News Agencies* (1980) and Jonathan Fenby's *The International News Services* (1986)[3]—focused on the rise of the Western international news agencies and sought to show how these agencies were not as powerful as they appeared to be. In the context of the debate over international communication at UNESCO and the criticism of Western dominance of international news flows, these books were extremely timely and contributed significantly to the international discussion. The situation at UNESCO also inspired edited volumes on international news, namely Jim Richstad and Michael Anderson's *Crisis in International News: Policies and Prospects* (1981), Robert Stevenson and Donald Shaw's *Foreign News And The New World Information Order* (1984), and Andrew Arno and Wimal Dissanayake's *The News Media In National and International Conflict* (1984)[4]. But even though these texts recognized international news's status as an international problem, none of them explored political decision-making about international news, except within the confines of the few years of the NWICO debate.

The three most recent books that deal at least in part with global news are those of Johan Galtung and Richard Vincent's *Global Glasnost: Toward a New World Information and Communication Order* (1992), George Gerbner et al's *The Global Media Debate* (1993), and Kaarle Nordenstreng and Herbert Schiller's *Beyond National Sovereignty: International Communications in the 1990s* (1993)[5]. They all are biased in favor of resurrecting the NWICO. Indeed, the NWICO was the most powerful inspiration and the point of reference for much of the academic research done on global news flows. The debate at UNESCO and the UN between government officials of various ideological postures toward news media, and the North American and European media's biased reporting on UNESCO—to kill the perceived threat to their press freedom—provoked enquiry into international news. So most of the research that has ever been done on international news was published within the decade of the NWICO debate between the mid-1970s and mid-1980s. Galtung and Vincent put the international news flow literature into two categories: "attempts to understand and predict volume and direction of news";[6] and attempts "to understand and predict factors and values determining news flow."[7] Both categories include a lot of quantitative research, especially content analyses, but Galtung and Vincent reported a move towards qualitative research in the second category, including the use of cultural studies techniques, rhetorical criticism and narrative theory.[8]

The NWICO debate and new international communication technology also inspired literature on the general character of the international communication system (including telecommunications and trade in cultural products, such as movies and TV programs), and this literature, of necessity, considered news. These writings also can be put into two categories. The first employs Marxist and dependency theories and shows how patterns of global news flows help to justify such theories.[9] The second, of a more recent vintage and antithetical to the first, pays homage to the "information revolution" and sees the new communication technologies eroding national sovereignties and fostering liberal-democratic freedoms.[10]

This book's professed goal to look at the "international politics of news" could (understandably) tempt many to believe that it is another academic investigation into those concerns about the ideological nature of international news. But the preceding chapters should have revealed that while ideology is not by any means ignored in this book, the focus here is about how actors in international politics have historically regarded news and used news in their international relations. The literature on the news media and foreign policy notwithstanding, no other work has attempted to put together in one place so comprehensive a set of ideas on this topic.

It is important to point out that the literature on foreign policy, especially as it relates to news media, has an entirely different set of preoccupations than does writing on international relations. Research in foreign policy tends to explore the strategic value to governments of news[11] or the impact that news has on the foreign policy-making process.[12] In contrast, research in international relations does not necessarily begin with the state, and it is more concerned with various ways in which states and all other actors (including international organizations, NGOs, and even private citizens) come together to conduct the affairs of international society.

Therefore, this book is as much about international relations as it is about mass communication. In particular, this book contributes to thinking in the field of international relations about international cooperation in an area that traditionally has been disregarded because it was perceived to be *low* politics.

By the 1980s the field of international relations (which had its North American and European origins in the research into peace studies following World War I) had a quite distinct hierarchy. At the top was the *high* politics of strategic studies, and at the bottom was the *low* politics of just about everything else. In the mid-1980s, in lamenting this state of affairs that had caused the neglect of research into international communication, Paul Wilkinson, professor of international relations at the University of Aberdeen, explained that the development of nuclear weapons spurred the popularity of strategic studies because more funding for such research was available. Similarly, international economic relations research became popular after the 1973 oil crisis.[13]

Indeed, by the time Wilkinson was writing, the receding of the nuclear threat, the revolution in international communication technologies, and the variety of economic problems had begun attracting considerable attention to *low* politics. Harvard University international relations theorists Robert Keohane and Joseph Nye already had proclaimed the coming of "complex interdependence." They said the three major characteristics of complex interdependence were : (1) multiple channels (e.g. conferences and NGOs) and rapid communications connecting societies; (2) the absence of a clear hierarchy of issues on the international agenda; and (3) the declining effectiveness of military force. Due to these characteristics, the political processes of complex interdependence were very different from those of the previous era of stark Cold War conflict. For example, because military force was less effective, the old strategy of linking military might to other issues as a means of reaching ends became obsolete in relationships of complex interdependence. Militarily weaker states were more able to pursue *linkage* of unrelated issues in order to achieve ends. International hierarchy was reduced as a result of this increased ability of weak states to pursue linkage in this way and the loss to powerful states of military force as an instrument of linkage. Also, international organizations played increasingly significant roles in the politics of complex interdependence because they provide fora for building alliances, mechanisms for agenda-setting and means of direct communication.[14]

The end of the Cold War, the expansion of the UN's peacekeeping operations, the growth of the Internet, and the addition of new international organizations seem to justify the theory of complex interdependence. The 1990s began with the member-states of the Conference on Security and Cooperation in Europe (CSCE) pledging in the Charter of Paris to begin "a new era of democracy, peace and unity" on the continent and later setting up the Organization for Security and Cooperation in Europe (OSCE). The eight years of contentious negotiations in the Uruguay Round of the General Agreement on Tariffs and Trade (GATT) that had begun in 1986 ended with the creation of the World Trade Organization (WTO).

The increased importance and prestige of studies in international economics, or international political economy, and the new attention to interdependence inspired a number of studies on the role of international regimes. Because the study of international regimes has been very much a preoccupation of American scholars, this has led to legitimate criticism of the research from across the Atlantic by British scholar Susan Strange.[15] Such criticism prompted Keohane and Nye to explain, in the second edition of their *Power and Interdependence,* that the idea of international regimes did not originate in the United States but had enjoyed a tradition of usage in international law long before American international political economists popularized its usage in the 1970s. The term itself is French, and we can find a 1924 European publication using the term in reference to international law.[16] Literature on international law published in the United States has discussed international regimes from as far back as the 1930s.[17] In the 1970s academic attention in the United States turned to exploring international regimes as order-maintaining entities in international relations, based on a popular belief in the United States that there had been an erosion of U.S. hegemony. Regime theory became an analytical tool for exploring the post-hegemonic era and understanding complex interdependence. Keohane and Nye credited their own use of the term "regime" to John Ruggie, who defined regimes as "sets of mutual expectations, generally agreed-to rules, regulations and plans, in accordance with which organizational energies and financial commitments are allocated."[18]

There is no consistent theory of international regimes but several theories. Stephen Krasner, editor of the most famous text on international regimes, could identify three major approaches: "modified structural", "conventional structural", and "Grotian".[19] A more recent study by Stephan Haggard and Beth Simmons found four theoretical types: "structuralist," "game-theoretic," "functionalist," and "cognitive."[20] Each theory has different assumptions about the role of regimes in international politics and the factors contributing to why regimes are formed.

The very fact that there is such a variety of approaches reflects the multiple new issues that caused increased attention to be focused on international political economy in the 1970s and 1980s. These issues include: the attempt to regain international economic order following the breakdown of the Bretton Woods system; the perceived loss of U.S. leadership in the world economy; the attempt by the global South to redistribute global wealth; and the consequences of the Organization of Petroleum Exporting Countries (OPEC) oil shocks. Writers focusing on one or another of these international economic problems have found new ways of looking at regimes or have criticized other approaches.

In previous work I have used regime theories—both agreeing and disagreeing with them—to interpret the structure of international communication, analyze the NWICO debate, and explain the connection between international communication and international power.[21] By looking at the international politics of news, this work builds on that previous work. For example, in *International Power and International Communication* I argued that international news was an area of international politics not covered by an international regime. This book reinforces that point by explaining why.

WHAT WE HAVE LEARNED

Our analyses in the preceding chapters have given us five conclusions about the international politics of news, or, more precisely, the political economy[22] of the news media in international relations. These conclusions will be dealt with in turn under the italicized headings below.

1. *Divergence between legal discourses and political discourses.*
My first observation is that there often is a wide gap between international legal discourses and international political discourses. Legal discourse refers not only to what international law says but also to the nuances of the international legal system, such as which principles and norms have the binding treaty status and which do not, and at which times national sovereignty is invoked by states. All interactions in which claims and counterclaims and responses are made, both by states and nonstate actors, are part of international political discourse. Therefore, the attempt by the British government to suppress the book *Spycatcher* was a part of international political discourse, and the rulings on the matters by the courts in Australia and Britain were part of international legal discourse.

The examination of the four areas dealt with in each of the four previous chapters reveals that international law concerning the news media were used as symbolic planks in establishing the post–World War II order. Through such instruments as the 1948 Universal Declaration of Human Rights (UDHR), the 1966 International Covenant on Civil and Political Rights (ICCPR), and the 1967 Outer Space Treaty, a set of liberal principles and ideals were set out for the new order. Propaganda for war was outlawed; propaganda for peace was encouraged; and censorship was discouraged. But states were careful to not surrender too much of their sovereignty in these areas to international law and international courts, and this accounts for why propaganda became a standard means of conducting international relations and censorship and harassment of journalists remained an international problem. States will only protect press freedom when it is in their interest to do so. And the NWICO debate revealed that powerful states will use the pretext of protecting press freedom to justify international policies when it is in their interests.

International news is certainly not the only area of international relations in which there is a divergence between the international law and the actual practices in international politics, but the divergence in this case has been the inspiration for an interesting pattern of activities by press freedom INGOs. (See below.)

2. The enigma of pessimism for press freedom in the "Information Age."
The responses of press freedom groups to the International Journalism Survey conducted for this book also reveal another divergence. This is the generally pessimistic view of the outlook for press freedom compared to the optimism and chest-thumping of those who tout the virtues of the information age and globalization. A majority of the groups that responded (six out of ten) said they were not optimistic that there would be less government censorship in the future. Similarly, a majority (seven out of ten) were not optimistic that there will be less physical harm and murders of journalists in the future. (See Appendix 9.) In their narrative responses they explained that they were pessimistic because of a number of factors, including the oppressive behavior of non-governmental groups (such as the Mafia and drug cartels), the inability of the law to secure journalistic freedoms, and the continuing prerogative of states to suppress journalists.

For those outside the press freedom and human rights lobbies there seems to be the simplistic assumption that the decline of communism, the end of Latin American military dictatorships, the growth of international capitalism, and the expansion of transnational telematic networks that are difficult to censor will produce a better state of affairs for press freedom and liberal-democratic freedoms generally.

However, the expansion of capitalism should not be confused with the growth of press freedom. Indeed, by the mid-1990s some of the fastest growing capitalist economies were housed in some of the more repressive states (in liberal-democratic terms). In explaining the Singapore government's ban on the waving of political banners by students, that country's prime minister, Goh Chok Tong, explained, "If you allow students to do so, then workers will begin to do so over the slightest grievance, and if you have several such demonstrations . . . the impression is created the government is not in control of the situation, that the place may become unstable, and that will have an impact on foreign investors."[23] The Singaporean government also was successful in suppressing two international publications—the *International Herald Tribune* and the *Far Eastern Economic Review*—that had published material it did not like. However, as our quotes in chapter 2 from U.S. Vice President Al Gore and the World Bank revealed, the expansion of the infrastructure of global capitalism is confused with the growth of press freedom and democracy. In his 1992 book, *The Twilight of Sovereignty*, Walter Wriston, the retired chair and CEO of Citicorp, declared:

> The global network is the essential infrastructure of that economy,
> and its use promises to make its users into a single worldwide com-
> munity sharing many tastes and opinions, styles of dress, forms of

> government, and modes of thought. These people, on the whole, will
> be internationalists in their outlook and will approve and encourage
> the worldwide erosion of traditional sovereignty. They will feel more
> affinity to their fellow global conversationalists than to those of their
> countrymen who are not part of the global conversation.[24]

Those with vested interests in maintaining and perpetuating capitalism are the
ones touting these ideas. Democracy and press freedom are seen as bonuses
in the growth of free markets. Cases of repression in such places as Singapore
and China are seen as anachronisms that will recede as the free markets take
hold. The press freedom groups, who labor "in the trenches," so to speak, are
not so sure of this.

3. The institutionalization of the international press freedom lobby.
Within a period of 20 years a number of new actors entered the international
discourse on the news media and international journalism. They were INGOs
(international non-governmental organizations) set up to represent the interests of news media owners and media workers. Eight of the fourteen major
international press freedom groups listed and described in Appendix 10 did not
even exist in 1970. Index on Censorship, the World Press Freedom Committee,
and the Human Rights Watch Free Expression Project originated in the 1970s.
Article 19, the Committee to Protect Journalists, the Canadian Committee to
Protect Journalists, IFEX, and Reporters Sans Frontières all were products of
the 1980s.

A number of factors account for the creation of these groups. The WPFC
was started directly because of the perceived need to protect press freedom
from expected attacks by UNESCO's proposed New World Information and
Communication Order (NWICO). All the international publicity about the
NWICO could have only channeled attention to the need to devote more
attention to press freedom. Also, the increase in press freedom organizations
was a consequence of the wider attention being given to human rights generally, fostered as it was by the United Nations and the creation of regional
human rights legal instruments that all covered press freedom. The European
Convention for the Protection of Human Rights and Fundamental Freedoms
came into force in 1953, the American Convention on Human Rights (covering North and South America and the Caribbean) in 1978, and the African
Charter on Human Rights and Peoples' Rights in 1986.

Another cause was technological. The potentially global media system created by the new technologies compelled consideration of press freedom issues
in a global context. Similarly, the INGOs, in the case of IFEX, have used the new
technologies as means to organize their concerns and lobby more efficiently.

The data collection of these organizations has enhanced the quality of discussion of press freedom issues. The practice of collecting statistics on the harassment and murder of journalists begun by the IPI was adopted and improved by the CPJ and RSF in the 1980s and 1990s. The creation of IFEX in 1992 provided a global communications network, linking these groups and other human rights groups, such as Amnesty International. As the International Journalism Survey revealed, communication strategies, such as negative publicity, letter-writing campaigns, and public education about the role of journalists, were found by the press freedom groups to be the most effective courses of action. (See Appendix 9.) By 1995 a number of other NGOs and INGOs were using the Internet as a relatively cheap, efficient means of global communication.[25]

This trend toward the creation of national and transnational coalitions is by no means unique to the international press freedom lobby. The separate arrangements, and even conferences, for NGOs at the 1992 Rio Earth Summit, the 1994 UN Global Conference on the Sustainable Development of Small Island Developing States, and the 1995 UN Fourth World Conference on Women, were testimony enough to the growing significance and influence of such groups in a plethora of areas, such as the environment, women's concerns, and indigenous people's rights.

4. Extra-legal rule-making for press freedom.
The failure of the international system to protect the professional integrity and physical safety of journalists, combined with the better organization of the press freedom lobby, have produced attempts by some of the INGOs to create international press freedom rules. The full text of three of these are provided in the appendices of this book. They are: the Declaration of Talloires, 1981 (Appendix 6); the Charter for a Free Press, 1987 (Appendix 4); and the Declaration of Chapultepec, 1994 (Appendix 5).

It is significant that these three documents were produced by organizations representing primarily media owners and executives, and that these bodies both were based in the United States, because they reflect the dispositions toward press freedom of such groups and the peculiar American approach to press freedom. The Declaration of Talloires and the Charter for a Free Press both were the work of the WPFC, while the Declaration of Chapultepec was created by the IAPA.

The documents reflect distinctly American concerns because, as was noted in chapter 6, the American groups are not at all tolerant of the idea of "permissible restrictions" and the three documents are likewise clear in their abhorrence of all forms of censorship. In being primarily concerned with the broad concept of "press freedom," as opposed to a narrow focus on the physical protection of journalists, the three documents are true to the character of lobbying by organizations that primarily represented owners and executives. Protecting the professional integrity and physical safety of journalists is only one dimension of ensuring press freedom, in the view of such groups. They also require governments to not pursue policies that will harm the material situation of their operations, such restrictions on access to newsprint, prohibitive tariffs, and curbs on advertising. All three documents reflect such concerns.

The contents of the Declaration of Talloires and the Charter for a Free Press, and the circumstances leading to the conferences that produced them, suggested they were a defensive strategy against anticipated threats to press freedom by UNESCO. The Declaration of Chapultepec was similarly another defensive move, because the IAPA drafted it on the assumption that democracy in Latin America was fragile and that the societies that only recently had been run by autocratic military rulers needed a reminder about the role of a free press. Within a year the IAPA was successful in getting 12 heads of state from North and South America to sign the document, including the presidents of Mexico, Argentina, Colombia, and the United States.[26] But it is questionable whether governments, by virtue of their signing such a declaration, would suddenly honor press freedom commitments any more than they had the human rights treaties they had already signed. Such documents can seem farcical if the persons who sign on are known to be contemptuous of the principles, but they at least serve the symbolic purpose of being instruments that can be cited whenever there are violations.

Three features of the declarations of Talloires and Chapultepec and the Charter for a Free Press stand out: their assumption that press freedom and individual freedoms are one and the same; their singular focus on government restrictions; and the intolerance of any grounds for restricting what the news media can report.

"Denying freedom of the press denies all freedom of the individual," the Declaration of Talloires asserts. The Charter for a Free Press begins with the sentence: "A free press means a free people." And, similarly, the Declaration of Chapultepec says, in its first article, that "No people or society can be free without freedom of expression and of the press." The separation between the press and people, or between the owners of media and the media workers, that is recognized by journalists' organizations is not acknowledged. It seems that by making a free press and a free populace one and the same the drafters of the documents were attempting to maximize the chances of their principles being taken more seriously. However, the entire discourse about the responsibilities of the press is based on the assumption that the press's interests are not nec-essarily one and the same with those of the public it is supposed to serve.[27]

The singular focus on government restrictions ignores the growing threat to press freedom from non-governmental sources, especially criminal groups. The WPFC documents in particular emphasize the need to have "indepen-dent" news media. The stress is in stark contrast to UNESCO documents that stress the need for both "independent" and "pluralistic" media. According to the Declaration of Windhoek (See Appendix 7), the term "pluralistic" press describes "an end of monopolies of any kind and existence of the greatest possible number of newspapers, magazines and periodicals reflecting the widest possible range of opinion within the community." It is understandable that media owners would tread gingerly around the question of whether media independent of government also are pluralistic because a worldwide trend by the mid-1990s was the increasing concentration of media ownership.

The grounds for press freedom restrictions provided for in international law, such as national security and maintaining public order, are completely missing from the three documents. Freedom from censorship is viewed as an absolute right. "Censorship and other forms of arbitrary control of informa-tion and opinion should be eliminated; the people's right to news and infor-mation should not be abridged," the Declaration of Talloires asserts. There is similar language in article 1 of the Charter for a Free Press and Article 5 of the Declaration of Chapultepec. This feature of the documents is the clearest indi-cation of the frustration the American groups feel about the inadequacies of the status quo concerning press freedom.

Despite the inability of the international community to establish an inter-national regime for the protection of journalists, it is interesting that the groups primarily representing journalists are less willing to issue interna-tional declarations such as those described above. When they do, such docu-ments usually are the products of UNESCO and UN-sponsored conferences. In the 1970s and 1980s the Prague-based International Organization of Journalists (IOJ) was at the forefront of such initiatives, which always espoused the principles of the NWICO. The IOJ became less prominent when the Communist Bloc collapsed and it was expelled from Czechoslovakia in the wake of charges that it was a Communist front.

5. *Diverse approaches to press freedom.*
Our investigation reveals that it is very misleading to assume uniformity in approaches to press freedom. The European tolerance for "permissible restric-tions" compared to the American intolerance is one distinction that can be made. And it is difficult at this time to understand the full texture of the

FIGURE 7.1
THE NEWS REVOLUTION MODEL

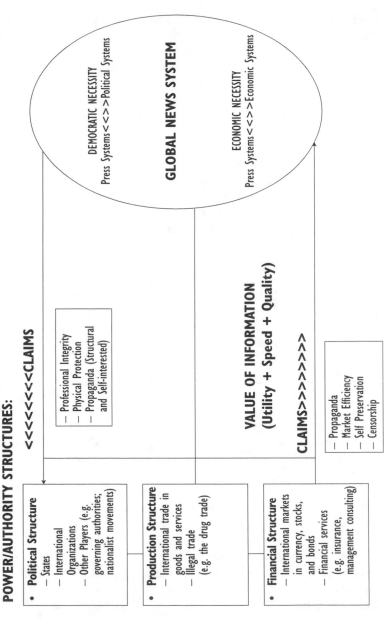

POWER/AUTHORITY STRUCTURES:

<<<<<<<CLAIMS

- **Political Structure**
  - States
  - International Organizations
  - Other Players (e.g. governing authorities; nationalist movements)

- **Production Structure**
  - International trade in goods and services
  - Illegal trade (e.g. the drug trade)

- **Financial Structure**
  - International markets in currency, stocks, and bonds
  - Financial services (e.g. insurance, management consulting)

- Professional Integrity
- Physical Protection
- Propaganda (Structural and Self-interested)

VALUE OF INFORMATION
(Utility + Speed + Quality)

CLAIMS>>>>>>>

- Propaganda
- Market Efficiency
- Self Preservation
- Censorship

DEMOCRATIC NECESSITY
Press Systems<<>>Political Systems

GLOBAL NEWS SYSTEM

ECONOMIC NECESSITY
Press Systems<<>>Economic Systems

worldwide discourse on press freedom because groups from other regions have been either reluctant or unable to project their ideologies as much as the North American and European groups have. In chapter 6 it was suggested that the peculiarities of European history and society help to explain why the Europeans generally are not as intolerant of permissible restrictions as are the Americans. Likewise, it is logical to expect that southern-hemispheric press freedom groups are inclined to make more allowances for concerns about social and economic development in their attitudes to press freedom.

The discussion in the preceding section also reveals the nuances of the international discourses about the news media. There are clear differences and preoccupations often separating or uniting the main actors—states, INGOs, journalists, media executives and owners, and the general public.

THE NEWS REVOLUTION MODEL

What we come up with after the investigation done in this book is "The News Revolution Model" depicted in figure 7.1. It is both a description of the international news system's political economy and a theory of the international relations of that system.

The model refines the conception of how the news media figure in international relations. It is a departure from the simplistic, technologically deterministic approaches of authors and thinkers already quoted in this book. It does not conceive of the news media as being merely at the cusp of a struggle between the forces of democracy and autocracy. It does not view the technological revolution as ending the discourse on censorship. And, most importantly, it takes account of the institutionalization of the international press freedom lobby, a factor that often is completely ignored in writings on the international news system.

The label "Global News System," and the oval that contains it, refers to the system of companies, organizations and people that produce the world's news. This includes wire services, radio and TV broadcasters, journalists, translators, magazines and newspapers, *as well as* the trade union, human rights and industry groups that represent their collective interests. The concept *does not* refer to sources of news outside the news media, such as political spokesmen or publicity departments of firms. These can be included in the idea of a news system, but in the model such actors are viewed as being outside the news system, making "claims" on it.

The labels "Democratic Necessity" and "Economic Necessity" at the top and bottom ends of the oval refer to the two bodies of ideas used to justify the existence of the news media. The term "Democratic Necessity" is borrowed from

Mukherjee,[28] but it is used here in quite a different way. Mukherjee used it to refer to the test used to justify any restrictions on human rights that are deemed necessary in a democratic society. For example, while there may be a right to possess arms, the restriction of that right can be said to pass the criterion of democratic necessity because the restriction is in the interest of public safety. But in the context of the News Revolution Model, the label "Democratic Necessity" simply describes the body of reasons used to justify the existence of the news media. These reasons are said to be necessary for democracy. The news media are necessary in liberal democracies because of the three basic roles they are expected to perform in such political systems: (1) as watchdogs on government; (2) as conduits for the two-way flow of information between the people and their government; and (3) as a source of information in the so-called free marketplace of ideas. Others have formulated the role of news media in democracies in ways that are different but that communicate essentially the same ideas. For example, the term "surveillance function" has been used to describe the work of the press instead of the term "watchdog."[29] It is also important to stress that the label Democratic Necessity does not refer only to liberal-democratic systems. Even Communists use the term "democratic," such as in the notion of "democratic centralism." And Communist conceptions of the democratic necessity of the news media are quite different from those of liberal-democrats. In the Communist conception, the media are to perpetuate party ideology and mobilize the populace. The Marxist notions of base and superstructure recognize the strategic function of information and ideas in political organization.[30] So, as figure 7.1 illustrates, press systems and political systems always interact with each other.

Even if there is not agreement that news media are necessary for democratic purposes, they also can be justified on grounds of "Economic Necessity." The press system and the economic system interact at a basic level whenever the media carry advertising. At a more sophisticated level, the media perform the information functions needed for the trade, currency, equities, and bond markets to perform. The Singaporean prime minister, in the quote given above, was also referring to the vital function the media play in attracting or deterring capital. News of political instability scares away investors. More positive news attracts them.

The model reflects the nuances of how the flow of news and press freedom figures in international politics by identifying more than just states as the sources of authority or forces acting on the media. Instead of merely states, the sources of power and authority are said to be structures. They are three: a Political Structure; a Production Structure; and a Financial Structure. My idea of structures in the international political economy is borrowed, in modified form, from Susan Strange. In *States and Markets*[31] Strange identified four primary structures of the world political economy: a Knowledge Structure; a Production Structure; a Security Structure; and a Financial Structure. In contrast, the News Revolution Model subsumes Strange's Security and Knowledge structures into the notion of a Political Structure. What Strange claims to be the Knowledge Structure is also covered by my conception of the role "Propaganda" plays in the News Revolution Model.

The Production Structure is "the sum of all the arrangements determining what is produced, by whom and for whom, by what method and on what terms."[32] The idea of the Production Structure depicted in the model also refers to the world trading system in services and tangible goods, and the trading system in illegal goods. The Financial Structure is "the sum of all arrangements governing the availability of credit plus all the factors determining the terms on which currencies are exchanged for one another."[33] The model's version of the Financial Structure is not limited to the credit system, but also includes the international currency, stock and bond markets, and could also include some financial services that can be categorized under the Production Structure.

The Political Structure refers to the states, international organizations, and other actors that play governing or military/security roles in international politics. The Political Structure is the set of relationships between entities seeking power and the arrangements set up to give and take power. So the Irish Republican Army (IRA) can be categorized as belonging to the Political Structure. So too can the World Trade Organization (WTO), but the WTO also can be placed in the Production Structure.

Just as in Strange's model of political economy, these structures are conceived in the News Revolution Model as interacting with each other to produce the set of circumstances that define the world political economy. But in specific relationship to the global news system they are best conceived of as exerting "claims."

The News Revolution Model regards the relationship between the Global News System and the Power/Authority Structures of the international political economy as one of an exchange of claims. So the news media's efforts to get rid of censorship and get better protection of journalists are really claims they make on those entities with the power, authority and means to change matters. Propaganda is also a claim to the extent that the term, in the context of the model, refers to the media's promotion of information and ideas that perpetuate their interests. So the positions taken by certain news media against the NWICO (in their reporting and through official statements) that were described in chapter 4 were means of propagating self-interested ideas. These media also perpetuate their interests (many times subconsciously) by relaying the structural propaganda that was described in chapter 3.

The set of claims listed at the top of the model are not by any means exhaustive. They are merely a sample of what the news media want. This list varies according to the type and location of the media. For example, the Declarations of Talloires and Chapultepec, and the Charter for a Free Press are really lists of claims. The annual reports of the CPJ and RSF are others.

Likewise, the list of claims the Power/Authority Structures make to the news media is not at all complete. States, companies, international organizations and other actors like to manage what information the news media disseminate about them. They do this, inter alia, through censorship and propaganda. Like the news media, these actors seek self-preservation, and the actors operating in the economic marketplace are particularly concerned with getting information that will help them make efficient decisions.

In addition to the exchange of claims, the global news system has a relationship with the authority structures through all the processes that determine the value of information. This part of the model is a reflection of the ideas contained in chapter 2. It was emphasized there that the character of international news flows has historically reflected the configurations of international trading and investment relationships. But we noted then that this fact was of limited utility in explaining the evolution in the content and value of international news over time. For answers to that we must look at all the forces that give international news its value, namely, those that enhance news' utility, speed, and quality.

The News Revolution Model takes us from the stage of merely describing the wonders of new technologies and assuming positive political consequences from the so-called information revolution to a clear explanation and understanding of how the news media function in international relations. The trade in claims and the dynamics determining the value of information are means of explaining the behavior of press freedom organizations and the strategic behavior of news organizations such as Reuters. The model is not the last word on the matter, but it is certainly a beginning.

Appendix 1

United Nations Document A/RES/41/39 (20 November 1986)
"Question of Namibia"
(Extract)

D

Dissemination of information and mobilization of international public opinion in support of the immediate independence of Namibia

The General Assembly,

Having examined the report of the United Nations Council for Namibia and the relevant chapter of the report of the Special Committee on the Situation with regard to the Implementation of the Declaration on the Granting of Independence to Colonial Countries and Peoples,

Recalling its resolution 1514 (XV) of 14 December 1960, containing the Declaration on the Granting of Independence to Colonial Countries and Peoples,

Recalling its resolutions 2145 (XXI) of 27 October 1966 and 2248 (S-V) of 19 May 1967, as well as all other resolutions of the General Assembly and of the Security Council relating to Namibia,

Underlining the fact that, twenty years after the termination by the General Assembly of the Mandate of South Africa over Namibia and the assumption by the United Nations of direct responsibility for the Territory, the racist regime of South Africa continues illegally to occupy the Territory in violation of the relevant resolutions and decisions of the United Nations,

Underlining that 1987 will mark the twentieth anniversary of the establishment of the United Nations Council for Namibia as the legal Administering Authority for Namibia until independence,

Taking into consideration the Final Communiqué of the Seminar on World Action for the Immediate Independence of Namibia, held at Valletta from 19 to 23 May 1986,

Taking into consideration also the Declaration of the International Conference for the Immediate Independence of Namibia and the Programme of Action on Namibia adopted by the Conference,

Gravely concerned at the total black-out of news on Namibia imposed by the illegal South African regime,

Gravely concerned at the campaign of slander and disinformation against the United Nations and the liberation struggle of the Namibian people for self-determination and national independence led by the South West Africa People's Organization, their sole and authentic representative,

Stressing the urgent need to mobilize international public opinion on a continuous basis with a view to assisting effectively the people of Namibia in the achievement of self-determination, freedom and independence in a united Namibia and, in particular, to intensify the world-wide and continuous dissemination of information on the struggle for liberation being waged by the people of Namibia under the leadership of the South West Africa People's Organization,

Reiterating the importance of intensifying publicity on all aspects of the question of Namibia as an instrument for furthering the mandate given by the General Assembly to the United Nations Council for Namibia,

Recognizing the important role that non-governmental organizations are playing in the dissemination of information on Namibia and in the mobilization of international public opinion in support of the immediate independence of Namibia,

1.Requests the United Nations Council for Namibia, in co-operation with the Department of Public Information of the Secretariat and in consultation with the South West Africa People's Organization, the sole and authentic representative of the Namibian people, in pursuance of its international campaign in support of the struggle of the Namibian people for independence:

(a) To continue to consider ways and means of increasing the dissemination of information relating to Namibia in order to intensify the international campaign in favour of the cause of Namibia;

(b) To focus its activities towards greater mobilization of public opinion in Western States, particularly the United States of America, the United Kingdom of Great Britain and Northern Ireland and the Federal Republic of Germany;

(c) To intensify the international campaign for the imposition of comprehensive and mandatory sanctions against South Africa under Chapter VII of the Charter of the United Nations;

(d) To organize an international campaign to boycott products from Namibia and South Africa, in co-operation with non-governmental organizations;

(e) To expose and denounce collaboration with the racist regime of South Africa in all fields;

(f) To organize exhibitions on Namibia and the struggle of the Namibian people for independence;

(g) To prepare and disseminate publications on the political, economic, military and social consequences of the illegal occupation of Namibia by South Africa, on legal matters, on the question of the territorial integrity of Namibia and on contacts between Member States and South Africa;

(h) To produce and disseminate radio and television programmes designed to draw the attention of world public opinion to the current situation in and around Namibia;

(i) To produce and disseminate in both the English language and the local languages of Namibia radio programmes, designed to counter the hostile propaganda and disinformation campaign of the racist regime of South Africa;

(j) To produce and disseminate posters;

(k) To ensure full coverage through advertisements in newspapers and magazines, press releases, press conferences and press briefings of all activities of the United Nations regarding Namibia in order to maintain a constant flow of information to the public on all aspects of the question of Namibia;

(l) To prepare and disseminate a thematic atlas on Namibia;

(m) To reproduce and disseminate the comprehensive economic map of Namibia;

(n) To produce and disseminate booklets on the activities of the Council;

(o) To update and disseminate widely a compendium of resolutions of the General Assembly and of the Security Council relating to Namibia and relevant documents of the Movement of Non-Aligned Countries and the Organization of African Unity, as well as decisions, declarations and communiqués of the front-line States on the question of Namibia;

(p) To publicize and distribute the indexed reference book on trans-national corporations that plunder the human and natural resources of Namibia, and on the profits they extract from the Territory;

(q) To produce and disseminate widely, on a monthly basis, a bulletin containing analytical and updated information intended to mobilize maximum support for the Namibian cause;

(r) To produce and disseminate, on a weekly basis, an information newsletter containing updated information on developments in and relating to Namibia, in support of the Namibian cause;

(s) To acquire books, pamphlets and other materials relating to Namibia for dissemination;

(t) To prepare, in consultation with the South West Africa People's Organization, a list of Namibian political prisoners;

(u) To assist the South West Africa People's Organization in the production and distribution of material on Namibia;

2. Requests the United Nations Council for Namibia to continue to organize, in co-operation with the Department of Public Information, media encounters on developments relating to Namibia particularly prior to the activities of the Council during 1987;

3. Requests the United Nations Council for Namibia to redouble its efforts to inform international public opinion of developments in Namibia in order to counteract the total news black-out on Namibia imposed by the illegal South African regime, which forbids foreign journalists from entering and reporting from the Territory;

4. Further requests the United Nations Council for Namibia to exert all efforts to counteract the campaign of slander and disinformation against the United Nations and the liberation struggle in Namibia carried out by South African agents from the so-called information centres established in several Western countries;

5. Requests the United Nations Council for Namibia to co-operate closely with relevant intergovernmental organizations in order to increase the awareness of the international community of the direct responsibility of the United Nations over Namibia and the continued illegal occupation of that Territory by the racist regime of South Africa;

6. Calls upon the United Nations Council for Namibia to continue to co-operate with non-governmental organizations in its efforts to mobilize international public opinion in support of the liberation struggle of the Namibian people, under the leadership of the South West Africa People's Organization;

7. Requests the United Nations Council for Namibia to prepare, update and disseminate lists of non-governmental organizations, in particular those in the major Western countries, in order to ensure better co-operation and co-ordination among non-governmental organizations working in support of the Namibian cause and against apartheid;

8. Requests the United Nations Council for Namibia to organize workshops for non-governmental organizations, parliamentarians, trade unionists, academics and media representatives at which the participants will consider how they can contribute to the implementation of the decisions of the United Nations relating to the dissemination of information on Namibia;

9. Decides to allocate the sum of $500,000 to be used by the United Nations Council for Namibia for its programme of co-operation with non-governmental organizations, including support to conferences in solidarity with Namibia arranged by those organizations, dissemination of conclusions of such conferences and support to such other activities as will promote the cause of the liberation struggle of the Namibian people, subject to decisions to be taken by the Council in each individual case in consultation with the South West Africa People's Organization;

10. Requests the United Nations Council for Namibia to continue to contact leading opinion makers, media leaders, academic institutions, trade unions, legislators and parliamentarians, cultural organizations, support groups and other concerned persons and non-governmental organizations and inform them about the objectives and functions of the United Nations Council for Namibia and the struggle of the Namibian people under the leadership of the South West Africa People's Organization;

11. Appeals to non-governmental organizations, associations, institutions, support groups and individuals sympathetic to the Namibian cause:

(a) To increase the awareness of their national communities and legislative bodies concerning South Africa's illegal occupation of Namibia, the liberation struggle being waged by the Namibian people under the leadership of the South West Africa People's Organization, the gross violation of basic human rights by the South African regime in Namibia and the plunder of the resources of the Territory by foreign economic interests;

(b) To mobilize in their countries broad public support for the national liberation of Namibia by holding hearings, seminars and public presentations on various aspects of the Namibian question, as well as by producing and distributing pamphlets, films and other information material;

(c) To expose and campaign against the political and economic collaboration of certain Western Governments with the South African regime, as well as diplomatic visits to and from South Africa;

(d) To intensify public pressure for the immediate withdrawal from Namibia of foreign economic interests that are exploiting the human and natural resources of the Territory;

(e) To continue and develop campaign and research work, in order to expose the involvement and operations of Western-based oil companies in the supply of petroleum products to Namibia and South Africa;

f) To step up their efforts to persuade universities, local governments and other institutions to divest themselves of all investments in firms doing business in Namibia and South Africa;

(g) To intensify the campaign for the immediate and unconditional release of all Namibian political prisoners and the granting of prisoner-of-war status to all Namibian freedom fighters, in accordance with the Geneva Convention relative to the Treatment of Prisoners of War and the Additional Protocol thereto;

12. Requests Member States to broadcast programmes on their national radio and television networks and to publish material in their official news media, informing their populations about the situation in and around Namibia and the obligation of Governments and peoples to assist in the struggle of Namibia for independence;

13. Requests all Member States to observe Namibia Day in a befitting manner, by giving the widest possible publicity to and ensuring the dissemination of

information on Namibia, including the issuance of special postage stamps for the occasion;

14. Requests the Secretary-General to direct the Department of Public Information to assist the United Nations Council for Namibia in the implementation of its programme of dissemination of information and to ensure that all activities of the United Nations on dissemination of information on the question of Namibia follow the policy guidelines laid down by the United Nations Council for Namibia as the legal Administering Authority for Namibia;

15. Requests the Secretary-General to continue to assist, as a matter of priority, the United Nations Council for Namibia in the implementation of its programme of dissemination of information;

16. Requests the Secretary-General to provide the United Nations Council for Namibia with the work programme of the Department of Public Information for the year 1987 covering the activities of dissemination of information on Namibia, followed by periodic reports on the programme undertaken, including details of expenses incurred;

17. Requests the Secretary-General to group under a single heading in the section of the proposed programme budget of the United Nations for the biennium 1986-1987 relating to the Department of Public Information, all of the activities of the Department relating to the dissemination of information on Namibia and to direct the Department to submit to the United Nations Council for Namibia a detailed report on the utilization of the allocated funds;

18. Requests the Secretary-General to direct the Department of Public Information to disseminate, in 1987, the list of Namibian political prisoners, in order to intensify international pressure for their immediate and unconditional release.

Appendix 2

United Nations Document A/RES/43/50 (5 December 1988)
"Policies of Apartheid of the Government of South Africa"
(Extract)

H

Dissemination of information against the policies of apartheid of the regime of racist South Africa

The General Assembly,

Recalling and reaffirming the legislative mandate of its resolutions 32/105 H of 14 December 1977, paragraph 4, and 33/183 I of 24 January 1979, in which it requested the Secretary-General to undertake, in co-operation with Member States, a regular programme of radio broadcasts directed at South Africa,

Recalling further its resolutions 13 (I) of 13 February 1946, 595 (VI) of 4 February 1952, 1335 (XIII) of 13 December 1958, 1405 (XIV) of 1 December 1959, 3535 (XXX) of 17 December 1975, 32/105 B of 14 December 1977, 33/115 of 18 December 1978, 34/181 and 34/182 of 18 December 1979, 35/201 of 16 December 1980, 36/149 of 16 December 1981 and 40/64 D of 10 December 1985, in which it requested the Secretary-General to intensify and expand radio programmes for broadcast to southern Africa,

Strongly convinced of the need to intensify and expand activities aimed at mobilizing world public opinion against the evil system of apartheid in South Africa,

Mindful of the important role of the United Nations and its specialized agencies in the dissemination of information against apartheid, as enshrined in the relevant General Assembly resolutions,

Bearing in mind the malicious propaganda activities of the racist regime of South Africa, which continues to commit numerous acts of military aggression and destabilization against the front-line States and other neighbouring States in the region, and the imperative need to effectively counter these activities,

Alarmed at the planned reduction in the establishment of the Anti-Apartheid Programmes Section of the Department of Public Information of the Secretariat,

Concerned at the continuous reduction in programme output over the years, and distressed at the prospect of the Department of Public Information's proposal to further reduce radio programmes directed at the people of South Africa and Namibia at this crucial period when the racist regime has escalated its disinformation campaign and mass media black-out,

Bearing in mind resolution 41/213 of 19 December 1986 regarding the restructuring of the administrative and financial functioning of the United Nations and, in particular, the need to ensure that reforms are implemented with flexibility and not have a negative impact on mandated and priority programmes,

Noting with appreciation that the Secretary-General has initiated radio programmes in co-operation with Member States whose broadcasts can be heard in southern Africa in the main languages spoken in South Africa, which are English, Afrikaans, Sesotho, Setswana, Xhosa and Zulu,

Taking into consideration that radio is the commonly and widely used as well as easily accessible medium of communication in the region,

1. Urges the Secretary-General to:

   (a) Intensify, increase and expand these radio broadcasts as well as the production of audio-visual material and to maintain, without interference, the unique linguistic features and characteristics of these programmes;

   (b) Provide all appropriate technical and financial assistance to radio stations of those Member States which are broadcasting or willing to broadcast to South Africa, in order to enable their radio transmitters to be heard inside South Africa;

   (c) Ensure regular monitoring and evaluation of the impact of these programmes;

   (d) Retain and commensurately increase the personnel in these programmes in accordance with the relevant resolutions of the General Assembly, in particular, resolution 42/220 of 21 December 1987;

   (e) Further strengthen and enhance these radio programmes by engaging, at the upper echelons of the Secretariat and senior policy-making and supervisory levels, personnel from the region who will readily understand, interpret and be responsive to developments in the region;

(f) Maintain these radio programmes as an exclusively separate entity for purposes of enhancing their effectiveness;

2. Appeals to all Governments, non-governmental organizations and the specialized agencies to co-operate with the Secretary-General in order to ensure the widest possible dissemination of information against apartheid, in particular, these radio programmes;

3. Expresses its appreciation to those Member States and international organizations which have provided the Department of Public Information of the Secretariat with their broadcasting facilities, as well as their contribution to the Trust Fund for Publicity against Apartheid, and request those which have not done so to do the same;

4. Requests the Secretary-General to report to the General Assembly at its forty-fourth session on the implementation of the present resolution.

Appendix 3

UNESCO's Mass Media Declaration

(Declaration on Fundamental Principles Concerning the Contribution of the Mass Media to Strengthening Peace and International Understanding, to the Promotion of Human Rights and to Countering Racialism, Apartheid and Incitement to War)

Adopted on 22 November, 1978, at the Twentieth Session of the General Conference of UNESCO held in Paris

PREAMBLE

The General Conference,

Recalling that by virtue of its Constitution the purpose of Unesco is to 'contribute to peace and security by promoting collaboration among the nations through education, science and culture in order to further universal respect for justice, for the rule of law and for the human rights and fundamental freedoms' (Art. I, 1), and that to realize this purpose the Organization will strive 'to promote the free flow of ideas by word and image' (Art. I, 2),

Further recalling that under the Constitution the member states of Unesco, 'believing in full opportunities for education of all, in the unrestricted pursuit of objective truth, and in the free exchange of ideas and knowledge, are agreed and determined to develop and to increase the means of communication between their peoples and to employ these means for the purposes of mutual understanding and a truer and more perfect knowledge of each other's lives'(sixth preambular paragraph),

Recalling the purposes and principles of the United Nations, as specified in its Charter,

Recalling the Universal Declaration of Human Rights, adopted by the General Assembly of the United Nations in 1948 and particularly Article 19 thereof, which provides that 'everyone has the right to freedom of opinion and expression; this right includes freedom to hold opinions without interference and to seek receive and impart information and ideas through any media regardless of frontiers'; and the International Covenant on Civil and Political Rights, adopted by the General Assembly of the United Nations in 1966, Article 19 of which proclaims the same principles and Article 20 of which condemns incitement to war, the advocacy of national, racial or religious hatred and any form of discrimination, hostility or violence,

Recalling Article 4 of the International Convention on the Elimination of all Forms of Racial Discrimination, adopted by the General Assembly of the United Nations in 1965, and the international Convention on the Suppression and Punishment of the Crime of Apartheid, adopted by the General Assembly of the United Nations in 1973, whereby the States acceding to these Conventions undertook to adopt immediate and positive measures designed to eradicate all incitement to, or acts of, racial discrimination, and agreed to prevent any encouragement of the crime of apartheid and similar segregationist policies or their manifestations,

Recalling the Declaration on the Promotion among Youth of the Ideals of Peace, Mutual Respect and the Understanding between Peoples, adopted by the General Assembly of the United Nations in 1965,

Recalling the declaration and resolutions adopted by the various organs of the United Nations concerning the establishment of a new international economic order and the role Unesco is called to play in this respect,

Recalling the Declaration of the Principles of International Cultural Cooperation, adopted by the General Conference of Unesco in 1966,

Recalling Resolution 59(I) of the General Assembly of the United Nations, adopted in 1946 and declaring:
'Freedom of information is a fundamental human right and is the touchstone of all the freedoms to which the United Nations is consecrated;

Freedom of information requires as an indispensable element the willingness and capacity to employ its privileges without abuse. It requires as a basic discipline the moral obligation to seek the facts without prejudice and to spread knowledge without malicious intent;

Recalling Resolution 110(II) of the General Assembly of the United Nations, adopted in 1947, condemning all forms of propaganda which are designed or likely to provoke or encourage any threat to the peace, breach of the peace, or act of aggression,

Recalling resolution 127(II), also adopted by the General Assembly in 1947, which invites Member States to take measures, within the limits of constitutional procedures, to combat the diffusion of false or distorted reports likely to injure friendly relations between States, as well as the other resolutions of the General Assembly concerning mass media and their contribution to strengthening peace, trust and friendly relations among States,

Recalling resolution 9.12 adopted by the General Conference of Unesco in 1968, reiterating Unesco's objective to help to eradicate colonialism and racialism, and resolution 12.1 adopted by the General Conference in 1976, which proclaims that colonialism, neo-colonialism and racialism in all its forms and manifestations are incompatible with the fundamental aims of Unesco,

Recalling resolution 4.301 adopted by the General Conference of Unesco on the contribution of the information media to furthering international understanding and co-operation in the interests of peace and human welfare, and to countering propaganda on the behalf of war, racialism, apartheid and hatred of nations, and *aware* of the fundamental contribution that mass media can make to the realization of these objectives,

Recalling the Declaration of Race and Racial Prejudice adopted by the General Conference of Unesco at its twentieth session,

Conscious of the complexity of the problems of information in modern society, of the diversity of solutions which have been offered to them, as evidenced in particular by the consideration given to them within Unesco, and of the legitimate desire of all parties concerned that their aspirations, points of view and cultural identity be taken into due consideration,

Conscious of the aspirations of the developing countries for the establishment of a new, more just and more effective world information and communication order,

Proclaims on this twenty-eighth day of November 1978 this Declaration on Fundamental Principles concerning the contribution of the Mass Media to Strengthening Peace and International Understanding, to the Promotion of Human Rights and to Countering Racialism, Apartheid and Incitement to War.

ARTICLE I

The strengthening of peace and international understanding, the promotion of human rights and the countering of racialism, apartheid and incitement to war demand a free flow and a wider and better balanced dissemination of information.

To this end the mass media have a leading contribution to make. This contribution will be the more effective to the extent that the information reflects the different aspects of the subject dealt with.

ARTICLE II

1. The exercise of freedom of opinion, expression and information, recognized as an integral part of human rights and fundamental freedom, is a vital factor in the strengthening of peace and international understanding.
2. Access by the public should be guaranteed by the diversity of the sources and means to information available to it. To this end journalists must have freedom to report and the fullest possible facilities of access to information. Similarly, it is important that the mass media be responsive to the concerns of people and individuals, thus promoting the participation of the public in the elaboration of information.
3. With the view of the strengthening of peace and international understanding, to promoting human rights and to countering racialism, apartheid and incitement to war, the mass media throughout the world, by reason of their role, contribute to promoting human rights, in particular by giving expression to oppressed peoples who struggle against colonialism, neo-colonialism, foreign occupation and all forms of racial discrimination and oppression and who are unable to make their voices heard within their own territories.
4. If the mass media are to be in a position to promote the principles of this Declaration in their activities, it is essential that the journalists and other agents of the mass media, in their own country or abroad, be assured of protection guaranteeing them the best conditions for the exercise of their profession.

ARTICLE III

1. The mass media have an important contribution to make to the strengthening of peace and international understanding and in countering racialism, apartheid and incitement to war.
2. In countering aggressive war, racialism, apartheid and other violations of human rights which are *inter alia* spawned by prejudice and ignorance, the mass media, by disseminating information on the aims, aspirations, cultures and needs of all peoples, contribute to eliminate ignorance and misunderstanding between peoples, to make nationals of a country sensitive to the needs and desires of others, to ensure the respect of the rights and dignity of all nations, all peoples and all individuals without distinction of race, sex, language, religion, or nationality to draw attention to the great evils which afflict humanity, such as poverty, malnutrition and diseases, thereby promoting the formulation by States of the policies best able to promote the reduction of international tension and the peaceful and equitable settlement of international disputes.

ARTICLE IV

The mass media have an essential part to play in the education of young people in a spirit of peace, justice, freedom, mutual respect and understanding, in order to promote human rights, equality of rights as between all human beings and all nations, and economic and social progress. Equally, they have an important role to play in making known the views and aspirations of the younger generation.

ARTICLE V

In order to respect freedom of opinion, expression and information and in order that information may reflect all points of view, it is important that the points of view presented by those who consider that the information published or disseminated about them has seriously prejudiced their effort to strengthen peace and international understanding, to promote human rights or to counter racialism, apartheid and incitement to war be disseminated.

ARTICLE VI

For the establishment of a new equilibrium and greater reciprocity in the flow of information, which will be conducive to the institution of a just and lasting peace and to the economic and political independence of the developing countries, it is necessary to correct the inequalities in the flow of information to and from developing countries, and between those countries. To this end, it is essential that their mass media should have conditions and resources enabling them to gain strength and expand, and to co-operate both among themselves and with the mass media in developed countries.

ARTICLE VII

By disseminating more widely all of the information concerning the universally accepted objectives and principles which are the bases of the resolutions adopted by the different organs of the United Nations, the mass media contribute effectively to the strengthening of peace and international understanding, to the promotion of human rights, and to the establishment of a more just and equitable international economic order.

ARTICLE VIII

Professional organizations, and people who participate in the professional training of journalists and other agents of the mass media and who assist them in performing their functions in a responsible manner should attach special importance to the principles of this Declaration when drawing up and ensuring application of their codes of ethics.

ARTICLE IX

In the spirit of this Declaration, it is for the international community to contribute to the creation of the conditions for a free flow and wider and more balanced dissemination of information, and of the conditions for the protection, in the exercise of their functions, of journalists and other agents of the mass media. Unesco is well placed to make a valuable contribution in this respect.

ARTICLE X

1. With due respect for constitutional provisions designed to guarantee freedom of information and for the applicable international instruments and agreements, it is indispensable to create and maintain throughout the world the conditions which make it possible for the organizations and persons professionally involved in the dissemination of information to achieve the objectives of this Declaration.
2. It is important that a free flow and wider and better balanced dissemination of information be encouraged.
3. To this end, it is necessary that the States facilitate the procurement by the mass media in the developing countries of adequate conditions and resources enabling them to gain strength and expand, and that they support co-operation by the latter both among themselves and with the mass media in developed countries.
4. Similarly, on a basis of equality of rights, mutual advantage and respect for the diversity of cultures which go to make up the common heritage of mankind, it is essential that bilateral and multilateral exchanges of information among all States, and in particular those which have different economic and social systems, be encouraged and developed.

ARTICLE XI

For this Declaration to be fully effective it is necessary, with due respect for the legislative and administrative provisions and the other obligations of Member States, to guarantee the existence of favorable conditions for the operation of the mass media, in conformity with the provisions of the Universal Declaration of Human Rights and with the corresponding principles proclaimed in the International Covenant on Civil and Political Rights adopted by the General Assembly of the United Nations in 1966.

Appendix 4

Charter for a Free Press

(January 1987)

A free press means a free people. To this end, the following principles, basic to an unfettered flow of news and information both within and across national borders, deserve the support of all those pledged to advance and protect democratic institutions.

1. Censorship, direct or indirect, is unacceptable; thus laws and practices restricting the right of the news media freely to gather and distribute information must be abolished, and government authorities, national or local, must not interfere with the content of print or broadcast news, or restrict access to any news source.

2. Independent news media, both print and broadcast, must be allowed to emerge and operate freely in all countries.

3. There must be no discrimination by governments in their treatment, economic or otherwise, of the news media within a country. In those countries where government media also exist, the independent media must have the same free access as the official media have to all material and facilities necessary to their publishing or broadcasting operations.

4. States must not restrict access to newsprint, printing facilities and distribution systems, operation of news agencies, and availability of broadcast frequencies and facilities.

5. Legal, technical and tariff practices by communications authorities which inhibit the distribution of news and restrict the flow of information are condemned.

6. Government media must enjoy editorial independence and be open to a diversity of viewpoints. This should be affirmed in both law and practice.

7. There should be unrestricted access by the print and broadcast media within a country to outside news and information services, and the public should enjoy similar freedom to receive foreign publications and foreign broadcasts without interference.

8. National frontiers must be open to foreign journalists. Quotas must not apply, and applications for visas, press credentials and other documentation requisite for their work should be approved promptly. Foreign journalists should be allowed to travel freely within a country and have access to both official and unofficial news sources, and be allowed to import and export freely all necessary professional materials and equipment.

9. Restrictions on the free entry to the field of journalism or over its practice, through licensing or other certification procedures, must be eliminated.

10. Journalists, like all citizens, must be secure in their persons and be given full protection of law. Journalists working in war zones are recognized as civilians enjoying all rights and immunities accorded other civilians.

This Charter for a Free Press represents provisions approved by journalists from 34 countries at the Voices of Freedom world conference on censorship problems in London, Jan. 16-18, 1987.

The conference was held by the World Press Freedom Committee, with the cooperation of the International Federation of Newspaper Publishers (FIEJ), International Press Institute, Inter American Press Association, North American National Broadcasters Association and the International Federation of the Periodical Press.

—World Press Freedom Committee

Appendix 5

Declaration of Chapultepec

Adopted by the Hemisphere Conference on Free Speech in Chapultepec,
Mexico City, Mexico, March 11, 1994

A free press enables societies to resolve their conflicts, promote their well-being and protect their liberty. No law or act of government may limit freedom of expression or of the press, whatever the medium. Because we are fully conscious of this reality and accept it with the deepest conviction, and because of our firm commitment to freedom, we sign this declaration, whose principles follow.

1. No people or society can be free without freedom of expression and of the press. The exercise of this freedom is not something authorities grant, it is an inalienable right of the people.

2. Every person has the right to seek and receive information, express opinions and disseminate them freely. No one may restrict or deny these rights.

3. The authorities must be compelled by law to make available in a timely and reasonable manner the information generated by the public sector. No journalist may be forced to reveal his or her sources of information.

4. Freedom of expression and of the press are severely limited by murder, terrorism, kidnapping, intimidation, the unjust imprisonment of journalists, the destruction of facilities, violence of any kind and impunity for perpetrators. Such acts must be investigated promptly and punished harshly.

5. Prior censorship, restrictions on the circulation of the media or dissemination of their reports, arbitrary management of information, the imposition of obstacles to the free flow of news, and restrictions on the activities and movements of journalists directly contradict freedom of the press.

6. The media and journalists should neither be discriminated against nor favored because of what they write or say.

7. Tariff and exchange policies, licenses for the importation of paper or news-gathering equipment, the assigning of radio and television frequencies and the granting or withdrawal of government advertising may not be used to reward or punish the media or individual journalists.

8. The membership of journalists in guilds, their affiliation to professional and trade associations and the affiliation of the media with business groups must be strictly voluntary.

9. The credibility of the press is linked to its commitment to truth, to the pursuit of accuracy, fairness and objectivity and to the clear distinction between news and advertising. The attainment of these goals and the respect for ethical and professional values may not be imposed. These are the exclusive responsibility of journalists and the media. In a free society, it is public opinion that rewards or punishes.

10. No news medium nor journalist may be punished for publishing the truth or criticizing or denouncing the government.

AUTHOR'S NOTE:

The Inter American Press Association, in its literature circulated in 1995 to promote the declaration, explained why it was needed:

> *The years of the 1980's brought revolutionary changes to public life in the Americas, with democracies replacing dictatorships. Members of the IAPA well understood that the success of these new democracies in solving their problems would depend on the ability of citizens to discuss them, and write about them, without fear of punishment. To find ways to protect this freedom of expression, IAPA organized the conference at Chapultepec. There the Declaration was written and adopted. The Declaration ignores national boundaries, and belongs to everybody.*

Appendix 6

Declaration of Talloires

A Statement of Principles to Which an Independent News Media Subscribes, and on Which It [sic] Never Will Compromise

The text of the Declaration of Talloires, adopted by leaders of independent news organizations from 21 nations at the Voices of Freedom Conference in Talloires, France, May 15-17, 1981—a statement of principles to which a free world media subscribes, and on which it [sic] never will compromise.

We journalists from many parts of the world, reporters, editors, photographers, publishers and broadcasters, linked by our mutual dedication to a free press,

Meeting in Talloires, France, from May 15 to 17, 1981, to consider means of improving the free flow of information worldwide, and to demonstrate our resolve to resist any encroachment on this free flow,

Determined to uphold the objectives of the Universal Declaration of Human Rights, which in Article 19 states, "Everyone has the right to freedom of opinion and expression; this right includes freedom to hold opinions without interference and to seek, receive and impart information and ideas through any media regardless of frontiers,"

Mindful of the commitment of the constitution of the United Nations Educational, Scientific and Cultural Organization to "promote the free flow of ideas by word and image,"

Conscious also that we share a common faith, as stated in the charter of the United Nations, "in the dignity and worth of the human person, in the equal rights of men and women, and of nations large and small,"

Recalling moreover that the signatories of the final act of the Conference of Security and Cooperation in Europe concluded in 1975 in Helsinki, Finland, pledged themselves to foster "freer flow and wider dissemination of information of all kinds, to encourage cooperation in the field of information and the exchange of information with other countries, and to improve conditions under which journalists from one participating state exercise their profession in another participating state" and expressed their intention in particular to support "the improvement of the circulation of access to, and exchange of information,"

Declare that:

1. We affirm our commitment to these principles and call upon all international bodies and nations to adhere faithfully to them.
2. We believe that the free flow of information and ideas is essential for mutual understanding and world peace. We consider restraints on the movement of news and information to be contrary to the interests of international understanding, in violation of the Universal Declaration of Human Rights, the constitution of UNESCO, and the final act of the Conference on security and Cooperation in Europe; and inconsistent with the charter of the United Nations.
3. We support the universal human right to be fully informed, which right requires the free circulation of news and opinion. We vigorously oppose any interference with this fundamental right.
4. We insist that free access, by the people and the press, to all sources of information, both official and unofficial, must be assured and reinforced. Denying freedom of the press denies all freedom of the individual.
5. We are aware that governments, in developed and developing countries alike, frequently constrain or otherwise discourage the reporting of information they consider detrimental or embarrassing, and that governments usually invoke the national interest to justify these constraints. We believe, however, that the people's interest, and therefore the interests of the nation, are better served by free and open reporting. From robust public debate grows better understanding of the issues facing a nation and its peoples; and out of understanding greater chances for solutions.
6. We believe in any society that public interest is best served by a variety of independent news media. It is often suggested that some countries cannot support a multiplicity of print journals, radio and television stations because there is said to be a lack of an economic base. Where a variety of independent media is not available for any reason, existing information channels should reflect different points of view.
7. We acknowledge the importance of advertising as a consumer service and in providing financial support for a strong and self-sustaining press. Without financial independence, the press cannot be independent. We adhere to the principle that editorial decisions must be free of advertising influence. We also recognize advertising as an important source of information and opinion.
8. We recognize that new technologies have greatly facilitated the international flow of information and that the news media in many countries have not sufficiently benefited from this progress. We support all efforts by international organizations and other public and private bodies to correct this imbalance and to make this technology available to promote the worldwide advancement of the press and broadcast media and the journalistic profession.

9. We believe that the debate on news and information in modern society that has taken place in UNESCO and other international bodies should now be put to constructive purposes. We reaffirm our views on several specific questions that have arisen in the course of this debate, being convinced that:

- Censorship and other forms of arbitrary control of information and opinion should be eliminated; the people's right to news and information should not be abridged.
- Access by journalists to diverse sources of news and opinion, official or unofficial, should be without restriction. Such access is inseparable from access of the people to information.
- There can be no international code of journalistic ethics; the plurality of views makes this impossible. Codes of journalistic ethics, if adopted within a country, should be formulated by the press itself and should be voluntary in their application. They cannot be formulated, imposed or monitored by governments without becoming an instrument of official control of the press and therefore a denial of press freedom.
- Members of the press should enjoy the full protection of national and international law. We seek no special protection or any special status and oppose any proposals that would control journalists in the name of protecting them.
- There should be no restriction on any person's freedom to practice journalism. Journalists should be free to form organizations to protect their professional interests.
- Licensing of journalists by national or international bodies should not be sanctioned, nor should special requirements be demanded of journalists in lieu of licensing them. Such measures submit journalists to controls and pressures inconsistent with a free press.
- The press's professional responsibility is the pursuit of truth. To legislate or otherwise mandate responsibilities for the press is to destroy its independence. The ultimate guarantor of journalistic responsibility is the free exchange of ideas.
- All journalistic freedoms should apply equally to the print and broadcast media. Since the broadcast media are the primary purveyors of news and information in many countries, there is particular need for nations to keep their broadcast channels open to the free transmission of news and opinion.

10. We pledge cooperation in all genuine efforts to expand the free flow of information worldwide. We believe the time has come within UNESCO and other intergovernmental bodies to abandon attempts to regulate news content and formulate rules for the press. Efforts should be directed instead to finding practical solutions to the problems before us, such as improving technological progress, increasing professional interchanges and equipment

transfers, reducing communication tariffs, producing cheaper newsprint and eliminating other barriers to the development of news media capabilities.

Our interests as members of the press, whether from the developed or developing countries, are essentially the same: Ours is a joint dedication to the freest, most accurate and impartial information that is within our professional capability to produce and distribute. We reject the view of press theoreticians and those national or international officials who claim that while people in some countries are ready for a free press, those in other countries are insufficiently developed to enjoy that freedom.

We are deeply concerned by a growing tendency in many countries and in international bodies to put government interests above those of the individual, particularly in regard to information. We believe that the state exists for the individual and has a duty to uphold individual rights. We believe that the ultimate definition of a free press lies not in the actions of governments or international bodies, but rather in the professionalism, vigor and courage of individual journalists.

Press freedom is a basic human right. We pledge ourselves to concerted action to uphold this right.

Appendix 7

**Declaration of Windhoek on Promoting an Independent
and Pluralistic African Press**

We the participants in the United Nations/United Nations Educational, Scientific and Cultural Organization Seminar on Promoting an Independent and Pluralistic African press, held in Windhoek, Namibia, from 29 April to 3 May 1991,

Recalling the Universal Declaration of Human Rights,

Recalling General Assembly resolution 59(I) of 14 December 1946 stating that freedom of information is a fundamental human right, and General Assembly resolution 45/76 A of 11 December 1990 on information in service of humanity,

Recalling resolution 25 C/104 of the General Conference of UNESCO of 1989 in which the main focus is the promotion of "the free flow of ideas by word and image among nations and within each nation";

Noting with appreciation the statements made by the United Nations Under-Secretary-General for the Public Information and the Assistant Director-General for Communication, Information and Informatics of UNESCO at the opening of the Seminar,

Expressing our sincere appreciation to the United Nations and UNESCO for organizing the Seminar,

Expressing also our sincere appreciation to all the intergovernmental, governmental and non-governmental bodies and organizations, in particular the United Nations Development Programme (UNDP), which contributed to the United Nations/ UNESCO effort to organize the Seminar,

Expressing our gratitude to the Government and people of the Republic of Namibia for their kind hospitality which facilitated the success of the Seminar,

Declare that:

   1. Consistent with article 19 of the Universal Declaration of Human Rights, the establishment, maintenance and fostering of an independent, pluralistic and free press is essential to the development and maintenance of democracy in a nation, and for economic development.

2. By an independent press, we mean a press independent from governmental, political or economic control or from control of materials and infrastructure essential for the production and dissemination of newspapers, magazines and periodicals.

3. By a pluralistic press, we mean the end of monopolies of any kind and existence of the greatest possible number of newspapers, magazines and periodicals reflecting the widest possible range of opinion within the community.

4. The welcome changes the increasing number of African States are now undergoing towards multi-party democracies provide the climate in which an independent and pluralistic press can emerge.

5. The world-wide trend towards democracy and freedom of information and expression is a fundamental contribution to the fulfillment of human aspirations.

6. In Africa today, despite the positive developments in some countries, in many countries journalists, editors, and publishers are victims of repression—they are murdered, arrested, detained and censored, and are restricted by economical and political pressures such as restrictions on newsprint, licensing systems which restrict the opportunity to publish, visa restrictions which prevent the free movement of journalists, restrictions on the exchange of news and information, and limitations on the circulation of newspapers within countries and across national borders. In some countries, one-party States control the totality of information.

7. Today, at least 17 journalists, editors or publishers are in African prisons, and 48 African journalists were killed in the exercise of their profession between 1969 and 1990.

8. The General Assembly of the United Nations should include in the agenda of its next session an item on the declaration of censorship as a grave violation of human rights falling within the purview of the Commission on Human Rights.

9. African States should be encouraged to provide constitutional guarantees of freedom of the press and freedom of association.

10. To encourage and consolidate the positive changes taking place in Africa, and to counter the negative ones, the international community—specifically, international organizations (governmental as well as non-governmental), development agencies and professional associations—should as a matter of priority direct funding support towards the development and establishment of non-governmental newspapers, magazines and periodicals that reflect the society as a whole and the different points of view within the communities they serve.

11. All funding should aim to encourage pluralism as well as independence. As a consequence, the public media should be funded only where authorities guarantee a constitutional and effective freedom of information and expression and the independence of the press.

12. To assist in the preservation of the freedoms enumerated above, the establishment of the truly independent, representative associations, syndicates or trade unions of journalists, and associations of editors and publishers, is a matter of priority in all the countries of Africa where such bodies do not now exist.

13. The national media and labour relations laws of African countries should be drafted in such a way as to ensure that such representative associations can exist and fulfill their important tasks in defense of press freedom.

14. As a sign of faith, African Governments that have jailed journalists for their professional activities should free them immediately. Journalists who have had to leave their countries should be free to return to resume their professional activities.

15. Cooperation between publishers within Africa, and between publishers of the North and South (for example through the principle of twinning), should be encouraged and supported.

16. As a matter of urgency, the United Nations and UNESCO, and particularly the International Programme for the Development of Communication (IPDC), should initiate detailed research, in cooperation with governmental (especially UNDP), and non governmental donor agencies, relevant non-governmental organizations and professional associations, into the following specific areas:

    (i)   identification of economic barriers to the establishment of news media outlets, including restrictive import duties, tariffs and quotas for such things as newsprint, printing equipment, and typesetting and word processing machinery, and taxes on the sale of newspapers, as a prelude to their removal;

(ii) training of journalists and managers and the availability of professional training institutions and courses;

(iii) legal barriers to the recognition and effective operation of the trade unions or associations of journalists, editors and publishers;

(iv) a register of available funding from development and other agencies, the conditions attaching to the release of such funds, and methods of applying for them;

(v) the state of press freedom, country by country, in Africa.

17. In view of the importance of radio and television in the field of news and information, the United Nations and UNESCO are invited to recommend to the General Assembly and the General Conference the convening of a similar seminar of journalists and managers of radio and television services in Africa, to explore the possibility of applying similar concepts of independence and pluralism to these media.

18. The international community should contribute to the achievement and implementation of the initiatives and projects set out in the annex to this Declaration.

19. This Declaration should be presented by the Secretary-General of the United Nations to the United Nations General Assembly, and by the Director-General of UNESCO to the General Conference of UNESCO.

ANNEX

INITIATIVES AND PROJECTS IDENTIFIED IN THE SEMINAR

I.   Development of cooperation between private African newspapers:
—to aid them in the mutual exchange of their publications;
—to aid them in the exchange of information;
—to aid them in sharing their experience by the exchange of journalists;
—to organize on their behalf training courses and study trips for their journalists, managers and technical personnel.

II.   Creation of separate, independent national unions for publishers, news editors and journalists.

III. Creation of regional unions of publishers, editors and independent journalists.

IV. Development and promotion of non-governmental regulations and codes of ethics in each country in order to defend more effectively the profession and ensure its credibility.

V. Financing of a study on the readership of independ
ent newspapers in order to set up groups of advertising agents.

VI. Financing of a feasibility study for the establishment of an independent press aid foundation and research into identifying capital funds for the foundation.

VII. Financing of a feasibility study for the creation of a central board for the purchase of newsprint and the establishment of such a board.

VIII. Support and creation of regional African press enterprises.

IX. Aid with a view to establishing structures to monitor attacks on freedom of the press and the independence of journalists following the example of the West African Journalists' Association.

X. Creation of a data bank for the independent African press for the documentation of news items essential to newspapers.

Appendix 8

International Journalism Survey

THE QUESTIONNAIRE

1. Please give the full name of the organization you are representing, as well as its acronym in English or in another language.

2. Is this an organization comprised mainly of (check one):

    Journalists ☐

    Media Owners and Executives ☐

    Others (explain): ....

3. Has your organization ever been involved in any international press freedom campaign on the behalf of any journalist, group of journalists, writers, or media workers in a specific country or region?   Yes ☐   No ☐

4. If your answer to question 3 was "yes", briefly describe the campaigns in which your organization has been involved. (If you have written documentation on the history of your work in this area attach it and return it with this questionnaire.)

5. What are the major international issues related to the work of journalists and the media that are of most concern to your organization?

6.   With regards to the specific issue of government censorship, which of the
     strategies listed below have been the most effective in bringing about change.
     Tick as many as you can.

Negative publicity ☐   Lobbying by organizations like yours ☐
Pressure from any foreign government ☐
Pressure from any government with which the government trades ☐
Pressure from the United States in particular ☐
Lobbying by international human rights groups ☐
Pressure from groups or individuals within the country ☐
Pressure from UN agencies ☐   Letter-writing campaigns ☐   Legal action ☐
Other strategies not listed above (explain):

7.   What are the major threats to the safety of journalists and writers today?

8.   What are the best means of ensuring that journalists and writers are pro-
     tected from physical violence and murder? Identify as many as you find
     necessary from the following list.

UN resolutions and declarations ☐   National laws ☐
Identification cards for journalists in war zones ☐
Declarations by organizations such as yours ☐
Public education about the role of journalists ☐
An end to international wars ☐   An end to civil wars ☐
No solution because threat of death is a hazard of the profession ☐
Other strategies not listed above (explain):

....

....

....

9. List below any international or regional declarations your organization has signed concerning press freedom and the rights of journalists or writers. (Please include the text of as many of these documents as you can when you return this questionnaire.)

10. Are you optimistic that there will be less government censorship in the years to come?   Yes ☐   No ☐

11. Explain briefly the reason for your reply in question 10.

12. Are you optimistic that there will be less physical harm and murders of journalists in the years to come?   Yes ☐   No ☐

13. Explain briefly the reason for your answer to question 12.

14. For purposes of verification and attribution, please give your name and position in the organization below.

    Name: ....

    Position: ....

Appendix 9

International Journalism Survey

LIST OF ORGANIZATIONS TO WHICH QUESTIONNAIRES WERE SENT

In addition to consulting the roll of organizations participating in IFEX, we checked directories (such as the *Europa Yearbook* and the *Encyclopedia of Associations*) to compile a list of non-governmental organizations engaged in the promotion of press freedom. Two main objectives guided the compilation of the list: (1) it should include all possible groups working to promote press freedom globally, rather than just in the regions where they were based; (2) every effort would be made to include organizations with such a vocation from as many parts of the world as possible.

AMNESTY INTERNATIONAL
CONTACT: CARLOS MIGUEL SALINAS,
GOVERNMENT PROGRAM OFFICER,
LATIN AMERICA AND THE CARIBBEAN

COMMONWEALTH JOURNALISTS ASSOCIATION
CONTACT: LAWRIE BREEN,
EXECUTIVE DIRECTOR

COMMONWEALTH PRESS UNION
CONTACT: ROBIN MACKICHAN, DIRECTOR

LATIN AMERICAN FEDERATION
OF PRESS WORKERS
CONTACT: SEÑOR ALFREDO JORGE CARAZO,
SECRETARY GENERAL

FEDERATION OF LATIN AMERICAN JOURNALISTS
CONTACT: LUIZ SUAREZ LOPEZ,
SECRETARY GENERAL

INTERNATIONAL FEDERATION
OF FREE JOURNALISTS
CONTACT: KRYSTYNA ASIPOWICZ,
GENERAL SECRETARY

THE INTERNATIONAL ORGANIZATION
OF JOURNALISTS (IOJ)
CONTACT: KAARLE NORDENSTRENG,
FORMER IOJ PRESIDENT

NORDIC FEDERATION OF JOURNALISTS' UNIONS
CONTACT: TORE SJOLIE, EXECUTIVE OFFICER

INTERNATIONAL CATHOLIC UNION OF THE PRESS
CONTACT: JOSEPH CHITTILAPPILLY,
SECRETARY GENERAL

WORLD ASSOCIATION OF WOMEN JOURNALISTS
AND WRITERS
CONTACT: PIERRETTE PARE-WALSH, PRESIDENT

WORLD FEDERATION OF JEWISH JOURNALISTS
CONTACT: GERSHON HENDEL,
SECRETARY GENERAL

COMMITTEE TO PROTECT JOURNALISTS
CONTACT: WILLIAM ORME,
EXECUTIVE DIRECTOR

PEN AMERICAN CENTER
CONTACT: SIOBHAN DOWD

ARTICLE 19
CONTACT: FRANCES D'SOUZA,
EXECUTIVE DIRECTOR

CANADIAN COMMITTEE TO PROTECT
JOURNALISTS (CCPJ)
CONTACT: WAYNE T. SHARPE,
EXECUTIVE DIRECTOR

FEDERACION INTERNACIONAL DE PERIODISTAS
(REGIONAL OFFICE OF THE IFJ–FIP)
CONTACT: KATIA GIL

FREE MEDIA MOVEMENT (FMM)
CONTACT: LUCIEN RAJAKARUNANAYAKE

FREEDOM HOUSE
CONTACT: LEONARD SUSSMAN

HUMAN RIGHTS WATCH
FREE EXPRESSION PROJECT
HUMAN RIGHTS WATCH (NEW YORK OFFICE)
CONTACT: GARA LAMARCHE

INDEX ON CENSORSHIP
CONTACT: PHILIP SPENDER

INSTITUTO PRENSA Y SOCIEDAD
(INSTITUTE FOR PRESS AND SOCIETY—IPYS)
CONTACT: KELA LEON

INTER AMERICAN PRESS ASSOCIATION
CONTACT: RICARDO TROTTI

INTERNATIONAL FEDERATION OF JOURNALISTS
  (IFJ)
CONTACT: BETTINA PETERS,
DEPUTY GENERAL SECRETARY

INTERNATIONAL FEDERATION
  OF NEWSPAPER PUBLISHERS
(FEDERATION INTERNATIONALE DES EDITEURS
  DE JOURNAUX—FIEJ)
CONTACT: ALI RAHNEMA

INTERNATIONAL PRESS INSTITUTE (IPI)
CONTACT: MICHAEL KUDLAK,
PRESS FREEDOM ADVISOR

JOURNALIST SAFETY SERVICE/DUTCH UNION
  OF JOURNALISTS (NVJ)
CONTACT: AMAIA ESPARZA

MEDIA INSTITUTE OF SOUTHERN AFRICA (MISA)
CONTACT: DAVID LUSH

REPORTERS SANS FRONTIERS (RSF)
CONTACT: ROBERT MENARD, DIRECTEUR

UNION DES JOURNALISTES DE L' AFRIQUE
  DE L'OUEST (UJAO)
WEST AFRICAN JOURNALISTS' ASSOCIATION
  (WAJA)
CONTACT: NDIAGA SYLLA, MADEMBA NDIAYE

LIST OF ORGANIZATIONS THAT RESPONDED

CANADIAN COMMITTEE TO PROTECT
  JOURNALISTS (CCPJ)
CONTACT: WAYNE T. SHARPE,
EXECUTIVE DIRECTOR

COMMITTEE TO PROTECT JOURNALISTS (CPJ)
CONTACT: BILL ORME, EXECUTIVE DIRECTOR

PEN AMERICAN CENTER
CONTACT: SIOBHAN DOWD

SOCIEDAD INTERAMERICANA DE PRENSA
INTER AMERICAN PRESS ASSOCIATION (IAPA)
CONTACT: RICARDO TROTTI

HUMAN RIGHTS WATCH (NEW YORK OFFICE)
CONTACT: GARA LAMARCHE

COMMONWEALTH PRESS UNION
CONTACT: ROBIN MACKICHAN, DIRECTOR

INTERNATIONAL FREEDOM OF EXPRESSION
  EXCHANGE
CONTACT: ISABELLE PATENAUDE,
ACTION ALERT COORDINATOR

INTERNATIONAL FEDERATION
  OF JOURNALISTS (IFJ)
CONTACT: BETTINA PETERS,
DEPUTY GENERAL SECRETARY

WORLD PRESS FREEDOM COMMITTEE (WPFC)
CONTACT: DANA BULLEN, EXECUTIVE DIRECTOR

FREEDOM HOUSE
CONTACT: LEONARD SUSSMAN

QUANTITATIVE REPORT ON RESPONSES*

TABLE 1:
INVOLVEMENT AND OPTIMISM

Question:	Yes	No	Unsure
Has your organization ever been involved in an international press freedom campaign?	10	0	0
Are you optimistic that there will be less government censorship in the future?	3	6	1
Are you optimistic that there will be less physical harm and murders of journalists in the future?	2	7	1

TABLE 2:
GOVERNMENT CENSORSHIP—STRATEGIES MOST EFFECTIVE IN BRINGING ABOUT CHANGE

With regards to the specific issue of government censorship, which of the strategies listed below have been the most effective in bringing about change?

	Percentage of responses identifying each
Negative publicity	70%
Lobbying by organizations like yours	100
Pressure from any foreign government	50
Pressure from any government with which the government trades	60
Pressure from the United States in particular	50
Lobbying by international human rights groups	100
Pressure from groups or individuals within the country	70
Pressure from UN agencies	50
Letter-writing campaigns	80
Legal action	70
Other strategies	80

TABLE 3:
MEANS OF ENSURING JOURNALISTS AND WRITERS
PROTECTION FROM VIOLENCE AND MURDER

What are the best means of ensuring that journalists and writers are protected from physical violence and murder?

	Percentage of responses identifying each
Negative publicity	70%
UN resolutions and declarations	40
National laws	60
Identification cards for journalists in war zones	40
Declarations by organizations such as yours	80
Public education about the role of journalists	80
An end to international wars	70
An end to civil wars	70
No solution because the threat of death is a hazard of the profession	20
Other solutions	90

*These tables do not reflect the nuances contained in the narrative replies given by all respondents. For a reporting and discussion of those comments see the relevant sections of chapters 5, 6 and 7.

Appendix 10

Profiles of Major International Press Freedom Organizations

Reporters Sans Frontières (RSF) was founded in 1985 and grew to seven branches in ten years. These branches were in Belgium, France, Germany, Italy, Spain, Sweden and Switzerland. By 1995 there were members of RSF in 83 countries. The organization works to help threatened journalists and censored media by conducting letter-writing campaigns on their behalf, providing legal assistance, supplying material assistance, hosting meetings, and publicizing their plight through its various publications. It has consultative status with UNESCO, the Council of Europe, and the UN Commission on Human Rights. Its main offices are in Paris.

Article 19, or the International Centre Against Censorship, was named for Article 19 of the Universal Declaration of Human Rights. It was established in 1986 and within ten years it had members in 32 countries, advocating the right to freedom to hold opinions without interference and to receive and disseminate information through any media. Article 19 works to eradicate censorship world-wide through its research program and through its network of contacts and correspondents for exchanging information about censorship. It is based in London.

The *Inter American Press Association* (IAPA) is a regional press freedom organization for North and South America. Its membership consists of newspapers, magazines, educators, and other individuals in allied fields. The main objectives of the IAPA are to guard the freedom of the press; to foster and protect the interests of the American press; to promote and maintain the dignity, rights, and responsibilities of journalism; to encourage uniform standards of professional and business conduct; and, finally, to exchange ideas and information that contribute to the cultural, material and technical development of the press. According to the Encyclopedia of Associations 1995-1996, the IAPA had over 1,300 members in 1995. These members strive for a strong friendship between editors and publishers around the world in order to engage in better understanding and goodwill between people. The organization was founded in 1942 and is headquartered in Miami, Florida.

Freedom House was founded in 1941. It is based in New York City. With over 2,000 members, Freedom House serves as a research and documentation center and a clearinghouse. As a way to strengthen free institutions at home and abroad, Freedom House distributes banned material from oppressed countries along with information on Caribbean, Central American, and Afghan issues. Over the last two decades Freedom House has worked directly with various countries around the world to promote an engaged U.S. foreign policy; to monitor human rights and elections; to sponsor public educational campaigns; to offer training and technical assistance to promote democracy and free market reforms; and to support the rule of law, free media, and effective local government.

Index on Censorship was founded in 1972 by Stephen Spender. Its aim is to protect the right to free expression. The journal, which is published every two months, reports on censorship issues from all around the world and publishes articles that add to the essential debates on those issues. Each issue contains a list of attacks on free expression compiled country by country. The Index operates an assisted subscriptions program that allows readers in South America, Africa, Asia, and the former Communist countries to receive the magazine free of charge. It is based in London.

The Toronto-based **Canadian Committee to Protect Journalists** (CCPJ) was founded in 1981. It is a nonprofit, non-governmental organization of more than 350 working journalists, editors, publishers, broadcasters, producers, technical support staff and interested citizens. The organization campaigns against censorship and abuses suffered by journalists, writers and media organizations around the world and in 1992 became a founding member of the International Freedom of Information Exchange (IFEX).

The **International Freedom of Expression Exchange** (IFEX) Clearing House links more than 100 organizations in over 40 countries. The main activity of the IFEX Clearing House is to operate an Action Alert network that works to defend freedom of expression and the rights of journalists, writers and media organizations. Whenever a case occurs, protest information is circulated around the world to participating organizations by electronic mail. These groups in turn fax their protests to governments, international organizations and others. Such concerted campaigns can be instrumental in securing the release of those imprisoned for their opinions or profession, or the lifting of restrictive laws. The Clearing House also publishes a weekly *Communiqué* that provides regular updates on worldwide developments in the freedom of expression community. It also assists groups around the world in conducting campaigns in response to attacks on freedom of expression.

The *International Federation of Journalists* (IFJ) is a worldwide organization of trade unions and associations of journalists. It was first set up in Paris in 1926 and was founded in its modern form in 1952. The IFJ is the world's largest organization of journalists, representing journalists in more than 90 countries. It fights for social and professional rights of journalists working in all sectors of the mass media. The IFJ is recognized by the United Nations and the international trade union movement as the representative voice of journalists worldwide. The IFJ has its headquarters in Brussels (Belgium) and has regional offices in Asia, Europe and Latin America.

The *International Press Institute* (IPI) is dedicated to: safeguarding freedom of the press; promoting the free exchange of news; and improving the practices of journalism. It was formed in 1951 and had over 2,000 members in 62 countries by the late 1980s. The organization consists of an executive board made up of leading editors and journalists from around the world; secretariats in Zurich and London under a director; and national committees in various countries that report directly to the director on developments in their area.

The *World Press Freedom Committee* (WPFC) was first organized in 1976 in response to the controversy at UNESCO over the proposed New World Information and Communication Order. It perceives its mission as being an ideological bulwark against communism and authoritarianism. It provides training and material assistance to news media needing them, especially those in the poorer countries of the southern hemisphere and the former Communist Bloc. Its funding comes primarily from North American media owners and publishers. Its offices are in Reston, Virginia, U.S.A.

The *Committee To Protect Journalists* (CPJ) was founded in 1981 and is based in New York City. The CPJ supports journalists around the world who have been subjected to human rights violations. It strives to keep U.S. and foreign journalists informed about such practices and organizes protests on behalf of those whose rights have been violated. The CPJ is concerned with government efforts to limit the ability of foreign correspondents and local journalists to practice their profession. Apart from the main objective of compiling and publicizing human rights abuses, the CPJ brings suppressed journalists to the United States for interviews and press conferences and sends delegations of journalists to areas of the world where there are especially serious and continuous problems.

Human Rights Watch began in 1978 with the founding of its Helsinki division. By 1995 it had five divisions covering Africa, the Americas, Asia, the Middle East, as well as the signatories of the Helsinki accords. The *Free Expression Project* is one of five collaborative projects conducted by Human Rights Watch. The others are on arms transfers, children's rights, prison conditions, and women's rights. The Free Expression Project explores the relationship between censorship and global social problems, investigates and analyzes restrictions on freedom of expression in the United States, and documents curbs on freedom of expression in other countries. It also gives grants to writers around the world who have been victims of political persecution. Human Rights Watch maintains offices in New York, Washington, Rio de Janeiro, and Hong Kong. It is an independent, non-governmental organization, supported by contributions from private individuals and foundations worldwide. It accepts no government funds, directly or indirectly.

The **Commonwealth Press Union** (CPU) (formerly called the Empire Press Union) was founded in 1909. Its membership is made up largely of media owners and executives from British Commonwealth countries. It aims to: uphold the ideals and values of the Commonwealth; promote understanding and goodwill within the Commonwealth through the press; advance the welfare of the Commonwealth's press and its employees; defend freedom of the press; and provide training for all branches of the print media. It is based in London.

The Paris-based **International Federation of Newspaper Publishers** (FIEJ) is comprised of national associations of newspaper publishers, press agencies, and independent publishers. It promotes and defends press freedom, including the economic independence of publishers. It fosters contact between newspaper executives, sponsors management and marketing seminars, and gives assistance to the press in developing nations. The FIEJ was founded in 1948.

Notes

CHAPTER 1

1. John M. Goshko, "U.N. Chief Stresses Need For Money," *The Washington Post*, Sunday, November 22, 1992, A1, A33.
2. An astute definition of "public opinion" is that of Michael Kunczik, who says it should be seen as a "social process," not a static phenomenon that can be measured reliably.

   > Public opinion comes about when many persons take the same view of a given issue and are aware of this sameness of view. This knowledge that others think like one does oneself is created in most cases by public statements, including of those the mass media. The statements made in the mass media generally have two functions. One is to enable the groups and/or political elites participating in the political process to communicate with each other, i.e. they create a focused public opinion. The other media function is to set themes which may become subjects of public discussion by selecting the themes they consider worth reporting, by leading articles, commentaries and so forth.

   From Michael Kunczik, *Images of Nations and International Public Relations* (Bonn: Friedrich-Ebert-Stiftung, 1990), 115.

3. For example, Lenin's "Twenty-One Conditions," presented to the Second Congress of the Comintern (July 19 – August 7, 1920), included: (a) strict guidelines for running the Communist press, and (b) the stipulation that refusal to do propaganda work would be seen as resignation from revolutionary action.
4. See Table 6.1.
5. Mort Rosenblum, *Coups and Earthquakes* (New York: Harper & Row, 1979).
6. Annabelle Sreberny-Mohammadi et al (eds.), *Foreign News in the Media: International Reporting in 29 Countries*, Reports and Papers on Mass Communication 93 (Paris: UNESCO, 1985), 52.
7. Anthony Smith, *The Geopolitics of Information* (London: Faber and Faber, 1980), 72.
8. Ajoa Yeboah-Afari, "Watching the Media," *West Africa*, Aug. 31, 1987, 1685.
9. Quoted in "Tourist Journalists," *The Japan Times*, March, 1981.
10. For a more in-depth discussion of the "Big Five" news agencies see Mark D. Alleyne, *International Power and International Communication* (London: Macmillan, 1995), in particular chapter 4, "The International Politics of News"; and Mark D. Alleyne and Janet Wagner, "Stability and Change at the 'Big Five' News Agencies," *Journalism Quarterly*, vol. 70, no. 1 (Spring 1993), 40-50.

11. Smith, 75. For more details on the history and development of Agence France-Presse see the typescript "From Havas To AFP: 150 Years of News Reporting" (Paris, 1985).

12. Smith, 83.

13. "Decree by the Russian Federation President on the Information Telegraph Agency of Russia," (January 22, 1992). Complete text relayed by *Federal News Service* (Washington D.C., Federal Information Systems Corporation, January 27, 1992).

14. Ludmila Alexandrova, "News Agencies Agree on TASS Information Pool" (text). Moscow, TASS in English, January 16, 1992. *Foreign Broadcast Information Service Daily Report—Soviet Union*, January 17, 1992 (FBIS-SOV-92-012; 25).

15. Quoted in Jonathan Fenby, *The International News Services* (New York: Schocken Books, 1986), 58. Also see Frank Bartholomew, "Putting the 'I' into UPI," *Editor & Publisher*, Sept. 25, 1982.

16. Reuters (Corporate Relations Dept.), *Reuters: A Background and Chronology of Key Events*, London: January 1990, 10.

17. Ibid.

18. See Bill McAllister, "UPI Will Transmit U.S. Agency's Material," *International Herald Tribune*, October 10, 1987.

19. Jean-Luc Renaud, "U.S. Government Assistance to AP's World-Wide Expansion," *Journalism Quarterly*, vol. 62 (Spring 1985), 10-16, 36. Also see Margaret Blanchard, *Exporting the First Amendment: The Press-Government Crusade of 1945 – 1952* (New York: Longman, 1986).

20. For details of Reuters's recent financial performance see *Reuters Holdings PLC Annual Report* (most recent year).

21. *Reuters: A Background and Chronology of Key Events*, 3.

22. William A. Henry III, "History As It Happens: Linking leaders as never before, CNN has changed the way the world does its business," *Time*, January 6, 1992, 27.

23. Marc Raboy and Bernard Dagenais, *Media, Crisis and Democracy* (London: SAGE, 1992), 6-7.

24. French television journalist Christine Ockrent is quoted as regarding CNN not as a champion of world dialogue but as a "U.S. channel with a global vocation, but which sees the world through an American prism." Henry III, 27.

25. See *Assignment Africa*. (videotape) New York: The Press and the Public Project, 1987. The term "Black Africa" is commonly used to refer to the part of the continent south of the Sahara where the vast majority of the population is black.

26. Mark D. Alleyne, *Travels With A Black Man* (New York: Bimshire Books, 1994), 54-59.

27. In a 1996 interview, Eason Jordan, Senior Vice President, CNN International News, described the lengths to which Muammar Qaddafi went to get access to CNN in the prelude to the Gulf War:

> A phone rang, a man on the phone speaking terrific English. He said his name was Muammar Qaddafi. Well, we had interviewed Mr. Qaddafi,

always in Arabic up to that point, and we thought it was a crank call, so
we hung up. Time and time again, this man claiming to be Qaddafi called
back, until finally we had ambassadors—Libyan ambassadors were calling
from all over the world, outraged, that we were hanging up on their great
leader, and we still didn't believe it, and so we challenged him. We said, "If
it's really you, Mr. Qaddafi, you will, at your expense, put up a TV satellite
feed and we'd like to see you for ourselves,["] and, sure enough, he did it.
. . . So, now we think twice before hanging up on a world leader.

In CNN News Transcript No. 241-11, "CNN Exec Says Iraq Was Told Phone
Needed for Video Link," January 16, 1996.

28. James F. Larson, "Television and U.S. Foreign Policy: The Case of the Iran Hostage
Crisis," *Journal of Communication*, vol. 36, no. 4, 108-30.
29. Telephone interview with Steve Haworth, CNN Public Relations, April 6, 1994.
30. World Service TV was started in 1991. By 1993 it was a 24-hour news and information service disseminated by separate feeds tailored to the interests of its
regional partners. For example, by early 1993 it was estimated to reach at least
nine million homes in Asia via the Star TV satellite package delivered on AsiaSat1.
Jeff Hazell, World Service TV's director of sales and distribution, said at that time
that the mission of World Service TV was "to be fully global by the end of 1993
using various joint venture partners." Meredith Amdur, "BBC World Service TV
looks west," *Broadcasting & Cable*, April 19, 1993, 35-36.
31. Peter Waldman, "Western-Style TV Fare Is Dished Out To Arab Viewers Via MBC
Satellite," *The Wall Street Journal*, March 5, 1992, A10.
32. See Rebecca Mead, "Money machine: Michael Bloomberg strikes it rich with his
brand of financial news; CEO of financial services firm Bloomberg L.P.," *New
York Magazine*, vol. 26, no. 46, November 22, 1993, 44 . Complete text relayed
by *Lexis/Nexis* (Dayton, Ohio: Mead Data Central, October 7, 1994); Carrie R.
Smith, "Crashing Bloomberg's party; Michael Bloomberg," *Wall Street &
Technology*, vol. 11, no. 9, January, 1994, 18. Complete text relayed by *Lexis/Nexis*
(Dayton, Ohio: Mead Data Central, October 14, 1994); "Medialink expands its
multimedia investor relations pipeline; Bloomberg, Medialink announce investor
relations multimedia service," *Business Wire*, October 11, 1994. Complete text
relayed by *Lexis/Nexis* (Dayton, Ohio: Mead Data Central, October 11, 1994).
33. Paula Dwyer, "Reuters Dives In—All The Way," *Business Week*, February 21,
1994, 46. Complete text relayed by *Lexis/Nexis* (Dayton, Ohio: Mead Data Central,
February 21, 1994).
34. See Hans-Henrik Holn and Georg Sørensen (eds.), *Whose World Order? Uneven
Globalization and the End of the Cold War* (Boulder, CO.: Westview Press, 1995).
35. Quoting the UN secretary-general, international legal scholar Oscar Schachter
explained the relationship between legal and political discourse this way:

These connecting highways—the concepts and principles of international
law—are a conspicuous feature of UN debates. As the Secretary-General
recently observed, "political discourse and the vocabulary of law mix cheer-
fully with one another . . . the dialectic between law and diplomacy is constantly at work." Perhaps it is not always "cheerful." The Secretary-General

went on to say that "the United Nations shows, better than any other organization, the competition States engage in to try and impose a dominant language and control the juridical ideology it expresses." We are thus reminded
that legal discourse is not divorced from political conflict. On the one hand,
the concepts of international law provide a necessary code of communication, and therefore greatly facilitate the institutionalization of international
society. On the other hand, international law is often relied upon by states
to resist the transfer of their power to international authority. We have to
look beyond international law itself to evaluate the likely consequences.

From Oscar Schachter, "The UN Legal Order: An Overview," in Oscar Schachter
and Christopher Joyner (eds.), *United Nations Legal Order* vol. 1 (Cambridge:
Cambridge University Press, 1995), 28-29.

36. See Holm and Sørensen, 192-93.
37. My definition of what exactly is a regime is borrowed from Stephen Krasner,
who defined regimes as

> ... sets of implicit or explicit principles, norms, rules, and decision-making pro-
> cedures around which actors' expectations converge in a given area of inter-
> national relations. Principles are beliefs of fact, causation, and rectitude. Norms
> are standards of behavior defined in terms of rights and obligations. Rules are
> specific prescriptions or proscriptions for action. Decision-making procedures
> are prevailing practices for making and implementing collective choice.

From Stephen Krasner, *International Regimes* (Ithaca: Cornell University Press,
1983), 2.

Chapter 2

1. This lexicographic reference is taken from *The Compact Edition of the Oxford
English Dictionary* (New York: Oxford University Press, 1971).
2. Mark D. Alleyne, *International Power and International Communication* (London:
Macmillan, 1995).
3. This is a quote from Harvey that is found in Waters. See Malcolm Waters,
Globalization (London: Routledge, 1995), 57, and D. Harvey, *The Condition of
Postmodernity* (Oxford: Blackwell, 1989), 293-95.
4. Waters, 63.
5. Donald Read, *The Power of News: The History of Reuters 1849-1989* (Oxford:
Oxford University Press, 1991). For additional information on the management
history of Reuters see the following Harvard Business School Case Studies (last
revised May 22, 1995): No. 9-595-113 "Reuters Holdings PLC 1850-1987: A
(Selective) History"; No. 9-595-114 "Reuters Holdings PLC: Network Renewal
and Product Integration (A)"; and No. 9-595-115 "Reuters Holdings PLC:
Network Renewal and Product Integration (B)."
6. Read, 7.
7. Ibid.
8. Ibid., 16.
9. Ibid., 34.

10. Ibid., 76-77.
11. Ibid., 159-60.
12. Ibid., 257, 271-72.
13. Ibid., 299.
14. Ibid., 300.
15. Ibid., 303.
16. Ibid., 311.
17. Michael W. Miller and Matthew Winkler, "Wiring Up: Computerized Trading Starts to Make Inroads At Financial Exchanges," *The Wall Street Journal*, April 24, 1989, A1, A6.
18. There were two main forces behind diversification: (a) declining profitability of hard news in text form; and (b) increased demand for communication and information to service expanding transnational structures of finance and production. This information must be of high quality (pictures, video, sound, analysis) and high velocity.
19. See Mark D. Alleyne and Janet Wagner, "Stability and Change at the 'Big Five' News Agencies," *Journalism Quarterly*, vol. 70, no. 1 (Spring 1993), 40-50.
20. Letter received from Robert A. Crooke, Vice President, Media Relations, Reuters America Inc., New York City, November 16, 1995.
21. Reuters Holdings PLC, *Annual Report 1994* (London: Reuters Holdings PLC, 1995).
22. Mark Wood, "Moving up the Media Value Chain," *News From Reuters*, 14 February, 1995, 1.
23. "Reuters Launches Financial TV Service In The US," News Release, Reuters America Inc., New York, May 24, 1995.
24. From 1937 to March 1967 Reuters had exchanged its world economic news for the Dow Jones service of North American financial news. In 1965 Dow Jones said it would market its ticker in Europe. Dow Jones later joined forces with AP, and their Economic Report was started on April 1, 1967.
25. Miller and Winkler, A1, A6.
26. George A. Hayter, "Telecommunications and the Restructuring of the Securities Markets," in Stephen P. Bradley, Jerry A. Hausman and Richard L. Nolan (eds.) *Globalization, Technology, and Competition: The Fusion of Computers and Telecommunications in the 1990s* (Boston: Harvard Business School Press, 1993), 151. In 1989 *The Wall Street Journal* was reporting that Reuters and Telerate were "scouring the world for . . . exchanges to automate." According to the newspaper

> They are circumspect about their ultimate goal, because it is so radical and would so profoundly disrupt the financial world's current power structures. But if electronic trading takes off, these companies and others like them may have a shot at becoming as powerful as the exchanges are today, in control of the infrastructure that links the world's markets . . . "Who's going to run the exchanges," asks Mr. [DuWayne] Peterson of Merrill. "The guys with the information."

From Miller and Winkler, A1, A6.

27. See Daniel Bell, *The Coming of Post-Industrial Society: A Venture in Social Forecasting* (New York: Basic Books, 1973, revised 1976).
28. Colin Cherry, *World Communication: Threat or Promise* (New York: John Wiley, 1971, revised 1978).
29. Another way of explaining this concept of *regeneration* is provided by Cherry, who says that "each further improvement in technical facilities not only satisfies an existing demand but creates new conditions which give rise to yet further increase in demand. Such 'regenerative growths' are typical of *service* industries of all kinds and are in distinction to the growths of *consumer* industries, in which demand may simply increase with increased wealth [,] merely to be satisfied. . . . Service industries, like capital investment, can be creators of new wealth." (90) In other words, service industries are regenerative, while many consumer industries are merely *income elastic*.
30. Bell used these figures which show an expanding service sector to support his argument that the OECD countries were becoming *postindustrial* societies. This concept that Bell popularized is in contrast to "pre-industrial" and "industrial". "A pre-industrial sector is primarily extractive, its economy based on agriculture, mining, fishing, timber and other resources such as natural gas or oil. An industrial sector is primarily fabricating, using energy and machine technology, for the manufacture of goods. A post-industrial sector is one of processing in which telecommunications and computers are strategic for the exchange of information and knowledge." Bell, (xix-xx.)
31. See Statistical Office of the European Communities, *Labour Force Survey* (Luxembourg; Office des Publications Officielles des Communautes Europeennes, 1988), 118-25.
32. Joan Edelman Spero, "Information: The Policy Void," *Foreign Policy*, vol. 48, (Fall), 1982, 139-56.
33. Robert Gilpin, *The Political Economy of International Relations* (Princeton: Princeton University Press, 1987), 199.
34. Elizabeth C. Hanson, "The Global Media System and International Relations," in Kanti P. Bajpai and Harish C. Shukul (eds.), *Interpreting World Politics* (New Delhi: Sage, 1995), 274.
35. Waters, 3.
36. Ibid.
37. Ibid., 42.
38. See Alleyne, 2-5.
39. Quoted in Nagy Hanna, Ken Guy and Erik Arnold, "The Diffusion of Information Technology," *World Bank Discussion Paper No. 281* (Washington, D.C.: The World Bank, 1995), 12.
40. Ibid., 10.
41. Marjorie Ferguson, "The Mythology about Globalization," *European Journal of Communication*, vol. 7, 1992, 73.
42. See Hans-Henrik Holn and Georg Sørensen, *Whose World Order? Uneven Globalization and the End of the Cold War* (Boulder, CO: Westview Press, 1995).
43. Read, 287. Despite this assertion by Read in Reuters's official history, a Reuters spokesman in 1995 denied that the company's business is so structured. "Reuters

puts significant resources behind maintaining a fully international news and television network of 138 bureaus around the world and distributes its information in 154 countries, not 3 or 7 or 12 or 25 or 52 countries, but 154," he stated. Letter received from Robert A. Crooke, Vice President, Media Relations, Reuters America Inc., New York City, November 16, 1995.

44. Rita Cruise O'Brien and G. K. Helleiner, "The political economy of information in a changing international economic order," *International Organization* vol.34, no. 4 (Autumn 1980), 446.

45. Ibid., 447.

46. Ibid., 457-58.

47. Walter S. Mossberg, "Beware What Passes For News When Wading Through Digital Data," *The Wall Street Journal*, Thursday, June 22, 1995, B1. On the same matter, an article in the magazine of the newspaper publishing industry noted that

> The principal benefit of the daily newspapers as an information source can be summarized in one word: editing.
>
> While there are no doubt many exceptions, most consumers do not want to edit their own newspapers. They want editorial judgment. They want someone to sift through the news of the day and tell them what is important: locally, nationally and internationally. At the moment, the typical four-section daily newspaper has the clear advantage in communicating what's news quickly and efficiently.

In Greg Martire, "The Information Superhighway: What Newspapers Should Know," *Editor & Publisher*, February 18, 1995, 56.

48. The end of news organizations' dominance of the definition of news has very real implications for the economic value of the information they disseminate. News organizations will become more pressed to provide a powerful justification for making others pay to receive their news. "News" must be presented with more expert knowledge and analysis by journalists, and it must be disseminated in such a way that the consumers have as much say as possible in the type of ways the "news" is packaged. In other words, it is not enough to say that a journalist is someone who knows how to collect information, edit and report it impartially. She must be someone with expert knowledge that assists the consumers of information who are likely to have the information in raw form before it is provided by the reporter.

49. See Mark D. Alleyne, "Thinking About The International System in the 'Information Age': Theoretical Assumptions and Contradictions," *Journal of Peace Research* vol. 31, no. 4 (November 1994), 407-24. Also see Fred S. Siebert, Theodore Peterson, and Wilbur Schramm, *Four Theories of the Press* (Urbana, IL: University of Illinois Press, 1956).

50. The World Bank, Telecommunications and Informatics Division, Industry and Energy Department, "Harnessing Information for Development—World Bank Vision & Strategy," Washington, D.C.: World Bank Home Page, World Wide Web (http://www.worldbank.org) 1995.

CHAPTER 3

1. L. John Martin, *International Propaganda: Its Legal and Diplomatic Control* (Gloucester, Massachusetts: Peter Smith, 1958, reprinted 1969), 12.
2. Jon T. Powell, "Towards A Negotiable Definition of Propaganda for International Agreements Related To Direct Broadcast Satellites," *Law And Contemporary Problems* vol. 45, no. 1 (Winter 1982), 3.
3. Elizabeth A. Downey, "A Historical Survey of the International Regulation of Propaganda," *1984 Michigan Yearbook of International Legal Studies* (New York: Clark Boardman, 1984), n.1.
4. 25 U.N. GAOR Committee on the Peaceful Uses of Outer Space at 7, U.N. Doc. A/AC.105/79 (1970), quoted in Powell, 27.
5. Adeno Addis, "International Propaganda and Developing Countries," *Vanderbilt Journal of Transnational Law* vol. 21, no. 3 (1988), 493.
6. Quoted in Donald Read, *The Power of News: The History of Reuters 1849-1989* (Oxford: Oxford University Press, 1991).
7. Kent Cooper, *Barriers Down: The Story of the News Agency Epoch*, 43, quoted in Herbert Schiller, *Communication and Cultural Domination* (White Plains, New York: M. E. Sharpe, 1976), 27.
8. Johan Galtung and Richard C. Vincent, *Global Glasnost: Toward a New World Information and Communication Order?* (Cresskill, New Jersey: Hampton Press, 1992), 9.
9. Ibid., 13-15.
10. Addis, 517.
11. Ibid., 533.
12. Martin, 89-90.
13. Edward W. Ploman, *International Law Governing Communication and Information: A Collection of Basic Documents* (London: Frances Pinter, 1982).
14. Martin, 80.
15. Ibid., 78.
16. See Garth S. Jowett and Victoria O'Donnell, *Propaganda and Persuasion* 2nd ed. (Newbury Park, California: Sage, 1992), 185-95.
17. UN document A/RES/37/92.
18. UNESCO General Conference, Resolution 4/9.3/2, 1978: Declaration on Fundamental Principles Concerning the Contribution of the Mass Media to Strengthening Peace and International Understanding, to Promotion of Human Rights and to Countering Racialism, Apartheid and Incitement to War.
19. 32 U.N. GAOR Committee on the Peaceful Uses of Outer Space (173d mtg.) at 42, U.N. Doc. A/AC.105/PV.173 (1977), quoted in Powell, 9.
20. Martin, 108.
21. See Mark D. Alleyne, *International Power and International Communication* (New York: Macmillan, 1995), chapter 5.
22. Hans Morgenthau, *Politics Among Nations* 5th ed. (New York: Knopf, 1973).
23. Ibid., 331.
24. Ibid., 332-33.

25. Morgenthau explained that:

> Diplomacy owes its rise in part to the absence of speedy communications in a period when the governments of the new territorial states maintained continuous political relations with each other. Diplomacy owes its decline in part to the development of speedy and regular communications in the form of the airplane, the radio, the telegraph, the teletype, the long-distance telephone. (525-26)

26. William A. Landskron, ed., *Annual Review of United Nations Affairs 1982* (Dobbs Ferry, N.Y.: Oceana Publications, 1983), 335.
27. Ibid., 337-38.
28. Between 1976 and 1995, 141 public documents of the United Nations actually mentioned the word "propaganda" in their text or had it as a key word in their indices. Of the 141, four were General Assembly resolutions concerning Namibia, and four were General Assembly resolutions about South African apartheid. This finding was arrived at from a key word search of the CD-ROM version of *Index to United Nations Documents 1976-1995*, in the Periodicals Room of the Library of Congress, Washington, D.C., October 18, 1995.
29. William A. Hachten and C. Anthony Giffard, *The Press and Apartheid: Repression and Propaganda in South Africa* (Madison: University of Wisconsin Press, 1984), 6-7, and also chapter 10.
30. Michael Kunczik, *Images of Nations and International Public Relations* (Bonn: Friedrich-Ebert-Stiftung, 1990), 155-65.
31. For more on this see Elaine Windrich, "South Africa's Propaganda War," *Africa Today* vol. 36, no. 1 (1st Quarter, 1989), 51-60.
32. See United Nations Documents A/RES/40/97 (1986); A/RES/41/39 (1987); A/RES/42/14 (1988); and A/RES/43/26 (1988).
33. See United Nations Documents A/RES/39/72 (1985); A/RES/40/64 (1986); A/RES/42/23 (1988); UN/RES/43/50 (1989); and A/RES/44/27 (1989).
34. UN Department of Public Information, (The United Nations Blue Books Series, Vol. 1) *The United Nations and Apartheid: 1948-1994* (New York: The United Nations, 1994), 62.
35. Ibid., 65.
36. See United Nations documents A/RES/40/148 (1986), and A/RES/41/160 (1987).
37. A sample includes: John R. MacArthur, *Second Front: Censorship and Propaganda in the Gulf War* (New York: Hill and Wang, 1992); Philip M. Taylor, *War and the Media: Propaganda and Persuasion in the Gulf War* (Manchester: Manchester University Press, 1992); Hamid Mowlana and George Gerbner, eds. *Triumph of the Image: The Media's War in the Persian Gulf: A Global Perspective* (Boulder: Westview Press, 1992); Susan Jeffords and Lauren Rabinowitz, eds. *Seeing through the Media the Persian Gulf War* (New Brunswick, N.J.: Rutgers University Press, 1994); Robert E. Denton, Jr., ed. *The Media and the Persian Gulf War* (Westport, CT: Praeger, 1993); and David Barsamian, *Stenographers to Power* (Interviews) (Monroe, Maine: Common Courage Press, 1992).

38. See Carol Matlack, "The Credibility Gulf," *National Journal* vol. 24, no. 30 (July 25, 1992), 1754; and Karl Waldron, "Spin Doctors of War," *New Statesman & Society* vol. 5, no. 213 (July 31, 1992), 13.

39. Kunczik, 116-17.

40. Indonesia, the Côte d'Ivoire, Turkey, Chile, Cyprus, India, Israel, Mexico, Portugal, Romania, South Africa, St. Lucia, Hungary, and Canada.

Chapter 4

1. Hedley Bull, "Justice in International Relations," University of Waterloo, 12-13 October 1983, Hagey Lectures.

2. Also, it is easier to conceive of distributive justice working in domestic societies where there are central governments with the means and authority to be the distributors. In contrast, it is harder to think of distributive justice working in international society where there is no central government. Apart from that problem, are questions about the kind of just distribution. "Is it a just distribution one among states or nations, or among individual persons?" Bull asked. "Does it consist in an 'end-state,' a just result of a process of distribution, or is it to be thought of as a just process or transaction?" See Bull, 16.

3. Jonathan Fenby, *The International News Services* (New York: Schocken Books, 1986), 23.

4. Comments of Frank Bartholomew, the United Press International (UPI) chairman, quoted in Fenby, 58.

5. Then they were AFP's predecessor, Agence Havas, as well as Reuters in London, and Germany's Wolff agency.

6. Fenby, 35.

7. George Kurian, "The World Press: A Statistical Profile," in George Kurian, ed., *World Press Encyclopedia* vol.1 (New York: Facts On File, 1982), 6.

8. Ibid.

9. Karl P. Sauvant, "From Economic To Socio-Cultural Emancipation: The Historical Context of the New International Economic Order And The New International Socio-Cultural Order." *Third World Quarterly* vol. 3, no. 1 (1981), 51.

10. Sauvant provides a list of the early strategies of development that all failed:

> The First UN Development Decade, launched with high hopes in 1961, fell short of its objectives; its extension in 1970 was viewed with dampened expectations. The Alliance for Progress, also launched in 1961 with similar hopes, quietly faltered. Another regional effort, the First Yaoundé convention of 1963, was replaced by the Second Yaoundé Convention and the Arusha Convention (1969), but the expectations associated with them were not fulfilled (in spite of the improved conditions negotiated in the latter two agreements). The UN Conference on Trade and Development (UNCTAD) had a promising start with its first meeting in 1964, but did not make considerable progress in its second (1968) and third (1972) sessions, thus only increasing the sense of frustration in the developing countries. The same can be said for the Group of 77 (G77), which had constituted itself in 1964 during UNCTAD I. (50)

11. UN GA Res.3201(S-VI) of 1 May 1974, paragraph 4, sec. (s).
12. Sauvant, 59.
13. Robert Cassen (Director of Queen Elizabeth House and former Staff Member of the Brandt Commission), "North and South," Lecture at Oxford University, Wednesday, March 2, 1988.
14. See Robert L. Rothstein, "Regime-Creation by a Coalition of the Weak: Lessons from the NIEO and the Integrated Program for Commodities," *International Studies Quarterly* vol. 28 (1984), 307-28; and his "Epitaph for a monument to a failed protest? A North-South retrospective," *International Organization* vol. 42, no. 4 (Autumn 1988), 725-48.
15. Colleen Roach, who worked for many years in the Communication Sector of UNESCO, describes Mustapha Masmoudi's role in the NWICO debate as "very important":

> Both his supporters and critics referred to him as no less than the "father of the NWICO." In 1976, it was Masmoudi, serving as Tunisian Secretary of States for Information, who gave the welcoming speech at the Tunis Non-Aligned news symposium where the term "International Information Order" was first pronounced. Later, as ambassador of Tunisia to UNESCO and a member of the MacBride Commission, he became the principle spokesman for the NWICO. He was notably responsible for the authorship of the well-known Non-Aligned document on the NWICO presented to the MacBride Commission in 1978.

Colleen Roach, "The Position of the Reagan administration on the NWICO," *Media Development* vol. 34, no. 4 (1987), 32-37.

16. "Declaration on Fundamental Principles concerning the contribution of the Mass Media to Strengthening Peace and International Understanding, to the Promotion of Human Rights and to Countering Racialism, Apartheid and Incitement to War." (Adopted by acclamation on November 22, 1978, at the Twentieth Session of the General Conference of UNESCO held in Paris.) [Emphasis added by Mark D. Alleyne.]
17. Mustapha Masmoudi, "The New World Information Order," *Journal of Communication*, vol. 29, no. 2 (Spring, 1979), 178. [Emphasis added by Mark D. Alleyne.]
18. International Commission for the Study of Communication Problems, *Many Voices, One World.* (London: Kogan Page, 1980), 254.
19. Ibid., 253.
20. Ibid., 266.
21. Vidya Charan Shukla, "Need For News Flow Code," in A. W. Singham ed., *The Nonaligned Movement in World Politics* (New York: Lawrence Hill & Co., 1977), 69.
22. See *UNESCO Reports and Papers on Mass Communication* No. 45, "Professional Training for Mass Communication" Paris: UNESCO, 1965.
23. Quoted in Kaarle Nordenstreng, Enrique Gonzales Manet and Wolfgang Kleinwachter, *New International Information Order Sourcebook* (Prague: International Organisation of Journalists, 1986), 10.

24. See Shukla, 69.
25. The dates of these conferences were: July 4-13, 1974, in Bogota, Colombia; June 24-30, 1975, Quito, Ecuador; and July 12-21, 1976, in San José, Costa Rica. Thomas McPhail reports that Latin America was selected as the venue for these conferences because it was home to "several excellent U.S.-educated researchers and scholars." Thomas McPhail, *Electronic Colonialism* (Revised Second Edition) (Beverly Hills: SAGE, 1987), 73.
26. UNESCO is governed by three basic organs: the General Conference, the Executive Board and the Secretariat. The General Conference is made up of delegates of all member-states. The Executive Board is elected by the General Conference from among the delegates and they serve four-year staggered terms on the Board. The Executive Board prepares the agenda of the General Conference and has oversight on the director-general's proposed program and budget. The Secretariat executes the day-to-day business of the organization.
27. James P. Sewell, "UNESCO: Pluralism Rampant," in Robert W. Cox and Harold K. Jacobson, eds., *The Anatomy of Influence* (New Haven: Yale University Press, 1974), 139-74.
28. Ibid., 142.
29. Ibid., 163.
30. Quoted in Colin Cherry, *World Communication: Threat or Promise* (New York: John Wiley, 1971, revised 1978), 197-98.
31. International Commission for the Study of Communication Problems, 212.
32. See "Resolution on the New International Information Order of the Fourth Meeting of the Intergovernmental Council for Co-ordination of Information Among Non-Aligned Countries" (Baghdad, June 1980).
33. UNESCO Res. 4/19—On the International Commission for the Study of Communication Problems (Belgrade, October 21, 1980), sec. VI, 14.
34. "Mass Media Declaration", (UNESCO General Conference Resolution 4/9.3/2, 1978) Article VI.
35. International Commission for the Study of Communication Problems, 233.
36. Ibid., 234.
37. Ibid., 255.
38. Ibid., 269.
39. Ibid., 239, n.1.
40. Also see Article 10 of the Council of Europe's Convention for the Protection of Human Rights and Fundamental Freedoms; and Article 13 of the American Convention on Human Rights.
41. International Commission for the Study of Communication Problems, 263.
42. Ibid.
43. Ibid., 263-64.
44. Ibid., 264.
45. Ibid., 260.
46. Ibid., 261.
47. Ibid., 270.

In stark contrast, the head of a similar commission convened by the International Telecommunication Union (ITU) to explore global telecommunication problems, Sir Donald Maitland, in an interview after his commission had finished its work, declared that "the role of the private sector is a theme running through our report." "The Missing Link," *Intermedia* vol. 13, no.1 (1985), 9. The Maitland Report noted that

> Decisions by telecommunications operators in developing countries to improve and expand their networks will create a major market for the owners of telecommunications technology and expertise, and the manufacturers of equipment. A more comprehensive world system will mean an increase in international traffic from which all operators will benefit. Where information flows so does commerce. The growth in world trade and other contacts will increase understanding among peoples. Effective and expanded telecommunications both within and between countries will make the world a better and safer place.

(From Independent Commission For Worldwide Telecommunications Development, *The Missing Link* [Geneva: ITU, 1985], 3-4). Instead of regarding the role of the private sector in the telecommunications development with suspicion, Sir Donald Maitland acknowledged that "telecommunications is to a great extent in private hands" and that 80 percent of telecommunications training was done by telecommunications operators and manufacturers in industrialized countries. "Missing Link," 10. The report suggested incentives that would not only continue such involvement by private companies but cause its expansion. For example, it was suggested that industrialized countries extend export/import financing and insurance coverage to their domestic suppliers of telecommunications equipment. Also, the commission wanted the World Bank to consider whether investment in telecommunications could qualify for protection under the Multilateral Investment Guarantee Agency. Independent Commission For Worldwide Telecommunications Development, 60.

48. UNESCO Doc. 22 C/3 (1981), 58. UNESCO 1979-1980: Report of the Director-General
49. UNESCO Doc. 23 C/3 (1984), 52-56. UNESCO 1981-1983: Report of the Director-General
50. UNESCO Doc. 24 C/3 (1986), 9. UNESCO 1984-1985: Report of the Director-General
51. Ibid., 11.
52. Ibid., 12.
53. Ibid., 12-13.
54. UNESCO Doc. 24 C/117, Report of Commission IV, Part I (Narrative), November 6, 1987, 6-7.
55. Quoted in Robert A. Kinn, "United States Participation in the International Telecommunication Union: A Series of Interviews," *The Fletcher Forum* vol.9 (Winter 1985), 51.

56. Mochtar Lubis, "A Commissioner's View," *International Herald Tribune*, July 10, 1980.
57. Curtis Prendergast, "The Global First Amendment War," *Time*, October 6, 1980, 62.
58. "Whose News Is Fit to Print?" *Newsweek*, June 16, 1986, 39.
59. See: Graham Storey, *Reuters' Century* (London: Parrish, 1951); Joe Alex Morris, *Deadline Every Minute* (Garden City, New York: Doubleday,1957); Oliver Gramling, *AP: The Story of News* (London: Kennikat Press, 1969); Kent Cooper, *Barriers Down: The Story of the News Agency Epoch* (Port Washington: Kennikat Press, 1942).
60. See: Oliver Boyd-Barrett, *The International News Agencies* (London: Constable, 1980); Jeremy Tunstall, "Worldwide News Agencies—Private Wholesalers of Public Information," in Jim Richstad and Michael H. Anderson, eds., *Crisis in International News* (New York: Columbia University Press, 1981); and Jonathan Fenby, *The International News Services*.
61. Fenby, 9-10.
62. Ibid, 4-5.
63. World Press Freedom Committee, *The Media Crisis . . .* (Miami: WPFC, 1981), 107.
64. Ibid.
65. McPhail, 110.
66. See also A. H. Raskin, "U.S. News Coverage of the Belgrade UNESCO Conference," and Colleen Roach, "French Press Coverage of the Belgrade UNESCO Conference," *Journal of Communication* vol. 31, no. 4 (1981), 175-87.
67. "Study Criticises U.S. Newspapers For Coverage of UNESCO Conference," (AP report) *International Herald Tribune*, March 16, 1981.
68. See (for example):
   - "Hands Off UNESCO," (editorial reproduced from *The Washington Post*), *International Herald Tribune*, September 30, 1980.
   - Rosemary Righter, "Third World Aim Is to Shackle the Fourth Estate, " *The Sunday Times*, October 19, 1980.
   - "International Big Brother" (editorial reproduced from *The Washington Post*), *International Herald Tribune*, October 21, 1980.
   - Leonard Sussman, "A Story of Two Belgrades," *The New York Times*, October 23, 1980.
   - "UNESCO As Censor" (editorial), *The New York Times*, October 24, 1980.
   - Paul Lewis, "UNESCO Battle: West A Loser?" *The Sunday Times*, October 26, 1980.
   - "New Order" (editorial), *The Daily Telegraph*, October 30, 1980.
   - "UNESCO's Threat to a Free Press" (editorial), *The Times*, October 30, 1980.
   - Paul Chutkow, "UNESCO Press Consensus: Wording Is Key," *International Herald Tribune*, November 1-2, 1980.
   - "Enough UNESCO" (editorial), *International Herald Tribune*, November 1-2, 1980.
69. "The Press: Credibility In Practice," *International Herald Tribune*, January 13, 1981.
70. C. Anthony Giffard, "Closing The Gap," *Africa Report*, March-April 1987, 64.
71. McPhail, 281, n. 6.
72. International Commission for the Study of Communication Problems, 279-80.

73. Ibid., 266.
74. Ibid., n.1, 266.
75. Ibid., 266.
76. Mort Rosenblum, "UNESCO Vs. Press Freedom," *International Herald Tribune,* February 25, 1980.
77. "Blocking Threat to Free Press," *International Herald Tribune,* May 12, 1980.
78. "UNESCO Ideologists Worry Reuter Head," *The Times,* February 22, 1980.
79. "UNESCO Report on World Media Is Denounced by Reuters Official," *International Herald Tribune,* March 1, 1980.
80. "The Truth In Chains," London Observer Service, release no. 40530, September 26, 1980 (article by Gerald Long, managing director of Reuters).
81. "UPI Board Expresses Concern," (UPI report), *International Herald Tribune,* October 28, 1980.
82. "Press Group Is Warned About UNESCO Report," *The New York Times,* May 27, 1980.
83. See "UNESCO Urged To Leave Press Alone," *The Guardian,* May 18, 1981; as well as World Press Freedom Committee, *The Media Crisis . . .* (Miami: WPFC, 1981), and World Press Freedom Committee, *The Media Crisis . . . A Continuing Challenge* (Washington, D.C.: WPFC, 1982).
84. "TASS Assails Western Media," (AP report) *International Herald Tribune,* May 20, 1981.
85. McPhail, 235.
86. Ibid.
87. Leonard S. Matthews, "Designing A Muzzle For Media," *Business Week,* June 15, 1981, 20.
88. Letitia Baldwin and Christy Marshall, "MacBride Report Gets UNESCO Hearing," *Advertising Age,* July 26, 1982, 59.
89. See the two books published by the WPFC and cited above.
90. "World Press Freedom Committee: A Coordination Group of National and International News Media Organizations," brochure sent to the author by the WPFC, October 1995.
91. Kaarle Nordenstreng, Enrique Gonzales Manet and Wolfgang Kleinwachter, *New International Information Order Sourcebook* (Prague: International Organisation of Journalists, 1986), 35.
92. Thomas McPhail has explained that

> the communication sector in UNESCO receives less than 10 percent of the budget, but clearly receives over 90% of the media coverage. The problem is further complicated because, in the Western nations, 90% of that coverage is negative. It is difficult, therefore, for either concerned individuals or governments to be supportive of UNESCO when the public at large is not favorably impressed, and when the uninitiated think that all UNESCO does is debate communication, and in that particular case deals with it in a negative and anti-Western fashion. (275)

93. The withdrawals of the United States, the United Kingdom and Singapore between 1984 and 1985 produced a U.S.$39 million deficit for UNESCO. UNESCO was

forced to cut its budget by 30 percent, suspend some programs and reduce staff by nearly 800. "UNESCO Board Meeting: M'Bow Seeks to Cover Deficit of $39 Million," *International Herald Tribune*, May 13, 1987.

94. UNESCO Doc. 24C/117, Report of Commission IV, Part I (Narrative), November 6, 1987, 9.

95. UNESCO's communication policies from 1990 to 1995 would be in three areas: Programme IV.1, "The free flow of information, and solidarity"; Programme IV.2, "Communication for development"; and Programme IV.3, "The socio-cultural impact of new communication technologies." The resolution adopted at the thirty-second plenary meeting of the Twenty-fifth General Conference, November 15, 1989, defined the types of activities to be undertaken under these headings. See UNESCO, *Records of the General Conference, Twenty-fifth Session, Paris, 17 October to 16 November 1989: Vol. 1 Resolutions* (Paris: UNESCO, 1990), 31-37. Programme IV.1 consisted of two parts: Subprogramme IV.1.1, "The free flow of ideas by word and image"; and Subprogramme IV.1.2, "Communication and solidarity." Subprogramme IV.1.1 involved

   (i)   encouraging the free flow of information, at international as well as national level;
   (ii) promoting the wider and better balanced dissemination of information, without any obstacle to freedom of expression;
   (iii) developing all the appropriate means of strengthening communication capacities in the developing countries in order to increase their participation in the communication process;
   (iv) advancing the mutual knowledge and understanding of peoples, through all means of mass communication and to that end recommending such international agreements as may be necessary to promote the free flow of ideas by word and image . . .

Subprogramme IV.2 sought

   (i)   to reinforce all the functions of the International Programme for the Development of Communication (IPDC) (mobilization of increased resources from the industrialized countries; intensification of its activities, particularly as regards the development of communication infrastructures, skills and capacities, in the developing countries; strengthening of international technical co-operation and particularly technical co-operation among developing countries);
   (ii) to explore all possible ways of increasing communication skills and capacities in the developed and developing countries . . .

Programme IV.2 aimed

   (a)   to establish linkages between communication and the development of societies;
   (b)   to train journalists and other communication professionals, particularly in the developing countries . . .

Programme IV.3's objective was

> (a) to study the economic and socio-cultural impact of new communication technologies (appropriate utilization of low-cost technologies and impact of the media on societies, culture and cultural identities);
>
> (b) to develop media education, by emphasizing the development of critical awareness, the ability to react to any kind of information received and the education of users to defend their rights . . .

96. UNESCO, *Records of the General Conference, Twenty-fifth Session*, 33-34.
97. Ibid., 34.
98. UN Resolution A/Res/36/149, 16 December 1981.
99. UN Resolution A/Res/44/50, 8 December 1989.
100. See UN Resolutions: A/Res/45/76, 11 December 1990; A/Res/46/73, 11 December 1991; A/Res/47/73, 14 December 1992; and A/Res/48/44, 10 December 1993.
101. United Nations Department of Public Information, *Yearbook of the United Nations 1991 Vol. 45* (Boston: Martinus Nijhoff Publishers, 1992), 82-87.
102. United Nations Department of Public Information, *Yearbook of the United Nations 1991 Vol. 46* (Boston: Martinus Nijhoff Publishers, 1993), 123-29.
103. "Letter: A Forceful Voice Calling for Independent Media," *The Independent*, May 3, 1993, 15. Complete text relayed by *Lexis/Nexis* (Dayton, Ohio: Mead Data Central, May 3, 1993)
104. UNESCO Press Release, "U.S. Contributes $45,000 to Communication Projects," New York, September 20, 1994.
105. This assumption was explicitly stated by Alain Modoux, Director of the Communication Division of UNESCO. He said that the organization "helps to set up media legislations according to democratic patterns and assists those states who request it to transform their government-controlled radio/television networks and news agencies into truly editorially independent public services." In the same document Modoux even rewrote history, in his effort to distance UNESCO from the old statist proposals. Despite evidence to the contrary, he declared that UNESCO's interpretation of the NWICO had been imposed by the Soviet Union. "The Soviet Union objective was to limit, if possible to hinder, the penetration of the big Western media, in particular the international news agencies, into the territories it controlled," he said. See Alain Modoux, "UNESCO From The Cold War To The New Communication and Information Technologies Era," (October 21, 1994) article posted on the World Wide Web Home Page of ORBICOM (The Network of UNESCO Chairs for Communications).
106. See, for example, the arguments of Edward Herman and Noam Chomsky, *Manufacturing Consent: The Political Economy of the Mass Media* (New York: Pantheon, 1988); and Robert G. Picard, *The Press and the Decline of Democracy* (New York: Greenwood, 1985).

CHAPTER 5

1. *The Compact Edition of the Oxford English Dictionary* (New York: Oxford University Press, 1971).
2. Editorial by Ursula Owen, *Index On Censorship* vol. 22, no. 7, July-August 1993, 1.
3. Sue Curry Jansen, *Censorship: The Knot That Binds Power and Knowledge* (New York: Oxford University Press, 1991), 14, and n. 1.
4. "Censors Through The Ages: Reaching for the red pencil," *The Economist*, December 26, 1992-January 8, 1993, 85.
5. *Ibid.*
6. According to Lahav:

> It is only in the mid-nineteenth century that John Stuart Mill developed his articulated and complex defense of free expression, and only in 1881 that France enacted a relatively liberal press law. Similarly, in the United States, it was only at the beginning of the twentieth century that the American Supreme Court began to pour liberal content into the First Amendment, and to articulate doctrines which would make the courts guardians of free speech. This development parallels the growth of the modern press. There is a historical correlation between the growth of modern newspapers and the democratization of politics, between the expansion of the market economy and the growing authority of an entrepreneurial urban middle class, and the development of modern press law. The growth of a democratized mass society and its increasing dependence on the press for information have encouraged the emergence of the press as powerful institution, as an essential intermediary between the government and the people that keeps the people informed about the government and informs the government what the people think and want, or where "the shoe pinches." From this vantage point, the press sees itself as an actor in the democratic marketplace, or as another pressure group in society.

Pnina Lahav, "Conclusion: An Outline for a General Theory of Press Law in Democracy," in Pnina Lahav (editor) *Press Law in Modern Democracies: A Comparative Study* (New York: Longman, 1985), 351.

7. Ibid., 350.
8. J. S. Mill, *On Liberty* (1859) in H. B. Acton, ed., *Utilitarianism, On Liberty and Considerations on Representative Government* (London: Dent, 1972), 83-84.
9. John Milton, "Areopagitica," in Charles W. Eliot, ed. *Essays, Civil and Moral and New Atlantis by Francis Bacon: Areopagitica and Tractate on Education by John Milton; Religio Medici by Sir Thomas Browne.* The Harvard Classics, vol. 3. (New York: P.F. Collier & Son, 1909), 383-407.
10. Curry Jansen, 73.
11. Ibid., 4.
12. See interview with Haile Gerima, *Index On Censorship* vol. 24, no. 6 1995, 136-139; as well as article by Adewale Maja-Pearce, pp. 140-42 in the same issue.
13. See John Blades, "Rushdie blows into the Windy City," *Chicago Tribune*, January 23, 1996, section 1, 10; Maureen O'Brien, "Statement on Rushdie Plight To Be

Distributed on Feb. 14 Marking 5th Year of 'Fatwa,'" *Publishers Weekly*, January 31, 1994, 13; and Janice Valls-Russell, "Muslim voices of courage; in defense of Rushdie," *The New Leader*, vol. 76, no. 14, December 13, 1993, 11.

14. *The Charlie Rose Show*, PBS, January 22, 1996.

15. See Howard Fields and Calvin Reid, "Clinton Waffling over Rushdie Meeting?" *Publishers Weekly*, December 6, 1993, 13, 18; and "Still not inhaling," (editorial) *The New Republic*, December 20, 1993, 8.

16. See Mark D. Alleyne, "Thinking About The International System in the 'Information Age': Theoretical Assumptions and Contradictions," *Journal of Peace Research* vol. 31, no. 4, 407-424.

17. Oscar Schachter and Christopher C. Joyner, eds. *United Nations Legal Order Vol. 1* (Cambridge: Cambridge University Press, 1995), 28-29.

18. Lahav, p. 354.

19. Schachter, p. 15.

20. Frank Rich, "Magical Rushdie Tour," *The New York Times* (national edition), January 20, 1996, 15.

21. See "How Spycatcher Was Brought In From The Cold," *The Sunday Times*, July 19, 1987, 10-11; and Frances Gibb, "Spy book judge accuses censors," *The Times*, August 14, 1987, 1.

22. See Mark D. Alleyne, "Letter From Britain: 'Spycatcher' secrets out in public," *The Sunday Advocate*, June 19, 1988.

23. "Islamic Tome Prophetic," *The Economist*, June 5, 1993, 102.

24. See Kara Swisher, "Cyberporn Debate Goes International," *The Washington Post*, January 1, 1996, 13, 16; "Worldwide Net, Worldwide Trouble," (Editorial) *The Washington Post*, January 5, 1996, A20.

25. Telephone interview with William Giles, Manager, Public Relations Planning, CompuServe, September 10, 1996.

26. Personal interview with William Orme, Executive Director, Committee to Protect Journalists, New York City, 29 September, 1995. See Appendix 9, International Journalism Survey.

27. The International Covenant on Civil and Political Rights was adopted by the UN General Assembly on December 16, 1966. As of December 31, 1994, 57 states had signed the Covenant and 129 were parties to it. The provisions of Articles 19 and 20 are just some of several in the Covenant that have provoked formal Reservations by signatories. For example, the Netherlands accepted Article 19 with the proviso "that it shall not prevent the Kingdom from requiring the licensing of broadcasting, television or cinema enterprises." The United States accepted Article 20 as long as it did not "require legislation or other action by the United States that would restrict the right of free speech and association protected by the Constitution and laws of the United States." See U.N. Doc. ST/LEG/SER.E/13, *Multilateral Treaties Deposited With the Secretary-General: Status as at 31 Dec. 1994*.

28. Danna Bullen, Executive Director, World Press Freedom Committee, written response to questionnaire of the International Journalism Survey, October 1995. See Appendix 9, International Journalism Survey.

29. The countries were: Australia; Austria; Canada; France; Germany; the Netherlands; Norway; Spain; Sweden; the United Kingdom; and the United States.

30. Sandra Coliver, "Comparative Analysis of Press Law in European and Other Democracies," in Article 19, *Press Law and Practice: A Comparative Study of Press Freedom in European and Other Democracies* (London: Article 19, March 1993), 188-189.

31. Haile Gerima, "Images of Africa," *Index On Censorship* vol. 24., no. 6, 1995, 137.

CHAPTER 6

1. Quoted in Karen DeYoung, "Somoza Guard Kills American," *The Washington Post*, June 21, 1979, A1.

2. Quoted in Linda Charlton, "ABC Reporter and Aide Killed By Soldier in Nicaraguan Capital," *The New York Times*, June 21, 1979, A12.

3. DeYoung, "Somoza Guard Kills American."

4. Quoted in Charlton, A12.

5. Karen DeYoung, "Vance Urges Somoza's Ouster From Power," *The Washington Post*, June 22, 1979, A1.

6. Reporters Sans Frontières, *1995 Report: Freedom of the Press throughout the World* (London: John Libbey & Company, 1995), 3.

7. Committee to Protect Journalists, *Attacks on the Press in 1994* (New York: CPJ, 1995), 268.

8. Reporters Sans Frontières, 4.

9. Committee to Protect Journalists, *Attacks on the Press in 1994*, 267.

10. Reporters Sans Frontières, 5.

11. For a discussion of this point, see Amit Mukherjee, "International Protection or Journalists: Problem, Practice, and Prospects," *Arizona Journal of International and Comparative Law* vol. 11, no. 2, 1994, 339-87

12. Quoted in Melissa A. Young, "Journalists Precariously Covering the Globe: International Attempts to Provide for Their Protection," *Virginia Journal of International Law* vol. 23, no. 1, (Fall 1982), 150, n. 89.

13. Committee to Protect Journalists, *CPJ Casework Manual* (New York: Committee to Protect Journalists, 1995), 1.

14. Amit Mukherjee, "International Protection or Journalists: Problem, Practice, and Prospects," *Arizona Journal of International and Comparative Law* vol. 11, no. 2, 339, n. 1.

15. See Charlton, A12; DeYoung, A1.; and "Probers Say Guardsman Admits Killing Newsman," *The Washington Post*, July 8, 1979, A10.

16. One writer noted that

> In September 1992, three years after the Ayatollah's death, the Saudi poet Sadiq Melallah was publicly beheaded for blasphemy, with nary a protest from the West. (Saudi Arabia is, after all, an ally; bitter comments run through For Rushdie [a book promoting freedom of expression] about the West's "hypocrisy," its choice of allies, and its reluctance to break off relations with Iran "just for an author.") That same year, the Egyptian novel-

ist Farag Fouda was assassinated by fundamentalists in Cairo for urging the disestablishment of Islam.

(Janice Valls-Russell, "Muslim Voices of Courage: In Defense of Rushdie," The New Leader vol. 76, no. 14 [December 13, 1993], 11.)

17. See Mukherjee, 340-41.
18. Ibid., 367.
19. The four Geneva conventions are: the Convention for the Amelioration of the Condition of the Wounded and Sick in Armed Forces in the Field; the Convention for the Amelioration of the condition of Wounded, Sick and Shipwrecked Members of Armed Forces at Sea; the Convention Relative to the Treatment of Prisoners of War; and the Convention Relative to the Protection of Civilian Persons in Time of War.
20. Melisa A. Young, 143-44.
21. See *The Right to Freedom of Opinion and Expression, Final Report,* UN ESCOR, Commission on Human Rights, Sub-Commission on Prevention of Discrimination and Protection of Minorities, 44th Sess., Agenda Item 4 of the Provisional Agenda, UN Doc. E/CN.4/Sub.2/1992/9 (1992); and the addendum to the report, E/CN.4/Sub.2/1992/9/Add.1 (1992).
Mukherjee interpreted these criteria this way:

> Legitimacy requires that the restriction have in view one of the goals of limitations expressly enumerated in the international treaties in the field of human rights. These goals include respect for the rights or the reputations of others and the protection of national security, public order, and public health. Legality requires that the restriction be prescribed by relevant domestic law. Democratic necessity requires that the restriction "respect for the principle of proportionality, as well as for the democratic principles of the rule of law, and human rights." (351)

22. According to Mukherjee,

> The U.N. Convention Against Torture enjoins each state party to "take effective legislative, administrative, judicial or other measures to prevent acts of torture in any territory under its jurisdiction," and to ensure that all acts of torture, attempts to commit torture, and acts by any person with constitute complicity or participation in torture are offenses under its criminal law "punishable by appropriate penalties which take into account their grave nature." However, according to the terms of the Convention, to be considered as "torture," the act has to be "inflicted by or at the instigation of or with the consent or acquiescence of a public official or other person acting in an official capacity." Thus, the Convention does not protect journalists facing physical violence if the violence is committed with the acquiescence of public officials but cannot be attributed to them as prescribed by the Convention or if the violence is perpetrated by people not under the effective control of the government. (357)

23. International Commission for the Study of Communication Problems, *Many Voices, One World* (London: Kogan Page, 1980), 235.

24. Sean MacBride, *The Protection of Journalists,* CIC Document No.90 (Paris: UNESCO, c.1978), 28, quoted in International Commission for the Study of Communication Problems, 236.

25. International Commission for the Study of Communication Problems, 236.

26. Ibid., 265.

27. Ibid., 264.

28. Ibid., n.1, 264.

29. Ibid., n.1, 237.

30. For a comprehensive discussion of the ideal of freedom of information in Western industrial countries see Patrick Birkinshaw, *Freedom of Information: The Law, the Practice and the Ideal* (London: Weidenfeld & Nicolson, 1988).

31. See Mark D. Alleyne, "Thinking About the International System in the 'Information Age': Theoretical Assumptions and Contradictions," *Journal of Peace Research* vol. 31, no. 4 (1994), 407-24.

32. See International Commission for the Study of Communication Problems, 8-9. For a discussion of colonial laws thwarting press freedom in the specific example of Barbados see Mark D. Alleyne, "The Dynamic of Southern Foreign Policy Making Concerning Communications—A Research Note," *International Communication Bulletin* vol. 29., nos. 1-2 (Spring, 1994), 8-13, 19. A more recent example is President Clinton's authorization of $1 million for "political actions" in Haiti, including the financing of newspapers. See Elaine Sciolino, "Mission to Haiti: CIA Reportedly Taking a Role in Haiti," *The New York Times,* September 28, 1994, A8.

33. "2,000 days of censorship," *The Irish Times,* August 11, 1994, 10. Complete text relayed by *Lexis/Nexis* (Dayton, Ohio: Mead Data Central, August 13, 1994); Dave Todd, "Canadian Writer in Hiding after Attack Ordeal Echoes Rushdie Case," *Toronto Star,* August 15, 1994, A3. Complete text relayed by *Lexis/Nexis* (Dayton, Ohio: Mead Data Central, August 16, 1994).

34. See Oscar Gandy, Jr., *The Panoptic Sort: The Political Economy of Personal Information* (Boulder, Colorado: Westview Press, 1993.) The term "panoptic" has been traced by Gandy to Jeremy Bentham's idea of a panopticon—an architectural design for a prison in which inmates can be kept under constant surveillance. Gandy's term of "panoptic sort" refers to the discriminatory procedures used by companies to sort potential customers based on their estimated value. Private information about individuals—such as credit history, marital status, and race—that are stored on computers are used in this sorting process. This surveillance and information advantage of companies means that the individual transacts business with companies from a position of disadvantage. Panoptic sorting practices also provoke the raising of questions about violations of personal privacy and discrimination.

Chapter 7

1. The 1948 UN Conference on Freedom of Information provided the opportunity for collecting in one place a comprehensive set of documents on the news media. See United Nations Department of Social Affairs, *Freedom of Information: Compilation,* vol. 1 "Comments of Governments" (Lake Success, N.Y.: United Nations, 1950).

2. See Kent Cooper, *Barriers Down: The Story of the News Agency Epoch* (Port Washington: Kennikat Press, 1942); Oliver Gramling, *AP: The Story of News* (London: Kennikat Press, 1969); and Graham Storey, *Reuters' Century* (London: Parrish, 1951).

3. Rosemary Righter, *Whose News? Politics, the Press and the Third World* (London: Burnett Books, 1978); Oliver Boyd-Barrett, *The International News Agencies* (London: Constable, 1980); Jonathan Fenby, *The International News Services* (New York: Schocken Books, 1986).

4. Jim Richstad and Michael H. Anderson, eds. *Crisis in International News* (New York: Columbia University Press, 1981); Robert L. Stevenson and Donald L. Shaw, *Foreign News and the New World Information Order* (Ames: Iowa State University Press, 1984); Andrew Arno and Wimal Dissanayake eds., *The News Media in National and International Conflict* (Boulder, CO: Westview, 1984).

5. Johan Galtung and Richard C. Vincent, *Global Glasnost: Toward a New World Information and Communication Order* (Cresskill, NJ: Hampton Press, 1992); George Gerbner, Hamid Mowlana, and Kaarle Nordenstreng, *The Global Media Debate: Its Rise, Fall and Renewal* (Norwood, NJ: Ablex, 1993); Kaarle Nordenstreng and Herbert I. Schiller, *Beyond National Sovereignty: International Communications in the 1990s* (Norwood, NJ: Ablex, 1993).

6. For example, Al Hester, "Theoretical Considerations in Predicting Volume and Direction of International News Flow," *Gazette* vol. 20 (1973), 82-98. Also see Hamid Mowlana, *International Flow of Information: A Global Report and Analysis.* UNESCO Reports and Papers on Mass Communication, 99 (Paris: UNESCO, 1985).

7. For example, Einar Ostgaard, "Factors Influencing the Flow of News," *Journal of Peace Research* vol. 2 (1965), 39-63; and Annabelle Sreberny-Mohammadi et al eds. *Foreign News in the Media: International Reporting in 29 Countries.* UNESCO Reports and Papers on Mass Communication, 93. (Paris: UNESCO, 1985).

8. See, for example, Myles Breen and Farrel Corcoran, "Myth in the Television Discourse," *Communication Monographs* 49 (1982), 127-36; and Richard C. Vincent, Bryan K. Crow, and Dennis K. Davis, "When Technology Fails: The Drama of Airline Crashes in Network Television News," *Journalism Monographs* no. 117 (1989).

9. See, for example, A. W. Singham and Shirley Hune, *Non-Alignment in an Age of Alignments* (Westport, CT.: Lawrence Hill & Co., 1986), 350-51; and Johan Galtung, "A Structural Theory of Imperialism," *Journal of Peace Research* vol. 8, no. 2 (1971), 81-117.

10. See, for example, Walter B. Wriston, *The Twilight of Sovereignty: How the Information Revolution Is Transforming Our World* (New York: Charles Scribner's Sons, 1992); and Michael J. O'Neill, *The Roar of the Crowd: How Television and People Power Are Changing the World* (New York: Times Books, 1993).

11. For example, see Robert S. Fortner, *Public Diplomacy and International Politics* (Westport, CT: Praeger, 1994).

12. See Arno and Dissanayake, eds. *The News Media in National and International Conflict.*

13. In J. M. Mitchell, *International Cultural Relations* (London: Allen & Unwin, 1986), x.

14. Robert Keohane and Joseph Nye, *Power And Interdependence* 2nd Ed. (Boston: Scott Foresman, 1989), chapter 2.

15. See Susan Strange, "*Cave! hic dragones*: a critique of regime analysis" in Stephen D. Krasner, ed., *International Regimes* (Ithaca: Cornell University Press, 1983); also her "The Bondage of Liberal Economics," *SAIS Review* vol. 6, no. 1 (Winter/Spring, 1986), 25-38; and *States and Markets* (London: Pinter Publishers, 1988).

16. See Fernand de Visscher, *Le Regime Nouveau des Détroits* (Brussels, 1924), in *Extrait de la Revue de Droit Internationale et de Legislation Comparée* (1924), nos. 1-2.

17. See reference to international regimes for Luxembourg and the Elbe River in L. Oppenheim, *International Law*, 5th Ed. (New York, 1937; edited by H. Lauterpacht), vol. 1, 207 and 366; David M. Leive, *International Regulatory Regimes* (Lexington: D. C. Heath, Lexington Books, 1976), 2 vols. There were also these articles in the *American Journal of International Law*: William L. Butler, "The Legal Regime of Russian Territorial Waters," 62 (1968), 51-77; Richard Young, "The Legal Regime of the Deep-Sea Floor," 62 (1968), 641-53; Leo J. Harris, "Diplomatic Privileges and Immunities: A New Regime Is Soon to Be Adopted by the United States," 62 (1968), 98-113; W. Michael Riesman, "The Regime of Straits and National Security," 74 (1980), 48-76; and John Norton Moore, "The Regime of Straits and the Third United Nations Conference on the Law of the Sea," 74 (1980), 77-121.

18. John Gerard Ruggie, "International Responses to Technology: Concepts and Trends," *International Organization* 29 (Summer, 1975), 569, quoted in Robert Keohane and Joseph Nye, *Power and Interdependence* , 250. Keohane and Nye also point to Richard N. Cooper, "Prolegomena to the Choice of an International Monetary System," *International Organization* 29 (Winter 1975), 64.

19. See Stephen Krasner, ed., *International Regimes* (Ithaca: Cornell University Press, 1983). The "conventional structural" view regards regimes as useless tools for analyzing the international system because international politics is essentially power politics, shaped by the most powerful states who exercise structural power over weaker states and are not constrained by the principles, norms and rules of international regimes. This outlook is best exemplified in the writings and theory of Susan Strange. "Modified structural" refers to the approach embodied in Keohane and Nye, *Power and Interdependence*, where international regimes are key variables in the world of complex interdependence because they are "the sets of governing arrangements that affect relationships of interdependence." International regimes are products of the international political structure ("the distribution of power resources among states"); but regimes in turn shape the political bargaining and decision-making that take place within the international system. For these reasons, Keohane and Nye devote the majority of their book to analyzing why regimes change and to case studies of regimes in bilateral and multilateral relationships. The terms "conventional structural" and "mod-

ified structural" are really new words for "realist" and "neorealist." Both realists and neorealists treat international regimes as *intervening* variables between the international power structure and desired outcomes. In contrast, the Grotian perspective respects international regimes as phenomena in their own right— *autonomous* variables. Regimes perform functions that are beyond the capability of states. States are confined because they are not the primary actors in international relations and international politics is very much the politics of transnational relations between elites and interest groups. States cannot on their own regulate such transnational relations; instead regimes provide (according to regime theorist Stephen Krasner) a "communications net [for transnational actors], embodying rules, norms, and principles which transcends national boundaries." This view is embodied in the writings of Oran Young, one of the most prolific writers on international regimes. See the following books and articles by Oran Young: *International Co-operation: Building Regimes for Natural Resources and the Environment* (Ithaca: Cornell University Press, 1989); *Resource Regimes: Natural Resources and Social Institutions* (Berkeley: University of California Press, 1982); *Resource Management at the International Level: The Case of the North Pacific* (London: Pinter, 1977); "The Politics of International Regime Formation: Managing Natural Resources," *International Organization* (Summer, 1989), 349-75; and "Science and Social Institutions: Lessons for International Resource Regimes," *International Challenges* vol. 8, no. 3 (1988) 5-8.

20. See Stephan Haggard and Beth A. Simmons, "Theories of international regimes," *International Organization* vol. 41, no. 3 (Summer, 1987), 490-517. Haggard and Simmons believe that while these approaches, in tandem, can tell us a lot about regimes, they all have their shortcomings. For example, hegemonic stability theory, a component of structuralism fails, to regard regimes as a fundamental part of "high politics and alliance strategy," and regimes do not necessarily benignly serve "international" collective interests as structuralists believe (503). Game theory fails to explain whether regimes will actually be formed, how they are institutionalized, and what rules and norms will compose them (506). Functional theories of regimes "assume highly convergent interests and downplay divergent ones, [and] they do not explore how regimes may institutionalize inequalities" (508). While cognitive theories pay attention to the role of information and ideology in the building of regimes—factors ignored by the other theories—they fail to explain how ideas and power interact.

21. See Mark D. Alleyne, *International Power and International Communication* (London: Macmillan, 1995); and Mark D. Alleyne, "The Political Economy Of International Communication In North-South Relations: A Case Study of the New World Information And Communication Order (NWICO) Debate c.1970 – c.1987," D.Phil. Thesis, University of Oxford, 1991.

22. The term "political economy" is problematical and requires some explanation here. It has been used to refer to different forms of academic investigation at different times in the history of the social sciences. The term was first used in the eighteenth century to describe the writings of such thinkers as Adam Smith, who enquired into the dynamics of wealth creation and the role of government in that

process. See Terry Curtis, "The Information Society: A Computer-Generated Caste System?" in Vincent Mosco and Janet Wasko, *The Political Economy of Information* (Madison: University of Wisconsin Press, 1988), 97-98. Most social science dictionaries consulted actually state that the term "political economy" was the original name for what is now referred to as the discipline of economics and make no distinction between the two fields of enquiry. See Alan Gilpin, *Dictionary of Economics And Financial Markets* 5th ed. (London: Butterworth, 1986); J. L. Hanson, *A Dictionary of Economics and Commerce* 6th ed. (London: Pittman, 1986); Arthur Seldon and F. G. Pennance, eds., *Everyman's Dictionary of Economics* (London: J. M. Dent & Sons, 1975); Byrne J. Horton, Julian Ripley and M. B. Schnapper, *Dictionary of Modern Economics* (Washington, D.C.: Public Affairs Press, 1948); David W. Pierce, gen. ed., *MacMillan Dictionary of Modern Economics*, 3rd ed. (London: MacMillan, 1986); and J. R. Winton, ed., *A Dictionary of Economic Terms* revised 3rd ed. (London: Routledge & Kegan Paul, 1951). The name "political economy" went out of vogue by the turn of the twentieth century and only reemerged after World War II. Within the field of international relations there has developed a body of thought called "international political economy."

International political economy has been plagued by the same problems of definition confronting political economy at the domestic level. Authors on international political economy interpret the subject in different ways. Political economist Charles Kindleberger, for example, has defined it as "the study of how the economy and polity work in settling questions of public policy." (Charles P. Kindleberger, *Power and Money* [London: MacMillan, 1970], 15.) For Edmund Dell it is the economic activities and relationships of political institutions. (See Edmund Dell, *The Politics of Economic Interdependence* [New York: St. Martin's, 1987].) Susan Strange says it concerns "the social, political and economic arrangements affecting the global systems of production, exchange and distribution, and the mix of values reflected therein." (Strange, *States and Markets*, 18.) My definition of international political economy is based upon these various ideas. I define international political economy as *the interaction of state (or other sources of authority) and market forces in fashioning the norms and values of international society.*

23. Quoted in William Safire, "Honoring Repression," *The New York Times*, July 10, 1995, A13; reprinted in edited form, under the headline "Honour for Singapore's PM raises storm," in *The Guardian* (London), July 19, 1995, 10.

24. Walter B. Wriston, *The Twilight of Sovereignty: How the Information Revolution is Transforming Our World* , 46.

25. See Marcus W. Brauchli, "U.N. Conferees Find A Global Connection Through the Internet," *The Wall Street Journal*, September 18, 1995, A7D.

26. "President Clinton Signs Declaration of Chapultepec," *Editor & Publisher*, April 15, 1995, vol. 128, no. 15, 10.

27. UNESCO's 1978 Mass Media Declaration and two statements on journalistic ethics produced under the auspices of UNESCO in 1980 and 1983 include a number of principles that assume the separation of the press from the people and the distinction between the interests of owners and media workers, including the right of reply, respect for privacy, and prohibitions on journalists promoting

racism, intolerance and war. See Kaarle Nordenstreng, Enrique Gonzales Manet, and Wolfgang Kleinwächter, *New International Information and Communication Order Sourcebook* (Prague: International Organization of Journalists, 1986). Similarly, the American and European human rights conventions and the ICCPR also declare the need for the media to balance rights with responsibilities.

28. Amit Mukherjee, "International Protection of Journalists: Problem, Practice, and Prospects," *Arizona Journal of International and Comparative Law* vol. 11, no. 2, (1994), 339-87.

29. See Joseph R. Dominick, *The Dynamics of Mass Communication* (Reading, MA: Addison-Wesley, 1983).

30. Lenin's so-called Twenty-One Conditions, presented to the Second Congress of the Comintern (19 July – 7 August 1920) included: strict guidelines for running the Communist press; and the stipulation that refusal to do propaganda work would be seen as resignation from revolutionary action. [For the original statement on base and superstructure, see Karl Marx and Friedrich Engels, *The German Ideology* (London: Lawrence and Wishart, 1970), 64.]

31. Strange, *States And Markets.*

32. Ibid., 62.

33. Ibid., 87.

Index

Universal Declaration of Human
Rights (UDHR), 15, 70, 96, 122,
130
Article 19 of, 100

V
Villeneuve, André, 23
Vincent, Richard, 40-41, 126

W
Wall Street Journal, The
on the automation of exchanges,
189*n*
Washington Post
report on Somoza criticism of the
press, 107-108
Wilkinson, Paul
on trends in international relations research, 127-128
Wilson, Harold, 98
Wolff, Bernhard, 6
World Press Freedom Committee
(WPFC), 68
description of, Appendix 10, 183
extra-legal rule-making of, 133-
135
funding, 83
on murders of journalists, 117
opposition to "permissible restrictions" on press freedom, 103,
115
origins of, 76, 132
protection stance, 113, 115, 119
Talloires conferences, 81-82
World Trade Organization (WTO),
128, 139
Wright, Peter, 97-98
Wriston, Walter
predictions for the information
age, 131-132

Y
Yeltsin, Boris
press reforms of, 7

Young, Melissa A.
on the protection of journalists,
113-114

Z
Zimmerman, Betty
on protection of journalists, 116